D0712160

BUENOS
AIRES

Map of central Buenos Aires

BUENOS AIRES

AIRES

THE BIOGRAPHY OF A CITY

JAMES GARDNER

St. Martin's Press
New York

www.stmartins.com

Map of central Buenos Aires is provided courtesy of the Buenos Aires City Board of Tourism and is used with permission.

Photograph on page iv of Buenos Aires's Hotel Majestic (c. 1910) is provided courtesy of the Archivo General de la Nación and is used with permission.

Library of Congress Cataloging-in-Publication Data

Gardner, James, 1960–
   Buenos Aires : the biography of a city / James Gardner.
 pages   cm
   Includes bibliographical references and index.
   ISBN 978-1-137-27988-0 (hardcover)
   ISBN 978-1-4668-7903-4 (e-book)
   1. Buenos Aires (Argentina)—History. 2. Buenos Aires (Argentina)—Intellectual life. I. Title.
   F3001.3.G38   2015
   982'.11—dc23
                                                                                                  2015018323

Design by Letra Libre, Inc.

Our books may be purchased for educational, business, or promotional use. For information on bulk purchases, please contact the Macmillan Corporate and Premium Sales Department at 1-800-221-7945, extension 5442, or write to specialmarkets@macmillan.com.

First Edition: December 2015

10 9 8 7 6 5 4 3 2 1

In Memoriam
Joachim Neugroschel
(1938–2011)
"a fellow of infinite jest"

CONTENTS

PREFACE

WHEN I ARRIVED IN BUENOS AIRES FOR THE FIRST
time, on February 1, 1999, I went looking for a history of the city that
would explain the genesis and evolution of its urban landscape. Having read excellent histories of Paris, London, Rome and New York, I
assumed that Buenos Aires, being one of the world's great urban centers,
must surely have a wealth of comparable books. But that was not the
case. Although I found many excellent volumes on the most obscure
aspects of the city, I found nothing that explained the grand strategy of
its development. In the more than sixteen years that have elapsed since
then, I did manage to find secondhand bookshops with a few out-of-
print volumes that served my purposes well enough, and in more recent
years some good books have appeared, but they are more devoted to the
history of the people of Buenos Aires—the Porteños, as they are called—
or to a detailed and scholarly examination of its urban planning than to a
readable account of its evolution. And all of them were in Spanish.

It was in this context that I finally decided to write the book that I
had initially set out to buy: a general history, for the general reader, of
Buenos Aires. It is necessary, however, to explain what this book is and
what it is not. It is a history of the city itself—as a city. By this I mean
that it engages every aspect of the subject as it touches upon the goal
of explaining how this aggregated mass of humanity came into being
and changed through time. For me, the most important element of the
story was its physical aspect, the laying out of the city's great grid, the
stylistic evolution of its wondrous building stock and the technological

development of its infrastructure. After that I was interested in the people who came to inhabit the city and the manner in which they did so. And although this book is also a history of what happened within the city, that aspect of the story has been incidental to my main interest and has been invoked mainly when historical events had some bearing on issues of urbanism.

It should also be emphasized that this is a history of the city of Buenos Aires, rather than of the province of Buenos Aires that surrounds it—an area roughly the size of England—or of what is called Greater Buenos Aires, a conurbation of 13 million souls who inhabit the areas directly outside the official limits of the capital. I have strayed only rarely beyond the strict borders of the capital, defined by Avenida General Paz to the west, the Rio de la Plata to the north and east, and the Riachuelo, a smaller river, to the south.

My book makes no claim to being a work of original scholarship or one intended for scholars. It is based entirely on my own observations drawn from years of extensive, delightful walks through the city and from a careful, even devoted reading of mostly secondary sources. Many excellent scholars, both in Argentina and abroad, have studied the minutest aspects of the city's history, from the paving of its streets and the introduction of electricity to the export of meat products and the architecture of its palaces. I have derived great insight and a wealth of information from all of these sources, without, however, doing archival research of my own. That would have resulted in a very different book and not the one that, I felt, needed to be written.

The great wonder and mystery of Buenos Aires is how it came to exist in the Western Hemisphere in the first place. I am aware of no other city in North, South or Central America that consciously sought to become a European capital, let alone that succeeded so well in this capricious quest. Even if Buenos Aires were not—as it is—a manifold of urban virtues and experiential delights, that achievement in itself would make a powerful claim on the world's attention.

INTRODUCTION

BUENOS AIRES AS CENTER OF THE UNIVERSE

BUENOS AIRES SHARES WITH A VERY SELECT GROUP of cities a quality that has been denied to the vast majority of them. It is a quality that goes beyond size, although that is a precondition, and beyond age, since some of these cities are exceedingly ancient while others are quite modern. It does not have to do with the beauty of the city or even with its eminence in human history. The quality in question is the ability to awaken in its inhabitants a vague and poetic sense of infinity and eternity converging upon a single place. To the historian and the journalist, this convergence is pure fiction, if not outright nonsense: every urban agglomeration, no matter how big, eventually runs headlong into its city limits, and even the most ancient cities of the earth were once empty fields. But it is the power and the prerogative of great cities in general, and of Buenos Aires specifically, to exert over the minds of their citizens the sense that, in some mysterious and unquantifiable way, they have always been there and always will be. "They tell me that Buenos Aires had a beginning," Jorge Luis Borges, the supreme poet of the city, writes in one of his most famous poems, "but to me it is as eternal as water and air." It is likewise the prerogative of the great city, in proud defiance of all the evidence of maps, that its physical dimensions can never be fully grasped. It is not for nothing that Borges chose Calle Garay in southern Buenos Aires as the setting for "El Aleph," his celebrated story about a mystic point in which the entire universe is contained, and from which every other point in the universe is simultaneously visible.

Corollary to these rare privileges of infinity and eternity, Buenos Aires has the power to conjure its inhabitants into believing that it stands at the center of creation, that it is nothing less than the center of the universe. And it does this not only through its size and history but also through the kinetic energy that it gives off and through an imperious self-regard that most other cities, however large or illustrious, simply cannot summon. Of all the cities that I have visited in my life, I have found this rare aggregate of qualities in only a very few, among them Paris and London, Rome and New York, and—to my initial surprise— Buenos Aires.

Perhaps the most emphatic assertion of Buenos Aires's status as the center of the universe appears in Leopoldo Marechal's novel *Adán Buenosayres,* which many critics consider to be the finest work of Argentine fiction. Roughly 800 pages long, it resembles, very much by design, Joyce's *Ulysses* in its plot, spirit and ambition. Published in 1948, this quintessentially modern novel is urban to its core, reveling in the street names and public squares of Buenos Aires, as well as in a hundred colorful characters whose general type would be instantly recognized by other *Porteños,* or "people of the port," as the citizens of Buenos Aires have always been called.

Consider this beautiful passage from the beginning of the novel (which, in my translation, I have slightly abridged):

Reader, if you had had the power of birds and had been able, from a great height, to take in a sparrow's view of the city [on that morning of April 28, 192-], I know full well that your breast would have swelled with automatic pride when you saw the vision that would then have presented itself to your faithful Porteño eyes. Black, sonorous ships, anchored in the port of Santa Maria de Buenos Aires, tossed upon its docks the industrial harvest of both hemispheres, the

colors and sounds of the four races, the iodine and salt of the seven
seas. An orchestra of trains entered the city or departed for the forests
of the north, the vineyards of the west, the farmlands of the center
and the pastures of the south.

Marechal's ambition is nothing less than to explore the human condition, in its ceaseless movement and infinite complexity, through the
expanding grid of Buenos Aires and its nearly fifty barrios. And yet,
crucially, he is not addressing mankind in general, but rather his fellow
citizens. It is very much as though we, the inhabitants of other lands,
are not hearing, but overhearing, the communication of one Porteño
with another. Obviously Marechal understood that no one outside of
Argentina would take especially kindly to his idea that Buenos Aires
was the center of the universe. But just as crucially, he did not care:
there were—and there remain—enough readers, enough cultural pride,
enough frantic, all-conquering energy and action in Buenos Aires to
support Marechal's claim of cosmic centrality—at least to his satisfaction and that of his compatriots.

Objectively speaking, I admit that Buenos Aires might seem to be a
poor candidate for the center of the universe. The city stands so far from
the general focus of the world's interests that even the Spanish crown,
which brought it into being over four centuries ago, largely ignored it
for the first two hundred years of its existence, considering it too far off
the map to warrant the slightest respect. Even today, in the age of jet
engines, most foreigners have only the vaguest notion of what goes on
down there. And so it may come as a surprise to readers who have never
visited Buenos Aires that, at some level of unspoken assumption, many
Porteños suspect that their city is not only the center of everything, but
a totality, an ontology, every bit as perfect as Paris or New York.

You come to understand the logic of this sentiment as you walk
through the city's teeming streets. It is possible to lose oneself in Buenos Aires, to disappear into it, to live one's entire life in it without once
feeling the need to travel beyond the great freeway of Avenida General
Paz, a road twenty miles long that delimits and nearly encircles the city.
This is the massive avenue that separates Buenos Aires from all that

is not Buenos Aires, a designation that includes everything from the contiguous counties (or *partidos*) of Avellaneda and Lanus to Greenland and Sumatra. But within the privileged limits of the avenue resides the universe of Buenos Aires, with barrios that even its inveterate natives may never have visited and streets whose names they will never learn. Within those borders live 3 million Porteños, a figure that does not include 10 million more who live just beyond Avenida General Paz in el Gran Buenos Aires, or Greater Buenos Aires.

One way to perceive this universality, to see it materialized, is to visit a local bookstore, of which there are many in the Argentine capital. Indeed, of all the cities I have visited, I have never found another with as many new or used bookstores as Buenos Aires. You find them in every barrio, whether it is residential or commercial, often two of them to a block. Some of these stores are recent arrivals, while others have occupied the same corner for more than a century. There are massive chain stores in the downtown area that offer lattes and the latest best seller, and tiny shops nestled in a side street of some remote barrio that sell remainders that have gathered dust since before the last dictator was sent packing. And if you look at their shelves, you will notice something you might not expect: an abundance of books about Buenos Aires itself. In other words, you will find exactly the sort of volumes you would find in the bookshops of Paris, London and New York: books about the best local cabarets and bars; books about the local parks; histories of each of the city's forty-eight neighborhoods; popular volumes that explain the names of the streets; scholarly works devoted to the city's labor relations in the 1930s; expensive, lavishly illustrated books devoted to the Belle Époque palaces of the Barrio Norte. And then there are what seem to be dozens of volumes with titles like *Mysterious Buenos Aires* or *Hidden Buenos Aires* or *The Unknown Buenos Aires*. Such an abundance of self-regard is unheard of in any other South American city, or in most cities anywhere else. Only cities with an invincible sense of their own worth and identity can support such publishing ventures.

Somewhere, I believe, Ezra Pound claims that it takes only five hundred committed souls to constitute a civilization. I am reminded of that in connection to Buenos Aires. One could describe the Porteños as

Virgil describes the denizens of the underworld: "They have their own sun and their own stars down there." Though the city, like the nation, is acutely conscious of cultural developments in the rest of the world, from literature and music to art and film, Buenos Aires has its own potent cultural center, from whose gravitational pull only the rarest artists, like Borges or the composer Astor Piazzola, escape to fame beyond the borders of Argentina. Buenos Aires has its revered poets and novelists of whom most of the world has never heard, as well as actors and classical musicians, statesmen and locals heroes, whom it cherishes with as great a love and loyalty as any Parisian or Londoner or New Yorker ever felt for the luminaries of his hometown.

It is a city teeming with memories, a city of ghosts and sites of tragic confrontation, a city that delights in remembering its vanished tea shops and carousels, as well as those theaters and nightclubs that continue to pulsate with a living joy. In Buenos Aires, nostalgia is an institution. You will find pedants who know everything about the city's obscurest rites and urban legends, as well as a whole infrastructure of tour guides who are happy to pad reality with the usual embellishments and inflated claims of their profession. As long ago as the 1880s, writers looked back longingly to an earlier Buenos Aires that had disappeared. To this day, José Antonio Wilde's *Buenos Aires desde setenta años atrás* (*Buenos Aires as It Was Seventy Years Ago*), published in 1881, remains a classic of the local literature, even though, typically, it is entirely unknown beyond the borders of Argentina.

This nostalgia is so strong that, even where no usable past exists, the poets of Buenos Aires are pleased to invent it. Consider Borges's famous poem "La fundacion mitologica de Buenos Aires" (The Mythological Foundation of Buenos Aires). Longing to create for his homeland the rich mythologies of his beloved Europe, Borges describes the first settlements of the Rio de la Plata in the following terms:

> Considering the matter closely, we must conclude that [the river] was bluish back then, / As though born of heaven . . . What is certain is that thousands upon thousands of men / Crossed a sea five moons wide/ Still teaming with sirens and dragons . . .

In a similar spirit, another fine Porteño poet, Silvina Ocampo, addresses Buenos Aires thus:

> Long before Solís and Mendoza [the earliest explorers of the region], many imagined you from afar. / Without knowing that you existed they invented you / amid ambiguous plains they yearned for you / a place without fevers or tyrants or serpents / with your eternal suns and your dew.

I have dwelt on the role of nostalgia in the Porteño psyche because, uniquely among the cities of Latin America, it rivals in strength, pride and persistence the urban consciousness of the great cities of North America and the Old World. But it is not necessary to have spent much time in Buenos Aires to sense that something is different about the place. It parts company with the other great cities of the world in one crucial respect: it has fallen short. It has not lived up to the dreams of its leaders one century ago. At the outbreak of the First World War, Argentina was the eighth-wealthiest nation on Earth, easily surpassing Canada and Australia by any standard of material progress. Today it struggles to remain in the top half of the list of nations. And despite the proverbial arrogance of the Porteños, despite the insistence of some—usually allied with the ruling party of the moment—that Argentina is doing fine, or would be if not for the interference of foreign and domestic enemies, despite all of that, everyone in Buenos Aires knows that things have been far better, that a great promise has been squandered. It is the tug-of-war between that pride and this realization that is the defining characteristic of the modern Porteño and the modern Argentine.

One century ago, the mood was very different; there was a febrile optimism about the future, a sense that Buenos Aires might soon become the capital of the wealthiest nation in the world. The stage was set, or so it seemed, and all the seats had been arranged. The Beaux Art palaces of its Gilded Age, its domed parliament and colonnaded academies, blazed with all the refinements that an imported classicism could impart to them. But then history took a wrong turn, and the fortunes of the nation, and with it those of the city, sank, never to regain that intensity of hope or promise. But in their collective psyche, the Porteños have never forgotten that tantalizing proximity to greatness. And I find in this fact a poignancy, a monumental human frailty, that endows Buenos Aires with a pathos and wayward nobility that make it uniquely worthy of the world's attention.

And so, I wish to reveal Buenos Aires as I have found it in its complexities and its imperfections, no less than in its manifold virtues. Traditional travel writing concerns only the virtues of a place, the things in it that are worth seeing. All the rest—the ugly little gas station, the rusting bridge that spans the train tracks, some dreary, rationalist development from the seventies—doesn't quite rise to the status of existence. They are to be thought away, like some discoloration in an otherwise beautiful Trecento fresco. If they are mentioned at all, it is only as something to be avoided. But what makes Buenos Aires interesting is Buenos Aires itself. As such, it should be approached—as, indeed, all cities should be approached—not as the sum of all the things in it that are worth seeing or all the restaurants and clubs worth patronizing, but rather as an indivisible totality that is compelling in its own right, and as compelling in its failures as it is in the splendor of its palaces.

To see Buenos Aires from the perspective of the tourist is one thing; to see it from the perspective of the urbanist is another thing entirely. In the former case, it is a kind of box that contains a number of objects more interesting than the box itself. One opens this box in search of certain things that one wants to see: in the case of Buenos Aires, El Obelisco, San Telmo and the Cemetery of Recoleta, steak asados, the wines of Mendoza and tango shows. But soon one learns that there are other things in Buenos Aires: a dreary stretch of working-class housing or a tangle of infrastructure too drab and boring to promise even that "edge" that coincides, at least for the moment, with a certain part of contemporary taste. As far as the traditional tourist is concerned, none of that is really Buenos Aires, at least not the part that he has come to see.

But if, having dispensed with this notion of Buenos Aires as a box, we begin to see it as a complex organism in its own right, then it starts to look very different and, I would argue, far more interesting. Suddenly no part of it is off limits. Surely the grand urban showpieces will continue to stand out, but the myriad interstitial passages as well will take on a relevance that is scarcely less important. In this totalizing view of the city, it is not the destination alone but rather the means of reaching it—or, in certain of the outer barrios, the absence of any destination to speak of—that rises to aesthetic and historical consequence. In such a reading of Buenos Aires, it is impossible to get lost, impossible to take the wrong train or hop on the wrong bus. Each step we take in this version of the city, each thing we see or do not see, is part of the total experience of Buenos Aires.

Consider, by way of example, the Avenida Juan B. Justo, one of the longest and ugliest thoroughfares in the city. No one has anything good to say about this avenue, and neither have I. It slings round the western half of Buenos Aires for nearly ten miles, its monotony rarely relieved by a decent park, a striking church or any picturesque conjunction of private homes. In fact, large parts of it are not really meant to be seen at all. No one walks along this avenue unless compelled by some unenviable necessity. Much of the ugliness of this avenue is due to its running, for part of its length, parallel to train tracks that were laid down before the avenue existed, tracks that not only harass the neighborhood with noise and stench but are largely concealed behind a thick and forbidding wall. That means that a good part of the avenue's eastern side is a dead zone, and death, urbanistically speaking, is contagious, infecting the circumjacent areas and making them decidedly less desirable as residential areas. And along much of its length you find those unmistakable monuments to urbanistic failure: tire shops and gas stations, which have taken up residence here because, of course, the rents are cheap.

It is a fair guess that few tourists ever see this avenue unless they are severely lost, and many a lifelong Porteño has grown old and never been here either. Can anything redeem this stretch of Buenos Aires? No beauty, to be sure.

But if you try to see this avenue in the light of thought, it will prove, I think, far more interesting. Ask most Porteños and they will tell you that their city is flat, standing as it does on the famed tableland of the pampas, except at the fringe where it tilts into what once was the Rio de la Plata. But this is not so. Although generally flat, it has prominences and recessions caused by the buckling of alluvial deposits that have descended, over hundreds of thousands of years, from the Andes toward the Atlantic Ocean. And one of these buckles is exactly coincident with the circuit of Avenida Juan B. Justo. Before humanity ever reached South America, the abundant rains in this part of the world coursed through the sluice of a stream called the Maldonado. For hundreds of years after the Spanish arrived, this stream lay exposed to the sky and served as the western boundary of Buenos Aires. And whenever a heavy rain fell, as it does so often in the city, the stream of the Maldonado would assume a dangerous, even deadly force: on more than one occasion it rushed forward and carried away some child who happened to be splashing around in it—one of the favored diversions of the locals in warm weather. But because the Maldonado, which also served as a natural sewer, was far removed from the center of Buenos Aires (then as now the Plaza de Mayo) few people chose or needed to live here. And so it made sense, when the railways arrived in the middle of the nineteenth century, to run the tracks through largely uninhabited areas of the city, like this one, in order to create minimal disruption.

Some decades after the tracks were laid down, however, the municipality decided to cover the Maldonado (*entubarlo,* in Spanish), resulting in the opening in 1937 of Avenida Juan B. Justo. But because the railway still runs near it, few people choose to live here. As for the Maldonado, it is still there. Buried beneath the asphalt of the avenue, it occasionally reminds the Porteños of its existence when, amid the torrents of January, it overflows its banks and menaces the ten barrios through which it passes, further inhibiting residential development in its vicinity. For the Porteño, Juan B. Justo is a blight upon the city. But in the eyes of the urbanist, it represents a fascinating reflex, as well as a direct and ongoing consequence, of those sedimentary deposits that flowed down from the Andes over the course of untold eons.

This urbanistic perspective on the city extends to its building stock as well. There is surely beauty on the streets of Buenos Aires, but its buildings offer a different satisfaction from those of Paris, Rome or New York. Buenos Aires does not possess great architecture. It offers an abundance of charming and pleasant buildings, indeed, extremely pleasant and extremely charming in their aggregate effect. But they are always derivative of something else, usually something from Paris if they were built before 1930, or from New York if they were built more recently. Since the very founding of Buenos Aires in 1580, or as soon as the Porteños undertook to build ambitious structures, this derivative-ness has been the essential fact about the city and its architecture. The earliest churches that survive, like San Ignacio, on Calle Bolívar, were vaguely derivative of Roman Baroque, filtered through the influence of Spanish colonial practice. The cathedral on Plaza de Mayo is inspired by French neoclassicism. Setting aside mid-nineteenth-century Gothic churches and institutional structures, the great flowering of palaces and *hotels particuliers* at the beginning of the twentieth century was the direct result of the École des Beaux-Arts in Paris. No less derivative were the Art Deco confections of the early thirties, the postwar rationalism of the International Style, the Postmodernism of the 1980s and the Deconstructivism of today.

None of this is to deny that Buenos Aires affords the pedestrian a powerful aesthetic stimulus on almost every block. Once we accept that Buenos Aires yields but few examples of truly world-class architecture, we begin to seek out and to delight in each unanticipated felicity of form and function: a colonnade, a cupola or an ancient, battered doorway that, in its extravagant pretentions, seems almost comical at first, until you succeed in finding the beauty in it. And when you do, it will be a beauty shot through, more often than not, with a poignant sense of the humanity of both the architect and his client: divided by a great ocean from Europe and the centers of their cultural longing, both did what they could, both did the best that they could, to create something noble and striking and impressive in the capital that they loved.

That doorway and ten thousand others like it are no less a part of Buenos Aires than the cathedral or Teatro Colón or even Avenida Juan B. Justo. All of these individual acts, taken together with the millions of souls who live out their lives along the city's labyrinthine grid, as well as all the souls who have ever lived within that grid or who ever will, are part of Buenos Aires the infinite city, part of Buenos Aires the center— on its own terms—of the universe.

ONE

CIVILIZATION OR BARBARISM

The Geography of Buenos Aires

THE PAST ISN'T PAST: IT HAS MERELY MOVED. IF YOU seek the bustling port city of nineteenth-century New York, the city that Herman Melville describes in the opening pages of *Moby Dick,* you will find it, improbably, six thousand miles to the south, in Montevideo, the capital of Uruguay. Amid ramshackle two-story houses, the old city comes to a peninsular point that strikingly recalls lower Manhattan before it was bulked up with landfill. The intuition of water—so effectively banished from the lives of most Manhattanites—is ever present there, as it once was in New York.

Fortunately, the thing one seeks is usually closer to home. This is because cities often seem to radiate, both spatially and temporally, from a central point out to the extremities. Thus what begins as an ultramodern downtown is apt to end up in water or an open field. In this sequence you can almost divine an echo of the Big Bang itself: the further out you go, the more archaic become the things you encounter along the way.

That is certainly true of Buenos Aires. The capital of Argentina was founded in 1580 when a contingent of sixty-five men and one woman, led by Juan de Garay, sailed south on the Paraná River from Asunción, now the capital of Paraguay, to establish a settlement along the estuary of the Rio de la Plata. This settlement arose near the Plaza de Mayo, between the streets now known as Yrigoyen and Rivadavia. For more than four hundred years, this area has been the spiritual center of Buenos Aires and of Argentina. One and a half centuries ago, the entire area was a place of low-lying brick houses assembled around a patio, such as you can still find, about a mile south of the center in the barrio of San Telmo. From two to four hundred years ago, it was made up of single-story adobe houses for which at least an approximation can be found in the outer barrios, not to mention the shanty towns of Villa 25 and Villa 31.

But to know how Buenos Aires appeared before Europeans settled the New World, indeed, before the first humans passed dry-shod over what is now the Bering Strait and began their millennial descent into Central and South America some thirty thousand years ago, it is sufficient to get on a train at Constitución Station and head thirty miles southeast to La Plata, the capital of the province of Buenos Aires. Midway between the two cities, if you look out the filthy windows, or better still, if you stand beside one of the doors that has been jolted open by the speed of the train, you will see before you, all the way to the horizon, the fabled pampas. Today these endless grasslands, unrelieved by a hill or often by so much as a tree, seem to be as far removed from Buenos Aires as the ice floes of the Tierra del Fuego. But in fact, the city and the province of Buenos Aires lie in the midst of the pampas, a vast plain, covering nearly 300,000 square miles, that sweeps down from the foothills of the Andes, engulfs the city and leaps over the Rio de la Plata into Uruguay and southern Brazil.

The pampas, whose name comes from the indigenous Quechua word for "plain," have inspired widely diverging assessments. Many visitors find beauty in them. A larger consensus seems to view them as somewhat tedious, given their general lack of geographical features or inflections. But from a certain perspective, if seen at noontime near the summer solstice, they can strike the visitor with the force of a nightmare, these suffocating, infinite plains that present themselves as dumb fact, these tall grasses in which you could get lost and never be found again.

Although the flora and fauna of the pampas have long since vanished from the Argentine capital, the flatness of the pampas remains its dominant topographical fact. Buenos Aires is a city of impressive beauty and magnificent parks, but it has few natural endowments. As the historian José Juan Maroni has written, perhaps too severely: "Buenos Aires derives little beauty or aesthetic value from its natural location. It consists of two juxtaposed plains. One is aquatic, the widest river in the world, with only one shore-line; the other is terrestrial, marked by the immense emptiness of the pampas. Both plains, of nearly the same level and hue, are separated by a straight coastline with almost no relief. If truth be told, it is a wearisome scene, of infinite and depressing monotony."

Roughly circular in shape and extending over seventy-eight square miles, Buenos Aires is bounded by Avenida General Paz for twenty miles to the northwest, while its southern limit is defined by a small river known as the Riachuelo and its eastern limit by the Rio de la Plata. From one end to the other, in any direction, is roughly a ten-mile walk, and it takes three and a half hours to traverse. Whereas New York's intricately splintered, indeed tattered, territory is interwoven with water in a thousand odd ways, Buenos Aires offers a fairly continuous and uniform density of buildings and occupants throughout. In this it also differs from Chicago, which similarly rises on a broad plain and is bordered by a large body of water to the east: Chicago's center is densely built up, but once beyond that area, it instantly becomes far smaller and quieter.

Buenos Aires may lie within the pampas, but it has always viewed them as its antithesis: while the pampas are (or were) the hinterland, the home of the gauchos, or cowboys, Buenos Aires has long seen itself as the "Paris of South America," the dazzling world capital that looks out across the Atlantic to Europe. The role of the pampas in forging a national identity is spelled out in one of the great polemics of the nineteenth century, *Facundo o Civilización y Barbarie* (*Facundo or Civilization and Barbarism*) written in 1845 by Domingo Faustino Sarmiento, who would later become president of Argentina. The very title of the work articulates, perhaps for the first time, a dichotomy between the city, Buenos Aires, and the hinterland that has resounded through all the subsequent history of the Argentine nation. For Sarmiento, there are the pampas and there is Buenos Aires: South America, with its crude and immemorial customs, Europe with its refinement and enlightenment. "If it is not the proximity of the indigenous savage," Sarmiento wrote, "that worries the residents [of the pampas], it is the fear of a tiger that stalks him or a snake that he might step on. This fear for one's very life, which is habitual and permanent in the countryside, stamps upon the Argentine character—it seems to me—a certain stoical resignation in the face of a violent death."

In stark contrast stands the Porteño: "The man of the city wears European clothes and leads a civilized life as it is known throughout the world. In the city are laws, notions of progress, means of instruction, some municipal organization, a regular government, etc. But once you leave the city, everything changes. . . . The man of the pampas, far from aspiring to imitate the customs of the city, rejects with disdain its luxuries and fine manners, as well as the attire of the city-dweller."

But although Sarmiento saw Buenos Aires as the antithesis of the pampas, in point of geographical fact it is a part of them. That is to say that the tall grasses that can still be seen midway between Buenos Aires and La Plata once extended all the way to the Plaza de Mayo. Almost all of the city of Buenos Aires sits on the pampas plateau, roughly thirty meters above sea level, just at the point where it descends toward the Rio de la Plata in a pronounced slope that is known locally as a *barranca*. These barrancas form a continuous fringe around the city, all the way from Belgrano, in the northwest of the city, to La Boca at its southernmost limit.

At the base of these barrancas once lay a sequence of sandy shoals and mud banks that stood between the plateau and the water. It was here, beside what is now the Casa Rosada (literally, the Pink House)— the official dwelling of the Argentine president—that black washerwomen used to gossip and sing as they did laundry in the river; here that young boys would splash around in the heat of summer; here that horses

Horses conveying voyagers from their ships to the port. (Archivo General de la Nación)

pulled carriages through the waters of the river, conveying passengers the final few hundred feet from ships that, due to the rock-filled shallows, had to remain far from the shore. In the absence of these horses, men of a requisite stoutness could be found to carry passengers ashore on their broad shoulders. Such was the life of Buenos Aires into the second half of the nineteenth century. It was the life of a vibrant port.

And yet the alert traveler who visits the city today will be instantly mystified to learn that the locals ever called themselves the Porteños, the people of the port, for he looks around and sees no port and no water. The tableland and the sloping barrancas are still there, but the water, it would seem, has vanished. Indeed, to an almost prodigious degree, Buenos Aires has banished water from its collective civic consciousness. In a perverse way, this is a remarkable achievement, given how central water once was to the merchants and sailors who lived beside the Rio de la Plata and haunted the taverns, warehouses and brothels that stood along what is now Avenida Leandro N. Alem and was once the shoreline and the river.

True, the persistent visitor will eventually encounter those sluices that stand, majestic and unused, in Puerto Madero, a man-made parcel of infrastructure that was completed in 1898 and is now less a port than a marina without vessels. In fact, there is considerable port life in Buenos Aires even today, but tourists, as well as locals, are discouraged from ever seeking it out. Starting in the 1850s, with the creation of the customs house that once stood where you now find Parque Colón, the municipal authorities built farther and farther out into the Rio de la Plata estuary. In the course of the ensuing century, they created a band of infrastructure two kilometers thick at its widest point. Today it consists of highways, railways, housing complexes, nature preserves, shantytowns and even a local airport, all of which stand between the Porteños and the water that once was so central to their identity. Rare is the native inhabitant who has ever visited those parts of the city that still function as a port and they are essentially inaccessible to mass transportation.

For the first two and a half centuries of its existence, the city of Buenos Aires was roughly one mile deep by two miles wide, as it sat on the western bank of the Rio de la Plata. The majority of its citizens lived within fifteen minutes' walk of the river, though more likely within five minutes' walk. Today many of their descendants will go for years without ever seeing the waters of the Rio de la Plata, unless they can afford to inhabit one of the high-rises of Avenida Libertador or Puerto Madero that, having turned their backs on the city itself, offer sight lines sufficiently elevated to see past the intervening layers of landfill clear to the river.

But if you have the wherewithal to make it all the way to the northernmost limit of the city, beyond Aeroparque Jorge Newbery and the Ciudad Universitaria, you will see, at long last, the Rio de la Plata estuary essentially as it must have appeared to the first Europeans who plied the river in 1512. And then many things about the city and its history may begin to make sense. Various writers have offered a depreciative assessment of the Rio de la Plata and its brownish waters, the result of mud deposits over tens of thousands of years from the confluence of the Uruguay and Paraná rivers. But to see those waters shimmering in the light of a summer afternoon, as small craft glide by nineteenth-century

Plaza Roma (now on Avenida Leandro N. Alem), c. 1880, looking out toward the Río de la Plata. Today high-rises occupy the area covered by water in the image. (Archivo General de la Nación)

buoys of an entirely superfluous loveliness, is to understand the almost hypnotic pull that the river must once have exerted on the earlier inhabitants of Buenos Aires. For the Río de la Plata is so wide that it resembles a sea more than a river, and Uruguay, thirty miles east on the opposing bank, is too far away to be made out.

Today only a few fishermen frequent this place, waiting in silence for a tug at their line. But then, water—in any other sense than the most utilitarian—has become so foreign to modern Buenos Aires that the city has almost no public fountains of any beauty or importance.

It was on the western bank of the Río de la Plata that Juan de Garay built the first permanent settlement known as Buenos Aires. Only a few days after the formal establishment of the city on June 11, 1580, he began to draw up the city's grid and thus, almost presumptuously, to impose a strict, quadrilateral order upon the fractious state of nature. The resulting blocks—perfect squares 140 *varas,* or 420 feet, to a side—remain intact to this day and have become a template

for the extensive growth of the city all the way to what is now Avenida General Paz. Nevertheless Buenos Aires as we see it today is not
a continuous grid, but a patchwork of interrelated grids that respond
to variations in terrain, as well as to shifting patterns of demographics
and development.

There is no more emphatic expression of Sarmiento's notion of the
city as Civilization itself than Garay's imposition of that grid upon the
rude and unruly landscape that he encountered. But Barbarism—as
Garay and Sarmiento would have conceived it—was ever present and
near at hand. Other than the fort that eventually rose on the Plaza de
Mayo, no defensive structure ever surrounded Buenos Aires as it did
Montevideo, in Uruguay, which was founded one and a half centuries
later by the citizens of Buenos Aires. Without such defense, Buenos
Aires stood exposed to the surrounding indigenous populations, whose
menace, even though it diminished over time, remained very real into
the nineteenth century. Only a few miles of grassland separated the
Porteños, in their estimable grid, from the often murderous hostility of
these indigenous peoples, who sometimes captured and enslaved European women and children. Some of these natives, it was believed, even
practiced cannibalism. And even as this threat subsided, there remained
abundant reason to fear wild beasts. As late as 1840, jaguars and cou-
gars were still startling the inhabitants of what are now the outer barrios
of Floresta and Belgrano.

Ultimately, of course, civilization won out, and today Buenos Aires
stands as perhaps the most conspicuous example of a grid in urban history. Although thousands of cities around the world are laid out in this
way, none of them, not even New York, pursues the logic of the grid as
insistently, or over as large a territory, as does Buenos Aires. The Manhattan grid is better known to the world, but it was imposed 231 years
later than that of Buenos Aires, and it stretches only from 14th Street
to 155th Street. The modern Buenos Aires grid is five times larger than
Manhattan's and fully fifty times larger than the grid Garay established
in 1580. Now really a collection of grids, it is punctuated by parks and
by interesting irregularities at the points where each of these individual
grids is joined to the others.

As remarkable as the size of the Buenos Aires grid is its persistence over more than four centuries. Most cities that came under Roman rule or were founded by Rome—among them Paris, London and Verona—were similarly endowed with a grid, as were most of the cities that the Spanish inhabited in the New World, including Lima, Guadalajara and San Juan. But over the course of centuries, most of these grids went to seed, and today it takes a practiced eye to discern anything of their original form. But in Buenos Aires that pattern remains as clean and clear as the day Juan de Garay imposed it.

At the same time, the Buenos Aires grid is different from more modern grids like Manhattan's. In a sense, an urban grid resembles a massive oriental rug that has been rolled out across the surface of a city. But the Buenos Aires grid was conceived in 1580, well before the industrial revolution, while the Manhattan grid dates to 1811, when that revolution was already under way. And so, while the Porteño grid almost feels as if it were woven by hand, Manhattan's grid exhibits a machine-made regularity that, once determined, can be replicated infinitely, without variation and in the sharpest detail. But just as a hand-made rug reveals shifts in emphasis and attention that result in minute variations of surface and design, so there are telling shifts in the makeup of the Buenos Aires grid. Consider the city's historic core from Callao to Puerto Madero and from San Juan to Santa Fe. From the air, or on a map, we seem to perceive a slight wobble in the facture, the weaving, of the city's street system: these shifts, though often imperceptible to the pedestrian, go back to the very foundation of the city.

And then there are those points where the grid falls apart due to the exigencies of the terrain. For a grid to function effectively, it should stand, ideally, on level ground. But, as we have seen, the level tableland of Buenos Aires eventually comes to a sudden halt where it descends, by means of a barranca, into what once were sand flats. At this point, in the days of Garay, the planar integrity of the plateau yielded suddenly to the waywardness of nature. It is one of the ironies of the history of Buenos Aires that the large and elegant area to the north, now known as the Barrio Norte, an area that seems so quintessentially Porteño, originally lay beyond the limits of Garay's grid. Even today, although the area is highly built up, strange things happen here to the Porteño grid: it goes haywire at precisely the point where the tableland of the pampas begins its descent into what once was the river.

For hundreds of years, this part of Buenos Aires, which now includes such tourist draws as the Plaza San Martín and the Cemetery of Recoleta, was either uninhabited or given over to farmland, villas and the occasional church. It was, for centuries, terra incognita, the last refuge of desperate men, of lunatics and thieves, of anchorites and runaway slaves. Overrun with willows, thistle and carob plants, it was teeming with insects, reptiles, rare birds and the occasional puma or jaguar. Here one did not encounter the flora and fauna of the pampas, over which Garay had set his implacable grid, but rather animals and plants that are native to sand and water.

✳

FROM THE PERSPECTIVE of European civilization, there is something wondrous in the settlements and cities of the New World. Surely there were indigenous settlements in pre-Columbian Latin America, and cities such as Mexico City and Cuzco in Peru—the seats of the Aztec and Inca empires respectively—were among the largest and most developed that the ancient world had ever seen. But many of the cities that the Spanish founded in South America, and all of the cities that they established in Argentina, emerged in regions where there were few if any settled populations.

This is especially true of the region that concerns us, the pampas and the Rio de la Plata. Here the sparse communities of natives, whether Araucanians or Mapuche, led a nomadic or seminomadic life that left little imprint upon the earth. And while native populations did exist in the vicinity of Buenos Aires, in no sense did the Spanish need to expel them from the area over which Garay imposed his grid, or to remove or accommodate any preexistent structures. And so, from an urbanistic or architectural perspective, you could say that the Spanish created Buenos Aires out of nothing.

For the first two and a half centuries of its existence, from its establishment in 1580 until the expulsion of Juan Manuel de Rosas, governor of the province of Buenos Aires, in 1852, the evolution of Buenos Aires generally resembles that of most of the other cities that the Spanish founded in the New World. Both in its building stock and in the customs and clothing of the Porteños, it bore the unmistakable stamp of its Spanish roots. But starting in 1852, the city began to part ways with the rest of the country: indeed, this became legally the case when, between 1852 and 1862, it actually seceded from the Argentine Confederation.

To an ever-greater degree, the urban model that Buenos Aires followed was Paris—the Paris of Baron Haussmann and the Second Empire. Henceforth Buenos Aires would be known throughout the world as "the Paris of South America." Surely other influences—like those of North American cities—became more evident in the course of the twentieth century. But the political order that ruled the city and the nation from the accession of Bartolomé Mitre as president of Argentina in 1862 all the way to the emergence of Juan Perón in 1946, was feverishly Francophile, and their Parisian predilection was joyously imposed upon the capital.

That a city as great and complex as Buenos Aires should have emerged out of nothing, at the edge of the pampas, is astounding enough. That it should have elected to re-create Europe in the New World, over the demolished and repudiated remains of its own colonial past—something that no other city in the Western Hemisphere ever attempted to do—makes it a prodigy among the world's urban centers. In this regard, one can only concur in the query attributed to Albert Einstein, on his visit to the city in 1925: "How did they manage to create out of nothing something that looks so much like Paris?" The delirious process by which that evolution occurred is the grand theme of the ensuing chapters of this book.

TWO

THE FOUNDING OF BUENOS AIRES

(1492–1541)

AT THE DAWN OF THE AGE OF EXPLORATION, IN THE last quarter of the fifteenth century, the imagination of Europe was fired by the quest to find a sea route to India, a faster and less laborious path than the land routes of the day, which passed through regions decidedly hostile to the Christian faith. So taxing was this five-thousand-mile trek through deserts and over mountains that the spices brought back from the East were literally worth their weight in gold. Christopher Columbus, however, believed that the Indies could be reached by sailing west. And so, when he first saw the island of San Salvador, in the Greater Antilles, on the morning of October 12, 1492, he had no doubt that he had reached the subcontinent. And he would go to his grave believing it.

But by the early years of the next century, it had become abundantly clear that the land that Columbus discovered was not India at all, but an entirely new and unimagined region of the earth. Accordingly, the new world ambitions of Spain (and Portugal) quickly changed from trading in spices to acquiring as much gold and silver as possible. And while gold was duly sent back to the coffers of Castile, the sum of its value paled in comparison with the silver that was found in the New World. This silver would sustain the empire of Spain for centuries to come.

It is in the context of this pursuit of silver that one must understand the birth of Buenos Aires. It stands on the banks of an estuary known as the Rio de la Plata, the River of Silver, in a land that would come to be known as Argentina, the Land of Silver. (The name Argentina first appears in 1602, in a lengthy narrative poem of that title by Martín del Barco Centenera, but it became the official name of the country only in 1860.) In both cases, the name expressed the fervid hope that the region would abound in the coveted ore. But that was not to be. And as soon as the Spanish monarchs came to appreciate the total absence of silver in this part of South America, they lost all interest in it—beyond the goal of impeding foreign powers, especially the Portuguese, from gaining a foothold. For more than two and a half centuries, the region of Buenos Aires was allowed to languish in penurious obscurity, systematically stunted and repressed by the Spanish crown and its viceroys and governors in the New World.

Rather, the center of Spanish interest in South America was Peru, especially the region known as Alto Peru or Upper Peru, which lies within the borders of modern Bolivia. A cold, windswept, treeless, grassless expanse of dust, this region would scarcely seem worth the trouble of defending it were it not for one thing: the mountain of Potosí, which rises out of its level plain in a nearly perfect cone and is quite literally filled with silver. Together with the mines of Mexico, this one mountain sustained the Spanish Empire well into the eighteenth century, when the annual yield from its veins of silver finally began to falter. To this day, its pocked and pitted surface, seen from the air, bears the indelible scars of five centuries of mining so assiduous that it is now fully one thousand feet lower than when the Spanish first scaled its dusty slopes in 1545.

Potosí was the great hive around which all the activity of the Spanish, their indigenous serfs and their African slaves was centered in South America. All roads led to and from Potosí. As for the cities nearer to the Rio de la Plata—Buenos Aires, Santa Fe, Tucuman, Corrientes, Asunción—they existed primarily to provision Potosí.

As it happens, the region traversed by the Rio de la Plata possesses almost incalculable natural wealth. But these resources, among them some of the richest topsoil in the world, meant little to the Spanish. Furthermore, Buenos Aires was on the opposite side of the continent to Peru, and travel from one region to the other was exceedingly slow. Before the arrival of the railways in the mid-nineteenth century, travel between Potosí and Buenos Aires—whether by horse or mule or on foot—took at least two months. And with Patagonia almost entirely uninhabited and unexplored into the 1800s, Buenos Aires was—for all that Spain and the rest of Europe cared—the southern limit of the known world.

But the lack of precious metals along the Rio de la Plata transpired only gradually, and before that happened, Spain exhibited some tentative interest in the region. The first Westerner to reach the Rio de la Plata, and indeed to name it, was Juan Díaz de Solís, starting in 1512. His tenure was short and signally unsuccessful: only a few weeks after his second voyage to the region, in 1516, he sailed up the river with a contingent of his men and was attacked, slain and possibly eaten by a tribe of Charrúa Indians. Four years later, Ferdinand Magellan passed by the Rio de la Plata, probably in the vicinity of modern Buenos Aires, but he did not tarry as he continued on toward his great goal, the Pacific Ocean. Several years after that, in 1527, Sebastian Cabot, a Venetian in the service of Spain, plied the waters of the Rio de la Plata and founded the short-lived settlement of Spiritu Santo, at the confluence of the Paraná and Carcarañá rivers. This was to be the first European township ever established in what is now Argentina.

As for Buenos Aires, it was destined to be founded twice, first by Pedro de Mendoza in 1536 and then by Juan de Garay in 1580. And it all began with a baseless dream. It was a dream of fabulous and illimitable wealth, and men would be moved to suffer almost inconceivable adversity, to murder and to be slain, in the service of this dream. At the center of the dream was a vaporous entity known as the White King, El Rey Blanco. The Spanish had heard rumors about him from the natives of the pampas. No one ever claimed to have seen the White King with his own eyes, but no one doubted that he lived somewhere far to the north, further up the Rio de la Plata and the Paraná than they had ever cared to venture, and beyond the mountains to the west. His name was meant to be taken literally: to the generally dark-skinned natives of the land, what most impressed itself upon the mind was the supernatural whiteness of the king's flesh. What inflamed the imagination of the Spanish, however, were the persistent rumors of his wealth in gold and silver. Historians seem to be divided as to whether this spectral being was the pure invention of awed superstition or whether it carried within it, though at a vast remove, some relation to the Inca king Huayna Capac.

Whatever the source or substance of the rumor, it was good enough for the Spanish, who wasted no time in committing the wealth of their empire to finding the White King. By then, nearly half a century after Columbus reached San Salvador, the new and virginal world that he had discovered was a playground for adventurers, not only from Spain and Portugal, but also from England and France. In 1494 Spain and Portugal signed the Treaty of Tordesillas, by which they presumed to divide between their two nations all the territories of the New World, whose true dimensions were barely imagined at the time. In his four voyages to the Western Hemisphere, Columbus was occupied exclusively with the Caribbean, which was almost as distant from the Rio de la Plata as it was from Spain. The only part of South America that he ever reached was the northern shore of Venezuela, on his third voyage in 1498. It would be another fifteen years before Balboa first set eyes on the Pacific, and twenty years more before Pizarro, in 1533, completed the conquest of Peru, thus inaugurating Spanish dominion in South America.

By this time, the Habsburg Holy Roman Emperor, Charles V, sat on the throne of Spain. And he was distinctly uneasy to learn that the ambitious João II, king of Portugal, was planning an expedition beyond the borders of Brazil, which Pedro Álvares Cabral had claimed for Portugal in 1500. Thus began the conflict that would persist, in one form or another, for the next three centuries and more, as the Spanish and their descendants agitated to thwart the ambitions of Portugal and its descendants in the area of the Rio de la Plata. And it is in the light of this evolving policy, no less than of the pursuit of bullion, that we must conceive the founding of Buenos Aires.

In 1534 Charles V granted the forty-seven-year-old Pedro de Mendoza, knight of Alcantara and of the Order of Santiago, permission to explore the territory around the Rio de la Plata and to establish a settlement there. Although historians usually date the founding of Buenos Aires to Juan de Garay's arrival on the west bank of the Rio de la Plata in 1580, in fact Pedro de Mendoza preceded him by nearly half a century. To achieve his goal, Charles gave Mendoza 1,500 men and thirteen ships, thus making his expedition the largest ever undertaken in the Age of Exploration. To put those figures in context, forty-four years later Garay's far more successful venture required only sixty-five men. And shortly before Mendoza set off on his voyage, Pizarro managed to conquer the vast Inca Empire with fewer than two hundred men and several dozen horses.

As was often the case with the conquistadors, Don Pedro undertook the voyage at his own expense, though only after Charles had promised him annuities of 2,000 ducats a year and the title of *Adelantado,* or governor. Unlike the relatively low-born Christopher Columbus, Mendoza was descended from one of the leading families of Spain: his brothers included the Spanish ambassador in Rome and the cardinal archbishop of Seville, and he counted the governors of Mexico and Peru as his cousins. Mendoza himself had already seen much of the world and had served in the imperial army during the infamous Sack of Rome in 1527. Whatever Mendoza's attainments, however, they were not, by themselves, enough to persuade Charles to grant him the coveted letter of mark that would allow him to undertake his voyage to the New World: it seems that there was no shortage of ambitious, well-born courtiers eager to explore the Rio de la Plata and to establish a settlement in those parts. Only through the intervention of one of Don Pedro's relatives, María de Mendoza, a woman of influence at court, did he finally win the commission. Before it was over, the voyage would cost him 40,000 ducats of his own money, with the banking firms of the Fuggers and Walsers providing additional funds, as well as ships manned by German sailors. The working assumption was that, if successful, Mendoza would gain far more than he had spent or borrowed. In addition, he would win the coveted right to call himself governor, captain general and chief justice of what was to be named New Andalusia. And although, in theory, this large territory would belong to the king, in practical fact it would almost be his.

In the so-called "Capitulación de Pedro de Mendoza" (a contract drawn up in 1534 by Charles V that spelled out his and Mendoza's obligations to one another), the emperor does not have much to say about the founding of towns or cities except in the most general terms. Mendoza is permitted and obliged "to found in said lands and provinces up to three fortresses of stone, in the areas and places that are most convenient and that appear to you and to our officers to be most necessary for the maintenance and pacification of said territory."

Much of what we know about the ensuing voyage comes from Ulrich Schmidl's *Wahrhafftige Beschreibung,* an eyewitness account published in 1567 and, according to the great naval historian Samuel Eliot Morrison, "one of the most popular travel books of the [sixteenth] century." An employee of the Walser family, Schmidl came from Straubing in Lower Bavaria. In seventy dense and poorly written pages, his narrative gives a fairly complete description of the colony from its foundation in 1536 to its ultimate abandonment five years later. In general it appears to be more accurate than not, even though Morrison has his doubts: "[Schmidl] was an unpleasant character, and I do not hesitate to give [the writings of Cabeza de Vaca] the palm for verity when the two conflict, as they often do." Nevertheless, the most important, indeed the most extraordinary, elements of Schmidl's narrative are beyond controversy.

Through Schmidl we learn the crucial detail that Pedro de Mendoza suffered from syphilis and that he was very sick. This disease was ravaging Europe in the first half of the sixteenth century, and its origins can probably be found in Western man's initial encounters with the indigenous peoples of the New World. Given the immense travails and privations of a transatlantic journey that was measured in months, rather than weeks, even for a man of exemplary health, we are uncertain whether to marvel more at Don Pedro's fortitude or at his folly in undertaking his voyage in the first place. Schmidl describes him as "always melancholy, weak and ill." Indeed, of the 1,500 men and women who set sail with him from Cádiz, only about 150 returned alive, and he was not among them.

Few other details of his life have survived, and they tell us little about the man that we would want to know. But amid the mud huts that surrounded him in his short-lived settlement on the Rio de la Plata, Don Pedro lived in relative comfort, exhibiting, according to the historians Romulo de Zabala and Enrique de Gandía, "a luxury that was uncommon in those parts." This luxury included an elaborately carved bed, a standard of the Order of Saint James, a crucifix, some elegant robes and, for his table, silver plates and utensils. But one item from the posthumous list of his effects compels our attention. In addition to a sword and rosary, as well as a volume of Virgil that was part of the baggage of any literate European of the age, Mendoza brought with him a work by Erasmus—we are not told which. The great Dutch humanist, the voice of reason and reformation, was enjoying something of a vogue in Spain during the 1530s, even though he was viewed with suspicion by the more established orders. That Mendoza should have carried this volume with him across the breadth of the ocean suggests certain intellectual stirrings, perhaps a tentative questioning of received ideas that endears him to us. Such and little more is the sum of all that we know about the founder of the first settlement of Buenos Aires.

Don Pedro set sail from Cádiz in October 1534. In January of the next year, at the height of the South American summer (since their seasons are the reverse of those in the Northern Hemisphere) he reached the Rio de la Plata with his 1,500 men, as well as a few women and about seventy horses that, as we shall see hereafter, were to have far greater importance in the history of Argentina than the men who brought them. The expedition sailed up the Uruguayan side of the Rio de la Plata to the small, heavily wooded island of San Gabriel, about three miles east of what is now Colonia, a settlement founded by the Portuguese in 1680. Mendoza did not proceed directly to the future site of Buenos Aires: it would be fully a year between his arrival in the Rio de la Plata and its foundation. Instead he sent out five of his men to scout the best place to build a fortress, and for some time it was an open question whether it should stand on what is now the Argentine, or western, side

Sixteenth-century depiction—largely fanciful—of the first settlement of Buenos Aires. (Archivo General de la Nación)

of the estuary or on the opposing Uruguayan side. After due delibera-
tion, Mendoza chose the former, near an insignificant tributary of the
Rio de la Plata known as the Riachuelo, the Spanish word for rivulet.
One reason for choosing the western bank was the calculation that the
Portuguese could not attack it by land.

All this we learn from Schmidl's narrative. What he failed to provide, however, was a precise record of where the fortress was located. In
the absence of archaeological evidence, the settlement has traditionally
been placed within an area roughly one mile in length, between what is
now Parque Lezama in San Telmo to the south and Calle Chile to the
north. If it was not placed in Parque Lezama, where a rather bombastic
late-twentieth-century monument has been erected to Mendoza, there
is some reason to believe that the settlement may have occupied what
is now the Plaza Dorrego, where, each Sunday, tourists flood the flea
market. What seems certain is that the fortress did not lie on the water.
Rather, in accordance with Spanish practice elsewhere in the empire, it
sat on an elevated plateau that rises some thirty meters above sea level.

A great deal of misunderstanding attaches to the name of Mendoza's settlement. According to one legend, supported by Schmidl, the
first Spaniard to reach the shore of the future settlement, one Sancho
del Campo, exclaimed, "Que buenos aires son los de este sitio!" (How
good the air is in this place!) But that is almost certainly nonsense. In
any case, a better and more accurate translation would probably be "fair
winds" or "favorable winds."

How Buenos Aires acquired its name is a little complicated. It was
customary among the conquistadors, wherever they landed in the New
World, to name their settlement after the saint whose feast day coincided with the day of its foundation. Just as Asunción in Paraguay was
officially named Nuestra Señora de la Asunción because it was founded
on August 15, 1537, the date of the Feast of the Assumption, so Nuestra
Señora del Buen Aire was founded on February 2, the feast of Our Lady
of the Fair or Favorable Winds. This name is connected to the Merce-
darian order of Santa Maria de la Merced, which was prominent in late
medieval Spain. When Jaime II of Aragon invaded the Sardinian city of
Cagliari in 1323, he founded a chapter of the order on a hill known as

Colle di Bonaria, or Buen Aire in Spanish. Some years later, on March 25, 1370, a storm ravaged the waters off Cagliari. Some sailors, in an effort to save their ship, threw their freight overboard, and instantly the storm subsided. All of the freight sank to the bottom of the sea, with the exception of a box that the sailors followed to the shore near Cagliari. They disembarked and tried but failed to open the box, until a child, who happened to witness their attempts, called on one of the Mercedarians, who opened it without difficulty. Inside was a statue of the Madonna, known thereafter as Nuestra Señora del Buen Aire, the protectress of mariners wherever in the world they might be. This incarnation of the Madonna was apparently dear to Mendoza, who founded his settlement on her feast day.

In founding Nuestra Señora del Buen Aire, Mendoza and his men almost certainly never imagined that they were creating a city, let alone a great city, that would last for centuries. Don Pedro was tasked with establishing a *fortaleza,* or fort by which to control the surrounding territory, to explore the estuary, to keep out the Portuguese and—as was still hoped in 1536—to exploit such reserves of silver and gold as the land might yet yield. There were many such forts throughout the Spanish dominions in the New World, and few were built to serve anything other than a defensive function.

The reader will recall that, in Charles's "Capitulación," he explicitly commanded Mendoza to build up to three fortresses of stone. Although there was considerable precedent for stone structures throughout the Spanish dominions in the New World, one would be hard put to find any useable stone on the pampas, especially in the vicinity of the Rio de la Plata. In fact, until the railway arrived in Argentina in the 1850s and made possible the movement of large quantities of stone over long distances, buildings in Buenos Aires were overwhelmingly formed from sun-dried clay and then brick. And so, when Mendoza fortified his settlement, he did so with thick clay walls that were scarcely six feet high and needed, according to Schmidl, to be repaired each morning. Yet within those walls Mendoza ordered the construction of four churches: those of Nuestra Señora del Buen Aire and Nuestra Señora de la Santa Trinidad, as well as a church for the Dominicans and another for the

Franciscans. As was not an uncommon practice at the time, these humble structures were made of wood from the ships that had brought Don Pedro and his men. For just as there was no stone on the pampas, so there were few trees to provide timber for construction. And since it was most unlikely that 1,500 settlers would ever need to embark at the same time, the settlement must have had more ships than it could possibly use.

Even in embryonic form, Don Pedro's settlement was fundamentally different from Buenos Aires in its second foundation. Mendoza's settlement was nothing more than an earthwork enclosure within which were arrayed, in no particular order, the four churches and a number of houses scarcely better than huts. The conspicuous absence of a *Cabildo,* or civic center, supports the idea that Don Pedro had given little thought to founding a city. According to historians Margarita Gutman and Jorge Enrique Hardoy, "The fact that [the first foundation] was not organized on a grid and that its lots were not divided in a systematic way, as was the case with such earlier settlements of the 1520s and 1530s as Puebla, Oaxaca, Guadalajara, Lima, Trujillo (in Peru), Quito, Cali and many more, seems to reveal some doubts about the convenience of establishing a definitive settlement in a territory so little known and of such doubtful prospects for success."

Those concerns were well founded, for the settlement was beset with problems from the start. It is noteworthy that when Columbus reached San Salvador, he encountered a docile and friendly population that fed the newcomers and even offered them such gold as they had. But the nation that rose to meet Pedro de Mendoza and his men on the Rio de la Plata was very different: these were the Querandí, a fierce and bellicose tribe. When the Spanish arrived, they solicited and received food from the locals, who supplied it with some measure of goodwill in the hope and expectation that the strangers would soon move on. In their arrogance, however, the Spanish expected the natives to continue providing for them indefinitely, which the indigenous people, naturally, were unwilling to do. Or perhaps they were unable, since the pampas—despite having a very fertile topsoil—bring forth little sustenance on their own. And so, after a few weeks of provisioning a host of 1,500 men and women, as well as horses, the Querandís refused to provide any more food. It was at this point that the Spanish tried to gain through coercion what they had previously gotten through goodwill: when the indigenous tribes simply ceased to show up with food, the Spanish went on the attack. This did not end well for them.

The Riachuelo is the small river that marks the southern limit of Buenos Aires and empties into the estuary of the Rio de la Plata. But a little farther inland, and for the remaining forty miles of its meanderings, this river is known as La Matanza. It passes through a *partido* (roughly equivalent to one of our counties) that is also named La Matanza (with a well-known university that is called La Matanza as well). The Rio de la Matanza, or the River of Slaughter, is so named because soon after Don Pedro's fort was completed, his brother Diego mounted an attack on the Querandís, who responded by ambushing him on the banks of the Matanza. To this day, the river's name recalls the savage manner in which Diego de Mendoza was cut down five centuries ago.

Here as well we find a crucial difference between the Querandís and those indigenous populations that Cortés encountered in Mexico and Pizarro in Peru. Two of the world's most splendid civilizations, the Aztec and the Inca, were conquered and enslaved by a few hundred Spaniards equipped with little more than horses and harquebuses. Having never before encountered horses or firearms, the natives prostrated themselves in terror before the Spanish, as though before superior beings if not gods. The Querandís, by contrast, were hunter-gatherers who lacked fixed dwellings, as well as art and those amenities of life that distinguished the great pre-Columbian kingdoms of Mexico and Peru. And yet when attacked by the Spanish, the Querandís defiantly stood their ground and answered the European rifles with flaming arrows of devastating effect. And though they had never before seen anything like a horse, they immediately contrived a definitively lethal response. Their weapon of choice was the bola, which would go on to have a long career among the gauchos who were—in part—the descendants of the Querandís. The bola consisted of a pair of stone balls joined by a rope. The Querandís had been using it for thousands of years to fell the occasional deer. But now this bola was deployed with unerring aim against the legs of the charging steeds, until horse and rider together were brought down.

And so it was that Diego de Mendoza and most of the men who had ridden out with him were killed beside the waters of the Matanza, with only a few of them managing to make it back to the safety of the fort. But presently a far more grievous threat arose. In general, Ulrich Schmidl is not to be trusted where numbers are concerned. We have no reason, then, to accept at face value his claim that 25,000 angry natives now rose up against the Spanish and laid siege to the fort on June 24, less than five months after its foundation. More likely, and more ominous, is his assertion that the besieging host no longer consisted only of Querandís, but of a confederacy of local tribes, including the Guaranís and Zechuruas.

The siege lasted over a month. Once the more conventional supplies were used up, the Spanish were reduced to eating rats, mice, pigeons and any shoe leather they could lay hands on. One day, in desperation, three men slaughtered and ate a horse, in punishment for which they were summarily hanged. At this point in his narrative, Schmidl relates that their corpses were left dangling and that, during the night, one or more of the inhabitants cut off parts of the corpses' legs and greedily consumed them. Schmidl claims to have seen the mutilated remains with his own eyes.

This account stands confirmed in the *Romance Elegiaco* of Luis de Miranda, one of Mendoza's lieutenants and the author of what appears to be the first poem written in Buenos Aires. Like so many of the tango lyrics of a later age, this fine poem is shot through with a tragic sense of life:

> *En punto desde aquel día*
> *Todo fue de mal en mal.*
> *La gente y el general*
> *Y capitanes.*
> *Trabajos, hambres, y afanes*
> *Nunca nos faltó en la tierra*
> *Y así nos hizo la guerra*
> *La cruel.*

*(Indeed, from that day forth, it was one suffering after another, for the
common folk, the general [Mendoza] and his captains. Labor, hunger
and toil never left us in that earth, and thus earth itself cruelly waged
war against us.)*

But his most embittered passage concerns the hunger that he and the
other settlers experienced: "What caused us even greater suffering was
the hunger, the most extreme ever seen. . . . The dung and feces that
some could not digest others ate in sadness, a horrible thing! It came to
such a pass that, as in Jerusalem, they even ate the flesh of man. What
we witnessed there was never seen in scripture, to eat the very flesh of
one's brother!"

It is often believed, mistakenly, that the first Buenos Aires vanished
after only a few months, due to the siege and the continuous aggressions
of the indigenous populations. In fact, although many of the Spanish
died during the siege, most survived, mainly because the hunger that
afflicted them began to afflict their besiegers as well, and so the siege
was lifted.

The settlement would last for another five years, and when it ended
it did so for reasons that had nothing to do with the hostility of the
local inhabitants. In part it survived thanks to the very humbleness of
its built structures. Without gunpowder and projectiles, the indigenous
peoples would have found it almost impossible to destroy the settlement completely. Though they presumably succeeded in setting fire to
some of the houses, with their flammable thatched roofs, these simple
structures, scarcely more complex than tents, could be rebuilt in a day
or two. Even the death of a significant portion of the inhabitants, tragic
though it was, probably had the pragmatic benefit of mitigating an unsustainable overpopulation relative to the existing food supply.

This problem of provisioning would hinder the growth of Buenos
Aires for centuries to come. Part of the problem, as we have seen, was
the absence of a naturally abundant food source. But mainly the problem was one of the settlers' own making. Why, we must ask, didn't
they simply grow and harvest more crops than the barest minimum?
Here we come up against the fact that Mendoza's voyage was perhaps

the most extraordinarily short-sighted in the entire Age of Exploration. Fully ten times the size of most other voyages to the New World, it had made no plans for provisioning its members once they arrived. A great many of the men and women who traveled with Mendoza were aristocrats. Unlike the proletarian bulk of most other voyages of that time, Mendoza and his men were part of the beau monde. "The fleet made a brave show," Morrison writes, "but one thing it lacked was know-how. Fernando de Oviedo, who saw it sail from Seville in August 1534, said that 'without doubt 'twas a company which would have made a good show in Caesar's army, or in all parts of the world.'" Together with these brave figures came scholars, lawyers and at least one surgeon and one barber. What was conspicuously lacking, however, were farmers, men who knew how to draw sustenance from the land. Indeed, the sort of men who were most likely to undertake such a voyage in the first place were precisely the sort who saw themselves as *hidalgos,* or gentleman soldiers, beneath whose dignity it was to till the fields with their own hands. What a Jesuit missionary, Miguel Herre (or Hesse), observed of Buenos Aires in 1727 could apply just as well to Buenos Aires in 1536: "In this part of the world anyone from Spain, or anyone who is white, is considered a nobleman. They are distinguished from the rest [of the inhabitants] by their language and attire, but not by their dwellings, which are those of beggars. But that doesn't diminish in any way their vaunting and their pride. They hold all skills in contempt. The man who has a skill and vigorously applies it is dismissed as a slave, while, on the contrary, the man who knows nothing and lives a life of leisure is accounted a gentleman and a noble."

Under such circumstances, the Spanish eked out a penurious existence beside the Rio de la Plata, sustaining themselves as they might with the fish they could catch in the shallows of the river, as well as the food they purchased from the local population and whatever else was brought over on the one or two ships that arrived each year from Spain. Though the settlement could hardly be said to prosper, it could surely have stumbled along in this way for some time.

The subsequent history of the first settlement of Buenos Aires is extremely unclear and reports tend to be partial, conflicting, ignorant and incomplete. We do know that the first Buenos Aires ceased to exist as of 1541. And we have reason to believe that the Querandís attacked several more times, and that, several more times, the Spanish rebuilt their settlement. Beyond that, however, we can only conjecture.

Charles V had granted Mendoza permission to build up to three settlements. And so, in 1537, one year after founding Buenos Aires, he sent his second in command, the lieutenant Juan de Ayolas, to establish what was to become yet another of the great cities of South America, Asunción, capital of modern Paraguay. This city, despite its depressed fortunes in more recent years, was destined to grow faster than Buenos Aires, in large part because its relations with the indigenous population were far more harmonious (as evidence whereof, modern Paraguay's population is predominantly Indian) and because the indigenous people, being less nomadic than those of the Rio de la Plata, had acquired some understanding of agriculture.

While Ayolas went north to establish the fort of Asunción, Don Pedro set sail for Spain with the intention of soliciting reinforcements for Buenos Aires. He placed his old friend Francisco Ruiz Galán in charge of the colony. Don Pedro never made it to Spain, however, but died en route somewhere in the Atlantic near the Canary Islands. He was fifty years old.

As for Ayolas, as he continued up the Paraná past Asunción, he went missing and was presumed dead. His second in command, Domingo Martínez de Irala, took over as governor of Asunción and acted as governor of the settlement on the Rio de la Plata. What happened thereafter is all confusion. Once news of Mendoza's death reached the ear of Charles V, he chose as his replacement Álvar Núñez Cabeza de Vaca, one of the most eminent and extraordinary men of the sixteenth century. His life was so full of incident that it must be told in brief.

Born in 1488 in Jerez de la Frontera, Cabeza de Vaca was twenty-three when he joined the Holy League against France, and he took part in the Battles of Ravenna and Puente de la Reina. But his greatest adventure began when, nearly forty years old, he sailed to the Americas with Pánfilo de Narváez in search of the fabled Fountain of Youth. Thus he became one of the first Europeans ever to set foot in what is now the United States when his expedition, sailing from Cuba, made landfall in Tampa Bay, Florida. But as the party crossed the Gulf of Mexico toward the mouth of the Mississippi, a storm arose and more than two hundred of the men perished. Only four survived, one of whom was Cabeza de Vaca. Undaunted, he continued west, thus becoming the first Westerner to explore Texas and New Mexico and Arizona. For the next eight years he lived among the native populations, learning their languages and using what medicine he knew to care for their sick. In the process he became so honored among them that they chose him as their shaman and, in ever growing numbers, accompanied him on his wanderings. For eight years he saw no Christians or Europeans. And when, in 1537, he finally returned to Spain, he wrote a book of memoirs, *Naufragios,* or *Shipwrecks,* that contains the first ethnological observations ever made of the indigenous peoples of the Gulf of Mexico.

Even in his fifties, Cabeza de Vaca was not ready to retire, and so he solicited and was awarded the title of Adelantado of the Rio de la Plata on Mendoza's death. He set sail late in 1540 and arrived in the Rio de la Plata in 1541. And when bad weather delayed his reaching Buenos Aires, he headed up the Paraná River to the famous Iguazú Falls, which he was thus the first Westerner ever to see and describe.

But when finally he came to Asunción, he learned that the settlement of Nuestra Señora del Buen Aire was no more, that it had been razed and its population had moved to Asunción, on orders of Domingo de Irala. We can only guess at the reason. Irala's "intentions," Gutman and Hardoy write, "have never been made clear." Cabeza de Vaca immediately had run-ins with Irala, who clearly saw the newcomer as a threat to his rule. Irala claimed, on grounds so spurious as to amount to insubordination, that he was unable to give up his power to Cabeza de Vaca because he held it during the absence of Juan de Ayolas and could not relinquish it until he had definitive news as to whether the man was still alive. Although Cabeza de Vaca was eventually installed as Adelantado, Irala soon contrived to have him arrested, and in 1544 Cabeza de Vaca was sent back to Spain in chains. Once he arrived there, however, all charges were dropped. He published a second volume of his memoirs in which he gave his side of the story and what he understood about the fate of the first Buenos Aires.

While Cabeza de Vaca was still stationed off the coast of Brazil,

Domingo de Yrala and Alonso Cabrera, a veedor [roughly, an accountant to the king], depopulated the port and people of Buenos Aires, which had been established on the Rio del Paraná [*sic*]. On learning this [in Asunción], I sailed to Buenos Aires with 140 men. All of those whom I encountered in said territory complained that the above mentioned pair had depopulated said port, and they said publicly that the pair had acted so that His Majesty would not learn of the death of Juan de Ayolas and of other Christians whose death was principally caused by Domingo de Yrala, since he had not properly governed the settlement, for which reason it was taken from his charge. Also it was alleged that he had so acted in order to profit from the merchandise left in Buenos Aires by Valencian merchants, silks, cloths and other things of great value; and also in order to inquire of the natives as to the location of gold and silver, so that, by sending it to His Majesty, he would win the governorship.

From the narrative of Cabeza de Vaca it becomes clear that, at the very least, Buenos Aires was not destroyed by any hostile natives. Indeed, if the passage is believed, the fact that Irala sought the help of the natives in finding silver and gold suggests that a certain modus vivendi had developed between the parties. It also appears circumstantially that, to the very end, Spanish merchant vessels, though few, were entering and leaving Buenos Aires, and that—in spite of their rugged existence—the first settlers had a taste for luxuries. Finally, from Cabeza's narrative we learn the startling fact that, even after the settlement had been depopulated, some Westerners (or Christians, as he calls them) continued to linger in the vicinity of the once and future Buenos Aires.

As for Cabeza de Vaca himself, he would never leave Spain again. As remarkable as were his achievements as an explorer, he accomplished one last thing that few other conquistadors could ever claim: he died at seventy, in his bed, of old age.

THREE

THE COLONIAL CITY

(1542–1776)

AT THE BUSY INTERSECTION OF AVENIDA LEANDRO N. Alem and Rivadavia stands a bronze statue of Juan de Garay, the founder of the second Buenos Aires. His suit of armor, spiked helmet and commanding posture have surely reminded more than one pedestrian of the Commendatore who, in the final act of Mozart's great opera, condemns the errant Don Giovanni to hell. Conceived in 1915 by Gustav Heinrich Eberlein, it is a monument of high-pitched late Romanticism: one almost expects that, at any moment, the eyes of its scowling countenance will glow to incandescence. The statue points downward to the ground where, more than four centuries ago, Garay planted *El Arbol de la Justicia,* the Tree of Justice, and ordered the construction of a fortress that would serve as the spiritual center of the new city and eventually as the moral matrix of the entire Argentine nation.

In late June 1541, soon after Domingo de Irala and Alonso de Cabrera razed the first Buenos Aires, the settlement of Pedro de Mendoza, its absence began to be urgently felt. "Buenos Aires was indispensable to mariners entering the Rio de la Plata," the historians Romulo Zabala and Enrique de Gandía have written. "After a long ocean-crossing, ships needed a port in which to reprovision in order to travel up the Paraná

River to Paraguay. Not having this port, however, they encountered enormous difficulties. . . . The error [of Irala] was apparent, and the Spanish kings tried by every means to undo it."

In the decades that followed, several efforts were made to reestablish Buenos Aires, but few got as far as sending a ship and crew south from Asunción. It was only when Juan Torres de Vera y Aragon, Garay's father-in-law, became governor in Asunción that things changed. Appointing Garay lieutenant governor, he charged him "in the name of the king and in my name to establish a city in the port of Buenos Aires."

And so, on June 11, 1580, thirty-nine years after the first Buenos Aires was destroyed, Garay refounded the city, probably within a mile of its original location. Garay gave the city a new name: *la Ciudad de la Santísima Trinidad y Puerto de Santa María del Buen Ayre*—the City of the Most Holy Trinity and of the Port of Saint Mary of the Fair Winds—since the second foundation coincided with the Feast of the Holy Trinity. To this day, writers sometimes refer to Buenos Aires as La Trinidad, much as New Yorkers call their city the Big Apple.

For Juan de Garay, Buenos Aires was but one episode in a life devoted to serving the cause of the Spanish Empire. Born into a family of conquistadors in 1528, he was not an aristocrat like Mendoza. His exact place of birth is subject to dispute, with both the Basques and Castilians claiming him as their own. Wherever it was, he did not stay long. At the age of fifteen, in 1544, he followed his uncle, Pedro de Zárate, to the New World and never returned to Spain. By all accounts, Garay was impetuous and impatient. On orders from the crown, he founded Santa Fe in 1573 and Buenos Aires in 1580, but only after he had completed his campaign to pacify the warring Guaraní tribes. No sooner had he founded the second Buenos Aires, however, than he returned to Santa Fe to quell a revolt of the settlers he had left behind. Soon afterward he went exploring the southern Rio de la Plata all the way to Mar del Plata, 250 miles south of Buenos Aires, before going in quest of the mythical City of the Caesars, rumored to exist in deepest Patagonia. Expecting a land of giants and ghosts, he found only the flatness of the pampas and a horde of Querandí Indians, who killed him in an ambush in 1583 at the age of fifty-four.

❊

"WE SHAPE OUR BUILDINGS," Winston Churchill once wrote. "Thereafter, they shape us." In its brevity and penetration, this statement is one of the finest things ever said about architecture and about urbanism as well. And its truth is borne out in Buenos Aires. Garay laid out the streets of his city along the western bank of the Rio de la Plata. There was nothing inevitable about his choice of this spot, nor any invincible necessity in his decision to lay out his grid in square blocks measuring 140 varas (420 feet) per side. But such were his specifications, and now, nearly four and a half centuries later, a city of millions moves along the circuit of streets that he arbitrarily specified. Through twenty generations, the Porteños have lived out their lives in such obedience to those specifications that, as the city has expanded far beyond its original dimensions, it has scrupulously preserved his measurements except where the terrain prevented it. How different the lives of the Porteños would be if their city had developed in an organic, nongeometric fashion; or if its blocks had been 80 varas to a side rather than 140; or if that grid had been laid down—according to the canonic practice of Spanish city planning—from northeast to southwest rather than along the north-south axis that dominates central Buenos Aires to this day.

The work of dividing the city into a grid required considerable surveying skill and was not completed until October 17, 1580, more than four months after the formal creation of the city. The original grid stretched from Avenida Independencia to Calle Viamonte on the north-south axis, while the river, along what is now Avenida Leandro N. Alem, bordered it to the east and Salta-Libertad marked its western limit.

From the start, this second Buenos Aires would be very different from the first. Though it contained a fort, it would not itself be fortified with an encircling wall. In part, the ambition to found a true city rather than the garrison that Mendoza had built reflected the new understanding by Spain that this part of its empire held little in the way of silver or gold and that the territory was far more important for its strategic value. Furthermore, a new king, Phillip II, now ruled in Madrid, and he was well versed in the latest developments in urban planning. Surely the form of the cities founded under his watch was largely dictated by functionalism; but these cities bore some trace of those new ideas about the city as a work of art that had first been elucidated by the Florentine intellectual Leon Battista Alberti more than a century earlier.

The ultimate archetype of the Buenos Aires grid, and of every other Spanish colonial grid, is the Spanish city of Santa Fe de Granada, founded in 1483. And although Columbus's short-lived Santo Domingo, established on Hispaniola in 1494, was the first grid city in the New World, grids became standard practice only with the publication, in 1573, of the so-called *Leyes de los Indios* (*Laws of the Indies*). Although their nine vast volumes sought to regulate every aspect of Spanish occupation of the New World, today they are remembered mainly for their chapters on urban planning.

These prescriptions included siting a city atop an elevated place, as Garay did when he set Buenos Aires some thirty meters above the level of the Rio de la Plata. He also made provisions for agriculture and cattle rearing, whose absence had proved so disastrous in the days of Mendoza. But the *Laws of the Indies* also addressed aesthetic concerns, advocating that houses be built in a uniform style (as was generally the case in Buenos Aires) and that the city have a central square, today's Plaza de Mayo. Most importantly and famously, however, the *Laws of the Indies* prescribed that cities be laid out in a grid, *a cordel y regal*, "according to string and ruler." Of all the hundreds of colonial settlements conceived according to the grid, none embodied the prescriptions of the *Laws of the Indies* better than Buenos Aires.

Contemporary Buenos Aires, like all important cities in the world, has a hierarchy of streets. But into the early nineteenth century, it was rather rare, anywhere in the world, for one street to be significantly broader or more beautiful than the others. Today, the potential monotony of the Porteño grid is greatly relieved, and the pedestrian's sense of its structure is greatly enhanced, by the broad avenues that divide it at roughly four-block intervals from north to south: Santa Fe, Córdoba, Corrientes and so on. But that refinement was first suggested only in 1827 by the Argentine president Bernardino Rivadavia, and it would

The flatness of Buenos Aires: las Cinco Esquinas (the Five Corners) at the intersection of Libertad, Juncal and Quintana, in 1870. (Archivo General de la Nación)

not begin to be put into practice until Torcuato de Alvear became *inten-dente,* a mayor of sorts, in 1883. In the three centuries before Alvear, the Buenos Aires grid must have seemed relentless in its uninflected regular-ity. When the young Charles Darwin arrived in 1832, he described it as "one of the most regular [cities] in the world. Every street is at right angles to the one it crosses, and the parallel ones being equidistant, the houses are collected into solid squares of equal dimensions." To make matters worse, most of the streets Darwin saw were without trees, pave-ment or sidewalks. If there was one saving grace amid this monotony, it was that the streets, even under Garay, were eleven varas wide, almost twice the width of the streets of contemporary Paris, London and Rome.

✱

WE KNOW THE NAME of every one of the sixty-five original set-tlers who stood beside Juan de Garay at the official founding of the city on June 11, 1580—or at least the heads of families, not counting their dependents and servants. Overwhelmingly they had been citizens of Asunción, presumably *criollos,* that is to say, born to Spanish parents in the New World. A few of them came from Spain and so were seen as being a step up from the criollos in the punctilious caste system that pervaded the Spanish Empire. Others are listed as Americans, presumably because they were of indigenous parentage. Of these sixty-five canonic settlers, all were men with the unique exception of one Ana Diaz.

We do not know exactly where Pedro de Mendoza founded the first Buenos Aires, but Juan de Garay surely did, since at least one of his companions, a Portuguese mariner named Antonio Tomás, had been a member of Mendoza's settlement before it was abandoned. After the initial settlers had removed to Asunción, the memory of the first settlement may have survived long enough for them to tell their children and grandchildren, some of whom decided, four decades on, to return to the site and found a second city over the remains of the first.

It is even possible that at least one structure from the time of the first settlement remained at the founding of the second. Among the more important and elegant barrios of the modern city is Retiro, in its northeast corner. The name, signifying a hermitage or place of retirement, is thought to date to the time when one of Mendoza's men killed another man and, ridden by remorse, took up residence here. Nearly two miles north of Mendoza's settlement, it was deserted then, except for the wild beasts that haunted the strand at the base of the barranca. Whatever the truth of the rumor, Retiro is the site of some of the oldest historical events in Buenos Aires, perhaps the only part of the city that, on Garay's arrival, preserved any traces of the initial settlement. What is certain is that a convent, known as the Ermita de San Sebastián, was established there in 1608, on what is today the Plaza San Martín, and that Agustín de Robles bought land there at the end of the seventeenth century and built a house on it that he named El Retiro, presumably to honor either or both of the previous settlements on the property. It is from the Robles house that the barrio takes its name.

Once the grid was securely traced and the city's patron saint, Saint Martin of Tours, had been selected, Garay set about distributing the lots in October 1580. Those lots in the center of the city, nearest to the

Eighteenth-century copy of a map of Juan de Garay's grid, with the lots and the names of their recipients. (Archivo General de la Nación) eventual site of the fortress, were considered the most valuable and so were divided into quarters, with each of the sixty-five original settlers receiving one of these parcels. In addition to this quarter-block, each settler received an entire block beyond the center for agricultural exploitation. It happens that we possess an eighteenth-century copy of the original chart of these distributions, with all the names intact. The most desirable lot was given to the governor of Asunción, Juan Torres de Vera y Aragon, who had authorized his son-in-law to found the city in the first place. This plot occupied the square between the fort and the Plaza Mayor. For himself Garay took the block next to that, on Rivadavia between Reconquista and 25 de Mayo: centuries later it would be the site of the first Teatro Colón, and later still, of the Banco de la Nación, whose second incarnation stands there today. Ana Diaz, the one woman who joined the expedition, received the lot that stands at the clamorous intersection of Florida and Corrientes, in the Microcentro, or downtown business district. Today it is the site of a Burger King. Lots were also assigned to the Franciscans and Dominicans and to the Hospital of San Martín.

And yet there was something almost comically presumptuous in that distribution. Even if you count all the dependents and servants who accompanied the initial settlers, the population would scarcely reach one thousand inhabitants, scattered across a territory that today is home to several hundred thousand. In reality, it would take more than two centuries to flesh out the grid, which, well into the eighteenth century, occupied an irregular territory scarcely ten blocks wide and three or four blocks deep. Along its east-west axis, it could be comfortably traversed in around six minutes; along its north-south axis, in a quarter of a hour. Even in Darwin's day, two and a half centuries later, when the population was forty times what it had been in 1600, the grid had large gaps lacking in architectural or even agricultural development. And so, for centuries to come, Buenos Aires was more like a village than a city.

Today the grid of Buenos Aires is a delightful thing. But for hundreds of years, it was nothing more than a relentless series of muddy, filthy streets. Each of them was the same length, with a spotty sequence of one-story adobe houses that were entirely without ornament. These streets lacked sidewalks and were littered with detritus that attracted roving dogs and not a few rats. Other than the central square beside the fortress, there was no public space or greenery, and few public buildings even aspired to the status of architecture. From out of this wearisome matrix a church might arise, towering above the surrounding structures and visible from any part of the city. But other than that, there was little to see. Garay himself seemed so uncertain of the success of his city that, according to Zabala and Gandía, he let it be known that "if it were necessary to move the city to a better location than the one it occupied, this could be done with the consent of the civic leaders (*los alcaldes y regidores*)."

———— ❋ ————

IN FACT, BUENOS AIRES WAS NOT intended for glory at all: it was founded, as we have seen, to serve a city greater than itself, Potosí, with its silver mines in Alto Peru. Buenos Aires was meant to play a small role in a vast empire that reached from modern Oregon down to the Straits of Magellan, a territorial extension of about 8,000 miles, not counting the Philippines or Spain itself. It was an empire of almost incredible size, nearly twice as broad, end to end, as the Roman Empire under the Antonines or the united Caliphate that reached, albeit briefly, from India to Morocco. It was, in territorial breadth, the largest empire the world would ever see.

So vast was the empire of Charles V that he divided it in half, creating in 1535 the Viceroyalty of New Spain, centered in Mexico, and in 1542 the Viceroyalty of Peru, which comprised most of South America, including modern Argentina. The principal port of the Viceroyalty of Peru was and must remain Lima. The Spanish were adamant about this, and the Viceroy in Lima was prepared to fight to preserve his primacy. By no means was Buenos Aires to become a center of commerce in its own right and thus a rival to Lima. To ensure that this never happened, the crown essentially closed Buenos Aires to almost all trade. Aside from selling the hide and fat of cows—but no other part, since meat had not yet become an exportable commodity—the Porteños were discouraged from the development of manufacturing. It was the ambition of the crown that the city remain little more than a market for the products and wares of Spanish manufacturers. It is a curious, almost unparalleled development in world history that a government should energetically suppress the native growth and prosperity of an important part of its dominion. As John Lynch has written, "With their port closed to direct commerce with Spain and their imports canalized through distant Lima, [Buenos Aires] languished on the periphery of the empire."

This is the point at which the story of Buenos Aires becomes boring, and it will remain so for two long and uneventful centuries. It is so boring that the leading historians of early Buenos Aires, Zabala and Gandía, feel compelled to avow, 435 pages into the first of two volumes devoted to the colonial city: "The 18th Century began for Buenos Aires with no extraordinary event that either slowed or accelerated the monotonous rhythm of its days." Surely some developments occurred: occasionally a pirate raid might stir things up, and it was not unheard of, during the feast of Saint Martin, for the Cabildo (the town hall and seat of local government) to stage a bullfight on what is now the Avenida 9 de Julio. But one could hardly claim that the city was thriving.

And so, almost from the moment that Garay founded his city to the creation of the Viceroyalty of the Rio de la Plata in 1776, the condition of Buenos Aires was one of permanent and systematic abasement.

In theory the crown wanted to attract settlers to Buenos Aires, but the closed port system that they imposed discouraged this goal and made it difficult for the Porteños to support themselves. In response to local pressure, the crown relented in 1618 to the point of allowing two ships a year to sail between Seville and Buenos Aires. These shipments, however, were at best irregular and often nonexistent. To make matters worse, in 1622 the crown undertook to seal off Buenos Aires from the interior settlements to the west by establishing a customs house in Córdoba to ensure that no products illicitly produced in Buenos Aires penetrated the hinterland, let alone reached Potosí. In consequence, Buenos Aires never developed, prior to achieving independence in 1816, the sort of merchant elite that arose in Lima. Furthermore, they were cut off from the capital markets, and the absence of wood and other forms of fuel in the vast and treeless pampas inhibited the development of larger industries.

The only industry that was officially permitted was the sale of cow hides and leather goods, to this day one of the most pervasive industries in Buenos Aires and across Argentina. The abundance and quality of the hides, as well as the skill with which the local craftsmen worked them, caused the products of the pampas to be eagerly sought as far away as North America and Europe, all the way to Russia.

Perhaps the most lucrative official source of profit, however, was the slave trade. Though Spain and its colonies made extensive use of slave labor throughout the colonial period, they rarely trafficked in slaves themselves, since they had never had any substantial presence in Africa, the source of the trade. For this assistance they looked to other nations: the Portuguese, the French and, eventually, the English. In 1701, France was granted the first official license, or *asiento,* for ten years, to sell slaves, mostly from the Congo and Angola. Their market stood in what today is the Parque Lezama in San Telmo, beyond what was then the city's southern limit. Afterward this asiento was transferred to the British, who kept it for nearly a century and held their auctions in what is now Plaza San Martín, to the north. There they remained until 1793, when the market migrated again, this time to Barracas, all the way in the south beside the Riachuelo. In each case, the traffic in slaves was conducted outside the official limits of the city.

Beyond the inherent viciousness of slavery as an institution, the lot of the slave who resided in Buenos Aires—as well as in the other cities of modern Argentina—was not quite as intolerable as, say, the slave labor in the mines of Potosí. In the Rio de la Plata there were, as yet, no big industries, certainly none that required the massive amounts of manpower that slave labor provided in the British colonies of North America. Most of the slaves in Buenos Aires were either domestic servants or craftsmen, like barbers and silversmiths, and they were allowed by law to seek redress of mistreatment by their owners. So great was the need for slaves within the city that, by 1800, as much as a quarter or even a third of the population was of African descent. This fact is all the more remarkable when you consider that by the end of the nineteenth century, there would remain almost no visible trace of the African population that once abounded in Buenos Aires. How that came to pass will be examined in a later chapter. For now, let it be said that the need for slaves was such that legal sales could not meet demand and had to be supplemented by the illegal trade, at which the Porteños soon became very adept.

For the prompt and natural consequence of Spain's ill-conceived suppression of commerce was that all the mercantile impulses of the Porteños shifted instantly to contraband. This would remain the chief business of Buenos Aires until 1776, when it finally became the capital of the new Viceroyalty of the Rio de la Plata. In the meantime, silver bullion and much else that was not supposed to be in Buenos Aires was delivered into waiting French, English and Dutch galleons that were not supposed to be docked in the Riachuelo, about a mile south of the city limits. Soon, it seemed, everyone was taking part in this contraband, including the Jesuits and even some of the magistrates who had been appointed precisely to shut down such illegal activities.

As a result, some of the Porteños grew very rich. But none of their fortunes went to beautifying the city. None of it, at least not before the establishment of the viceroyalty, went to constructing a park or noble avenue, a fine theater or an especially ornate church. In 1727, Michael Hesse, a German Jesuit resident in the port, wrote that "Buenos Aires is called a city, but many villages in Germany are bigger. . . . In itself, Buenos Aires is ugly. It has only three churches, of which ours [Sant' Ignacio] is the worst."

Not even elegant private dwellings, though they could have been easily afforded, rose to adorn the Porteño streetscape. Rather, all of this wealth was turned inward. In 1658, the French traveler Acarete du Biscay wrote admiringly that "the houses of the people are made of mud, because there is little stone in the region, all the way to Peru. All of the houses have one story and are very spacious. They have large patios and, behind each house, is a large garden with orange, lemon, fig, apple and pear trees." As for the houses of the upper classes, although their exteriors differed little from those of humbler rank, inside they were "adorned with wall-hangings, paintings, and other ornaments, as well as beautiful furniture, and all of those who are passably rich are served on silver plates and have many negro servants." A century later, one would have observed much the same thing.

The one area of legitimate commerce permitted to the Porteños was, as we have seen, raising livestock. Buenos Aires was cow country, since livestock thrived on the pampas to a degree that nearly strains credulity. Consider that livestock, with enough pasture and without natural predators, will double every three years. When Mendoza's settlement was abandoned in 1541, twelve horses were left behind, five of them mares. Between that date and the refounding of the city in 1580 was a span of thirty-nine years, or thirteen three-year generations. And so, when Garay returned to the site less than forty years later, those twelve domesticated horses had increased to 100,000 wild horses. Soon cattle were introduced into the pampas and they fared even better.

In due course, the physical remains of the cow, especially its hide and leather, became fully integrated into the lives and homes of the Porteños. Early on, doors, windows and roofs were often covered with hides; not just clothing but also furniture like chairs and cots was made out of leather.

Acarete du Biscay describes a remarkable spectacle. The entire wealth of Buenos Aires, he wrote, "consists of livestock, which multiply so prodigiously . . . that the Pampas are almost completely covered with them. . . . When I expressed my astonishment at the sight of such an infinite number of cattle, they told me of a stratagem they sometimes use when they fear an enemy invasion. They drive a great number of bulls, cows, horses and other animals toward the shore, making it completely impossible for any large number of men, even if they do not fear the fury of these animals, to open up a path through this great multitude of beasts."

In one sense, the degree of the Spanish monarchy's interest in Buenos Aires is manifested on every street corner. Everywhere you look you see—nothing. Nothing, in any case, from before 1800. If Buenos Aires had figured as prominently in the eyes of the King of Spain as Mexico City or Lima, it could boast today, as they do, a magnificent Baroque cathedral dominating its main square.

With the exception of a few churches and the Cabildo, truncated in the 1880s and remade in the 1930s, little survives from the time of the viceroys, let alone from before them. Almost all trace of that period of the city's history has vanished, not only because the Porteños came to reject its homely style, but also because it proved vastly insufficient to the city's frantic expansion, which started in the second half of the nineteenth century. In cities like Córdoba and Mendoza, where that expansion was far more measured, the evidence of Spanish dominion is much more substantial. For the most part, however, colonial architecture has vanished from Buenos Aires because it was not worth preserving in the first place.

Consider the massive fortress that once rose over the Plaza de Mayo (formerly the Plaza Mayor). It stood, as Juan de Garay had ordered, at the point where the *bañado,* the strand that separated the city from the river, was narrowest. Garay chose the site, but work on the fortress began only in 1594, more than a decade after his death. Officially named *La Real Fortaleza de San Juan Baltasar de Austria,* the Royal Fortress of Saint John Baltasar of Austria, it was built by the chief magistrate in the city, Fernando de Zárate, at the urgent behest of the king, who feared that the British, having only recently vanquished his invincible armada, now had designs on the Rio de la Plata.

The fortress was the dominant architectural fact of Buenos Aires from its second founding until 1853, when the demolition of the building finally began. Its drab, flattened roof was the first thing visitors saw of the city as they sailed past it toward the docks of the Riachuelo. Originally of baked earth, it was eventually recast in brick and stone, and it lasted just long enough to be photographed. On the evidence of the surviving image, it was almost unseemly in its ugliness, a mottled and irregularly shaped two-story structure with a flat roof. The forbidding brick wall that encircled it was engirded, along the Plaza Mayor, by a moat, but one without water, as though to make it seem even more baleful. Its main entrance was a perfectly cubic, barrel-vaulted blockhouse that emerged from its shapeless mass and communicated with the square by a drawbridge extended over the moat. We scan the photograph for any hint of grace, any leaven of ornament that might relieve its hulking mediocrity, but we come up empty-handed. It is as though—in the eyes of Spain—any concession to beauty or amenity would have been wasted on a settlement as insignificant as the port of Buenos Aires.

For hundreds of years, however, this plaza was the only public space in the city, beyond those *huecos* where carts from the countryside were parked or where the bones of cattle were discarded. Occupying the center of the city, it quickly established itself as the focus of civic attention. To this day, when a new president is elected, or the archbishop of Buenos Aires becomes pope, or some great tragedy befalls the republic, or anyone feels like protesting anything at all, the Porteños come pouring into the place that Juan de Garay arbitrarily chose, four centuries ago, as the site of his fortress.

The other public buildings were largely of a piece with the fortress. Concolorcorvo, the renowned Spanish travel writer, has left a description of the Plaza Mayor around 1750: "The plaza is unfinished and only the entrance to the Cabildo has doors. . . . They are building a great and mighty temple [the cathedral], but I don't believe it will be adorned in a manner that befits it, since the bishop is poor and his coffers do not contain more than a thousand pesos, as is the case with the other curates. The remaining churches are entirely common and ordinary."

And so it is that visitors to modern Buenos Aires will find few traces of the colonial city, the *Ciudad Indiana* as it is sometimes called. The Buenos Aires of myth and memory, of Beaux Arts palaces and tango, is a much later Buenos Aires, a different Buenos Aires. And except in the memories of a few of the more historically minded citizens, this period of the city's history has been entirely forgotten, if not repudiated, by the present generation of Porteños. The Ciudad Indiana lingers in their collective imagination—if at all—as a vague, colorless, odorless dream time, and even Mendoza and Garay occupy a station somewhere between a rumor and a myth.

But even if there are few physical remains from the time of the Ciudad Indiana, visible traces of it survive, and even more survives just beneath the observable surface. Several of the cardinal elements of Garay's plan have endured into the present: around the main square, directly across from the fortress, he placed a Cabildo, or town hall, whose later incarnation can still be seen on that very spot. To the northwest, across the Plaza de Mayo, the city's main church evolved into the cathedral, whose overblown neoclassical facade now dominates the plaza. It is the very cathedral where Pope Francis once served as cardinal bishop. As for the area of the fort that faced the square and was inhabited by the governor of the city, it would evolve, in the later nineteenth century, into the famed Casa Rosada, the official dwelling of the President of the Republic.

But the most important traces of the colonial city are systemic rather than physical. In terms of deep structure, of the infrastructure of roads and what we might call the infrastructure of religion, much of the colonial city remains tenaciously intact.

Even beyond the grid, even beyond the limits of the city during its first three centuries, movement was dominated by roads that were older perhaps than the earliest human presence in the Rio de la Plata, stretching back a thousand or even tens of thousands of years. These roads followed the natural lay of the land, which would have been reinforced by ancient hunter-gatherers seeking the path of least resistance. And so, of the main trails that led out from Garay's city through the country (much of it now within the greatly expanded city limits), the Camino del Bajo, or Low Trail, became the modern Avenida Las Heras; the Camino del Alto, or High Trail, became Avenida Sante Fe; and the Camino del Campo became Autopista Luis Dellepiane, one of the city's main highways. Although Buenos Aires today is a city of many lovely parks and plazas, it had none to speak of before the 1870s. And yet many of its finest plazas rise over the huecos, also called *baldíos,* that once dotted the landscape. These, as I have mentioned, were large and empty plots of lands, usually one or two blocks from end to end, that had never been cultivated.

And then there is what we might call the entire religious infrastructure of the city, the sequence of churches that, even if renovated or replaced, tend to survive with the most remarkable tenacity. Just as religious beliefs and conventions are apt to represent the most conservative and deeply rooted convictions in a human being, so churches tend to be among the most ineradicable elements of an urban landscape. The church of Nuestra Señora del Socorro, for example, has stood at least since 1750 at the corner of Juncal and Suipacha: once, when the Rio de la Plata came within a hundred meters of this spot, some fishermen who plied its waters raised a humble altar here, and that altar evolved into the noble building we see today.

These houses of worship, like most houses of worship, possessed an urbanistic importance that, today, is easily overlooked. In premodern times, even the humblest of such structures was apt to possess a relative sumptuousness, a specialness that impressed all who entered and that is nearly unimaginable amid the unrelenting barrage of visual stimulation that we endure today. However drab and utilitarian the rest of Buenos Aires was, its churches, with their pure white facades, their fanciful belfries, their columns and triangulated pediments, embodied the striving for something higher and finer. They were the architectonic equivalent of the Sunday best that the Porteños—like Christians everywhere—donned on the Sabbath. Indeed, in their beauty and in the ornateness of their decor, these houses of worship, rising between the monotony of the pampas and the monotony of the river, were, in all likelihood, the most beautiful thing a Porteño would ever see.

One of these churches, Sant' Ignacio, on the corner of Alsina and Bolívar, contains within it the oldest surviving structure of any kind in Buenos Aires. Dating to the 1680s, it is the only building that can be traced back, at least in part, to the seventeenth century. Sant' Ignacio springs directly from the source of European classical architecture and preserves some hint of its power. True, if this church stood on a street in Rome, in all likelihood you would pass by without giving it a glance. But it was, and it remains, one of the finest things in Buenos Aires.

The southern tower of Sant' Ignacio and part of its facade were added in 1685, shortly after the first brick foundry opened in Buenos Aires. In 1710, the German Jesuit Johannes Krauss redesigned the rest of the building, but he died in 1714, and so it was completed by Giovanni Battista Primoli and Andrea Blanqui. These two architects would also work on the churches of la Merced, San Telmo and Pilar, which are still standing in the capital. The fact that a German and two Italians built their churches on Garay's grid seems to foreshadow the internationalism that would define the architecture of Buenos Aires throughout the nineteenth and twentieth centuries. In that later age, architects from all corners of Europe would descend on the capital, which, in its swift and vertiginous expansion, needed all the help it could get. But for now, many quiet years would pass before Buenos Aires began to emerge from the unprepossessing shell of its colonial days.

FOUR

BUENOS AIRES, CAPITAL OF THE VICEROYALTY

(1776–1810)

AT EXACTLY THE MOMENT WHEN BRITAIN'S NORTH American colonies were revolting against the King of England, a similar ferment, set in motion by similar causes, began to be felt in the Rio de la Plata. If anything, the Porteños had more legitimate grievances than the colonists in Boston and New York. The citizens of Buenos Aires would have been happy to suffer nothing worse than the Stamp and Townshend Acts: they were inhibited in what they could manufacture or produce, what they could buy and from whom, what they could sell and to whom. Their only consolation was the relative ease with which they could flout the law. But even if most of them did not suspect it at the time, there was something irksome and base in this condition that had been imposed upon them: though it did not diminish their handsome illegal profits, it certainly inhibited their city's ability to reach full maturity.

And yet the restiveness that broke out into open revolt along the Eastern Seaboard of North America was forestalled in Buenos Aires by more than a generation, through the shrewdness of the Spanish crown. This was no longer the Hapsburg monarchy that had colonized much of the New World and that, for more than two centuries, methodically suppressed the fortunes of Buenos Aires. The War of the Spanish Succession ratified the Bourbon title to the Kingdom of Spain, and now a relatively enlightened monarch, Carlos III, ruled in Madrid.

Carlos recognized that, by the 1770s, the two-fold division of Spain's territories in the New World had become impossibly unwieldy and that the local governors and *corregidors* were bywords for corruption. And so, among other measures, he resolved to create four viceroyalties out of the existing two. In the northern half of his American possessions, the Viceroyalty of New Granada, consisting of modern Colombia and Venezuela, was carved out of the Viceroyalty of New Spain. In the south, much of the Viceroyalty of Peru was transferred to the new Viceroyalty of the Rio de la Plata. This jurisdiction contained all of modern Argentina north of Patagonia (at the time virtually uninhabited and unexplored) as well as modern Bolivia, Paraguay, Uruguay and the Cuyo region of Chile. But the port of Buenos Aires was to be the viceroyalty's heart and soul, the engine of its prosperity. For the first time since the city's founding, the regional primacy that it had won, both through its geographic situation and through the brisk, if illegal, traffic in contraband, would be enshrined in law.

Behind this great realignment were urgent geopolitical calculations. With the emergence, in the mid-eighteenth century, of France and England as the dominant nation-states of Europe, the balance of power shifted throughout the world. Because of Spain's alliance with France—England's ancient enemy—the British sought to challenge Spanish naval supremacy in the South Atlantic through an alliance with Portugal. That nation, in turn, was eager to expand southward from Brazil. To this end, they had founded Colonia do Sacramento in 1680, thirty miles east of Buenos Aires across the Rio de la Plata, and from there they were well positioned to threaten the entire eastern shore of modern Argentina. Suddenly the value of Buenos Aires became clear to the court of Madrid. In the words of Pedro Antonio de Cevallos, its first viceroy, Buenos Aires was Spain's "most important bastion in America, [a port] whose development we must encourage by every means possible. For here we will win or lose South America."

It was not fortuitous that the viceroyalty was established in 1776, the same year in which the North American colonies declared their independence from Great Britain. For some time, Spain had wanted to remove its main rivals, the Portuguese, from the Rio de la Plata. But the inveterate ties between Portugal and England, with its incomparable navy, made this nearly impossible. Suddenly, however, England's American colonies were in open revolt, tying it down in what would prove to be a long and costly war. Seizing his chance in October 1776, Cevallos, armed with 117 ships and nearly ten thousand Spanish soldiers, sailed across the Rio de la Plata and laid siege to Colonia. Within two weeks, the settlement had fallen to Spain and most of Cevallos's troops were sailing home. But nearly a thousand of them remained in Buenos Aires.

Despite these potent geopolitical considerations, however, the new viceroyalty was mainly a response to new economic realities. The yield from the silver mines of Potosí was beginning to falter and could no longer be counted on to sustain the Spanish state. As importantly, the Spanish crown finally recognized Buenos Aires as the de facto center of trade in the southern half of South America. As John Lynch has written, "If Spain did not appreciate the most natural route to South America, other European nations did. Drawn by the weakening of Potosí, the English, the Portuguese and the Dutch converged upon the Rio de la Plata."

The natural consequence of forcing all trade through Lima had been, as we have seen, to create in Buenos Aires a highly efficient trade in contraband, which the crown was powerless to stop and from which it derived no profit whatever. In consequence, Cevallos took the momentous step of redirecting Potosí's silver from Lima and Panama to Buenos Aires, and from there to Spain. With this one move, he reversed the economic model on which South America had run for 250 years. With the enactment of the *Ley de Libre Comercio* (the Free Trade Law) of 1778, the merchants of Buenos Aires, for the first time in their history, could trade openly, practice agriculture on a larger scale and traffic in the now fully legal sale of slaves. In time Buenos Aires would become the conduit by which most African slaves were introduced into the nation of Argentina, and by the beginning of the next century, as many as one Porteño in three were of African descent. The port city was like a ship that had stood becalmed and motionless for two hundred years: now a sudden wind filled its sails, and with all hands on deck, it finally began to move. In the words of James R. Scobie, "Domestic and external trade increased enormously, government revenues mounted, and social and cultural life experienced a new birth. This was, in reality, the birth period of the Argentine nation."

By 1800, Buenos Aires had a population of nearly 45,000 (up from 12,000 in 1750), thus making it one of the largest cities of South America. Suddenly the pedestrian would have found far fewer empty patches in the grid. A certain density was developing, an as yet inchoate tremor and hint of that bustle and commotion without which a city cannot truly be deemed a great city. Still, the physical condition of the Buenos Aires before independence remained unprepossessing in the extreme. It preserved the aspect of a small town and would continue to do so for another half a century and more, until the arrival of French taste began, finally, to dispel the torpor of colonial days.

For now, the new dispensation manifested itself more in political and commercial terms than in urban form. Certainly the first viceroys had more urgent matters to attend to than the beautification of their capital. But then, it may be doubted whether Spain, throughout the prodigious length and breadth of its empire, had ever exhibited any great interest in the beauty of its cities. In the thirty-four years of the viceroyalty of the Rio de la Plata, from 1776 to 1810, eleven viceroys, each of relatively short duration, had little time to effect dramatic changes in the cityscape of Buenos Aires. Still, one might have expected that the sudden influx of wealth among the merchant class would have expressed itself in the sort of ambitious private architecture that emerged during the booms of the 1890s and the 1920s. The economy prospered and men grew rich, but the very ethos of the place seemed to inhibit spending on sumptuous dwellings. It was almost as if no one even knew that that was an option.

Very few examples of eighteenth-century domestic architecture survive in the capital, but one does, and we have good photographs of two others. The former stands at 336 Saint Martin. Ordinarily it would have been a prime target for development, probably in the late nineteenth century and certainly in the twentieth: set in the heart of the financial district, it is surrounded by massive rationalist buildings from the 1960s and 1970s. But it survives because, for much of the second half of the nineteenth century, it was the home of the eminent Bartolomé Mitre, the first president of Argentina. The interior decor is nearly unique as a surviving example of a nineteenth-century Porteño dwelling of the haute bourgeoisie. As for the eighteenth-century facade and the structure of the interior, even today in its cleaned and renovated form, it is apt to strike visitors—and there are not many of them—as too drab and unadorned to be worthy of a nineteenth-century head of state or even of the eighteenth-century merchant for whom it was built in 1785. It is a simple one-story building with a flat roof, though the back, invisible from the street, has a second story added in the later nineteenth century. Other than a doorway and a few windows surrounded by a simple trim, the facade is almost entirely featureless, while the dominant structural feature of the interior is a central patio around which all the rooms were arranged. This has Iberian and even Roman precedents. The local term for this sort of structure is *casa chorizo,* or "sausage house," so named because each room, arranged around the central patio, opens into the next room like linked sausages.

Today the house at 336 San Martín stands in awkward isolation, but throughout the eighteenth century and most of the nineteenth, the endless repetition of such houses—or even less prepossessing ones—made up the entire residential stock of Buenos Aires. The relentless conformity of postwar American developments like Levittown on Long Island approximates, one imagines, the cumulative, mind-numbing tedium of an entire city formed of such structures.

Slightly more interesting is the *Casa de la Virreina Vieja* (the House of the Old Vicereine) from 1782, whose owner went to the trouble of adorning its facade with triangular pediments and a decorative attic.

This one-story building survived until 1913 at the corner of Belgrano and Peru, when the strikingly somber Edificio Otto Wulf rose over its demolished remains.

Consider an even older one-story house that, like the Casa de la Virreina Vieja, survives only in grainy, antiquated photographs. This building once stood on the corner of Belgrano and Avenida Paseo Colón, four blocks south of the fort and only a few feet from what was then the water's edge. The facade of Mitre's house has been so reverently maintained and plastered over that it gives a false idea of how such houses really looked in their day. The older house, dating at least as far back as 1754, was built for Domingo de Basavilbaso—a wealthy merchant—and predates the viceroyalty. The surviving photographs, of course, are from at least one century later, but as an indication of how slowly the city developed, there is little reason to suppose that the house, or the street on which it stood, had changed greatly in that time. If anything, the scene looks a little better in the nineteenth-century image than it would have in the eighteenth century, given that cobblestones have replaced compacted dirt and years of rubbish have been removed. The scarred surface of the house reveals bare brick where the plaster has fallen away. Unlike the flat *azotea* roof of the slightly later Mitre house—a sign of enviable modernity in its day—the pitched roof of Basavilbaso's house bristles with irregular tiles that express perfectly the spirit of the colonial town.

There is, however, something odd and noteworthy about the structure. At its western edge is a doorway that would seem absurdly grandiose for a palace, let alone for a simple one-story house. That doorway, with its three finials and the lilting curves of its pediment—a distant echo of Borromini's Roman churches—is actually a not-unlovely instance of Iberian Baroque or even rococo design. It was tacked on by the second viceroy, Juan José de Vértiz, who, in the name of the king, rented the building in 1779 as the new *aduana,* or customs house, of the port of Buenos Aires. As odd as his inability to find or build a more imposing structure for such an important magistracy is the fact that it continued to serve as the *aduana* up to 1857, when it was finally replaced by the Aduana Taylor, a building nearly one hundred times its size.

But however louche that doorway might seem, it has the extraordinary distinction of being, as far as we know, the first time in the history of Buenos Aires that a building other than a church was conceived or reconceived for aesthetic effect. It was not much, a simple frill superimposed upon the entrance of a dull pile, but it was a start. And although the viceroyalty lasted only until 1810, it is quite clear that the viceroys felt that something must be done to raise the standard of the local building stock.

Only one eminent building was completed during this period, a massive arcade known as the Recova, or covered market place. This noble structure would become, for better or worse, a symbol of the viceroys, from its construction in 1804 until its demolition eighty years later. And although, for subsequent generations, the Recova embodied the heavy, almost feudal heritage of the Spanish dominion, it was, in fact, quite progressive in its day. Completed toward the end of the viceroyalty, shortly before the Porteños gained their independence from Spain, the Recova was the most ambitious structure ever built in Buenos Aires up to that time.

Eastern facade of the Recova, completed in 1804. (Archivo General de la Nación)

The Porteño building replaced an informal market where, virtually since the founding of the city, tradesmen had gathered to hawk their wares and produce. In due course, however, such raucous commerce came to offend the sensibilities of an increasingly refined citizenry. In 1774, before the viceroyalty was even established, the governor, the same Vértiz who would become the second viceroy in 1778, advocated that an imposing building should occupy the site. But nothing was done on that occasion, nor would it be done ten years later, when the idea was briefly revisited. Only in 1801, after Joaquín del Pino became viceroy, was action finally taken. Based on plans by the architect Juan Bautiste Segismundo, a massive arcaded structure was completed in 1804, cutting across the entire Plaza Mayor.

A forerunner of the medium-sized malls that, in more modern times, have arisen throughout the city—Abasto, Alto Palermo, and Gallerias Pacifico—the Recova consisted of forty shops under forty arches, twenty facing the fortress and twenty facing the Cabildo. It bore little relation to any contemporary architectural developments in Europe, its design being very much an example of the Spanish colonial style. And yet for the first time in Buenos Aires, one has the feeling that one is in the presence of real architectural intelligence. Even if the architect disregarded French or Italian precedent, he succeeded, in his provincial way, in achieving something memorable, something impressive. There is a rare degree of idiosyncrasy, even anticlassicism, in the insistent regimentation of the twenty single-story arches that contrast so abruptly with the triumphal arch in the center, the Arco de los Virreyes, crowned by a fluttering of finials. Even though, with its bay divisions and its clean, clear coursing lines, this pale structure could hardly have been simpler, how beguiling it must have seemed to eyes accustomed only to the mud and mediocrity of colonial Buenos Aires!

Because the Recova survived into the 1880s, it is documented in a number of good photographs. They are invaluable records, but they are indifferent as photographs. A far better record of the building is the lovely watercolor by Carlos Pelligrini, a French émigré and one of the more renowned artists and architects in mid-nineteenth-century Buenos Aires. In his painting, we see the structure at early morning, with diffused sunlight rising out of the east from beyond the fortress and the Rio de la Plata. As our eye descends the Calle Defensa, on one side we see the Recova Nueva (completed in 1818) and the twin belfries of San Francisco farther south. And we begin to understand, to feel the influence that this showpiece of a building must once have exerted on the center of the city. It had an undeniable majesty to it. For once, everything seems to come together to suggest, as was surely not yet the case, that Buenos Aires was a full-fledged, beautiful city.

But even now some changes, however subtle and episodic, were starting to alter the fabric of the capital. As early as 1772, the surveyor Cristobal Barrientos made the first usable map of the northern portion of the city, including the quintessential Porteño barrios of Retiro and Recoleta. Shortly afterward, the engineer Cardozo began to open up roads through this area, formerly the abode of outcasts, anchorites and the occasional jaguar, but increasingly dominated by farmsteads and the summer retreats of the gentry. This was the first substantive expansion in the city's history. A path that had long conveyed the discalced friars from the city to the Church of Nuestra Señora del Pilar—next to what would become the famous Cemetery of Recoleta—was broadened into the Calle Larga, or Long Road, the antecedent of today's elegant Avenida Quintana. In the process, the *mataderos* or slaughterhouses that once populated these parts were relocated to Barracas, south of the city on the banks of the Riachuelo. Although Barracas would not officially become part of Buenos Aires for another hundred years, this act of relocating the *mataderos* would depress its fortunes down to the present day. Long after the slaughterhouses disappeared, the area remains somewhat undesirable.

❋

IN SPANISH AMERICA IN GENERAL, and in Buenos Aires specifically, governors displayed a nearly total indifference to anything other than the most basic functioning of the urban centers that sustained their far-flung empire and that existed principally to exploit the natural resources of the land. Other than a main square created to call the citizens to assembly or to arms, there were apt to be neither parks, nor trees, nor fountains, nor ornate palaces for the king's magistrates, nor so much as a decorative cornice or door handle on the exteriors of the houses of private citizens. In Buenos Aires, each citizen adorned his life as best he could. Voltaire, who in the thirteenth chapter of *Candide* sends his eponymous hero to Buenos Aires together with his beloved Cunegonde, famously enjoins us to cultivate our own gardens. And that is exactly what the Porteños did, and that was virtually all they could do. The garden that grew behind their house, or in the patio of their house, was about as much green as they were likely to see. No street had trees, there were no parks, and the few theaters that existed in later colonial times were purely the result of private enterprise. Beyond that there were the immemorial diversions of port cities, the brothels and taverns that catered to transient merchants and sailors.

But under the viceroyalty that began to change. The most important measure adopted at this time was the construction of the Paseo

Paseo de la Alameda, subsequently the Paseo de Julio, in one of the earliest surviving photographs of Buenos Aires, c. 1846. (Archivo General de la Nación)

de la Alameda in 1780, by order of the viceroy Vértiz. His predecessor, Viceroy Cevallos, had indeed proposed such a thing as early as 1761, when he was the governor of Buenos Aires, but those plans had come to nothing. A tree-lined walkway, it ran along the river on land reclaimed from the mudflats of the bañado, where now we find Avenida Leandro N. Alem. One of the earliest photographs ever taken in Buenos Aires depicts this avenue in the time of Juan Manuel de Rosas, by which date, admittedly, it had undergone some modifications. And while it might seem unfair to judge the Alameda from an image that has survived in poor condition and seems to have been shot under an overcast sky, nevertheless, the walkway—more than sixty years after it was built—looks quite uninviting. Its tree-lined copse forms a stuttering line rather than a continuous one, while the grass looks patchy and unappealing, the seating spare and insufficient. But such cavils miss the point. There is something momentous about this image: it reveals to us the first public space ever created in Buenos Aires specifically for the pleasure of its citizens. It was to be a refuge from the clamorous getting and spending of the capital. Here at last was a place where men and women from all levels of society could stroll and be seen. And although the Alameda was relatively small, stretching a mere three blocks from Lavalle to Perón—a distance that could be traversed in six minutes—it was immediately embraced by the Porteños. For the first time in their history, a part of Buenos Aires, the waters of the Rio de la Plata, was being offered to the citizens in an almost purely formal way, as something beautiful in and of itself. One other enhancement of the general dreariness of Buenos Aires under the viceroys was the construction of a bullring on what was then the outskirts of the city, in Retiro, on the southern side of what is now the Plaza San Martín. Completed in 1801, a few years before the Recova was built, it arose in the exact spot where, for decades, the British South Sea Company had sold African slaves. It is the spot where you now see the statue of the poet and orator Esteban Echeverría. The Plaza de Toros was a comparatively large structure, far larger than the simple wooden bullring that had been built in the Hueco Monserrat in 1791 and that had just recently been demolished. In its drab adequacy, it presaged today's

River and Boca stadiums, which command and divide the loyalties of the modern Porteños.

The bullring consisted of a massive, two-tiered and two-toned octagonal drum, composed entirely of brick, whose topmost rim achieved a vaguely Mozarabic effect through a series of discreet battlements. It was able, almost incredibly, to accommodate ten thousand men—since men alone were allowed to attend bullfights. Given that the population of Buenos Aires numbered forty-five thousand souls, roughly half of them presumably female, it would seem to follow that nearly half of the male population was potentially in attendance at these bullfights, paying anywhere from 15 centavos to 2 reals for the satisfaction. But the Plaza de Toros did not last long. In 1819, three years after independence, the authorities outlawed bullfighting in Buenos Aires—the first of many attempts by the new magistrates to repudiate their Iberian roots—and the bricks that had gone to building the bullring were reused to construct, a few hundred feet north of it, the Cuartel del Artilleria, a barracks that would itself disappear half a century later.

But for now, with the completion of the Recova, the Retiro bullring and the Alameda, it was clear that change was afoot in Buenos Aires. In theory, the elevation of Buenos Aires to the status of a capital, furnished with the new amenities I have described, should have been a boon to all its citizens. But these benefits proved to be a mixed blessing. Under the Hapsburgs and the earlier Bourbons, even if the condition of Buenos Aires had been debased, at least its merchants were left alone and its magistrates, through the indifference of the crown, enjoyed a fair degree of home rule. The Creole citizenry—no longer Spanish, but the offspring of the Spanish—had effectively been independent for a century or more. Now, however, they had to look on as a whole superstructure of Spanish bureaucrats was imposed upon their city and its trade, effectively ousting the Porteños themselves from their former positions of power. As yet, the yearning for independence remained primordial and inchoate. But resentment toward these Spanish bureaucrats would be kindled to conflagration in the space of a single generation. By the second decade of the next century, it would become quite clear to most

Porteños that they and the Spanish, like the North American colonists and the British, no longer belonged to the same nation. And although, for now, there was no manifest hostility toward the troops garrisoned in Retiro, their coercive presence did not pass unnoticed by the local population.

FIVE

INDEPENDENCE

(1806–1829)

FOR MORE THAN TWO CENTURIES, FROM SHORTLY after the second founding of Buenos Aires in 1580 down to the first British invasion of 1806, the history of the city is not only somewhat colorless and dull but singularly lacking in vivid personalities—indeed, in any personalities—who might assist in weaving an historical narrative.

And yet, no sooner has the nineteenth century begun than everything changes. Suddenly the sepia tones of colonial times burst into a riot of full-bodied color and dramatic chiaroscuro. The history of the city to this point has been almost torpid, notwithstanding the occasional incursion of pirates or indigenous peoples. It has been played out mostly by faceless merchants and bureaucrats. But the opening years of the nineteenth century bring forth more personalities—violent, passionate, principled or otherwise—than the historian can easily accommodate. Liniers, Lavalle, Saavedra, Rivadavia, San Martín: these are the men—and they were all men—whom the Argentines still refer to as *los próceres,* the leaders, the eminences. Granted, most of them are unknown outside of Argentina. But inside the country, and especially in Buenos Aires itself, they are names to conjure with.

For there is this important urbanistic dimension to them, as well: these are the men who have given their names to the thousands of streets and avenues of the capital, to its parks, plazas and barrios. To read the history of the city and the nation after acquiring some familiarity with the Porteño grid is often to experience a very pleasant shock of recognition: So *that* is whom Avenida Rivadavia and Plaza Vicente López are named for!

We must not underestimate this distinction of having a street named in one's honor. The average Porteño—like pedestrians everywhere—is so far from knowing or caring about the origin of street names that it would never occur to him to inquire into it. But each day these Porteños, in their millions, traverse the mighty Avenida Pueyrredón, stretching from Rivadavia to Libertador, and there is, for the estimable Juan Martín de Pueyrredón, the hero of Perdriel, some measure of immortality in that. Indeed, if one has a touch of the poet, one can almost imagine that these eminent men of action and high purpose, Beruti and Alvear and Alberdi, have sustained an Ovidian metamorphosis: transformed into the streets that bear their names, they continue to serve the republic long after their words and deeds have been forgotten by an ungrateful populace.

It is possible for a city to be the sort of great city that I defined in the opening chapter, without, however, being the scene of great historical events. London and New York are surely great cities, and important historical events have surely occurred within their limits. But the most important historical events that influenced them and the nations to which they belong have tended to occur at some remove from these capitals, usually on a field of battle in open country. One misses that indissoluble bond between the historical act and the tangle of urban streets and public spaces in which it played out. This quality, however, is present to the highest degree in Paris and Rome, and in Buenos Aires as well. In writing about the Argentine capital one recalls the words of Cicero: "Wherever we walk, we tread upon history." Of course, the history of Rome and Paris is the history of the world, whereas the history of Buenos Aires is the history of Argentina and, occasionally, of Uruguay. But within the infinite universe of Buenos Aires itself, these events possess as sublime an importance as any site in Athens or Paris or Rome.

With regard to Buenos Aires, many of the most notable events in its history, and that of Argentina, occurred in the Plaza de Mayo: it was here that Juan de Garay planted the Tree of Justice on founding the city. It was here that rogue members of the air force bombarded the supporters of Perón on June 16, 1955, and here that the Mothers of the Plaza de Mayo gathered in the early 1980s to protest the disappearance of their sons and daughters. Similarly, the second British invasion in 1807 was routed near the Plaza San Martín, where it descends toward the Retiro train station. And many of the streets of the capital became theaters of historical action amid the sundry convulsions of 1810, 1946 and 2001.

Consider this account, by Enrique German Herz, of a skirmish during the so-called Revolution in the Park of 1890: "At the southwest corner of Lavalle and Libertad, on the roof of a house that then belonged to a gentleman named Martinez, stood twenty men from the 10th Infantry and three artillery men. . . . At Viamonte 1248, near the Palacio Miró, stood Celindo Castro in command of twenty-five men. . . . The first shots were discharged, shortly after nine in the morning, at the corner of Corrientes and Paraná." Most foreigners who read this passage will feel mystified by the recitation of streets they have never visited. But if you listen closely and with a hint of sympathy, you may hear the poetry, the music of these names. In truth, the first quarter of the nineteenth century marked the city of Buenos Aires spiritually more than urbanistically or architecturally. A few buildings were erected and a few came down, but the convulsions of the time distracted an entire generation from any extensive urban development. As a British ambassador, Woodbine Parish, wrote, "The old government considered money laid out in beautifying the city as so much thrown away upon the colonists, and the new government has been as yet too poor to do more than has been absolutely necessary; what has been done, however, has been well done, and does credit to the republican authorities."

But in assessing such a city from an urbanistic perspective, we must remember that it is, obviously, more than the sum of its streets and structures. There is another kind of structure to cities, a vast superstructure of moods and vague sentiments that a city engenders in its citizens and that they reflect back upon it. And what, in its most general terms, was this mood that dominated the city in 1806? It was a response to the fervor of the age, to the passion that convulsed the entire Eurocentric cosmos. The rise of democratic movements and the bourgeoisie played out in many ways throughout the world. In Europe, this was the age of revolutions; in South America, the age of independence. And it would permanently stamp the city of Buenos Aires. The landscape of the capital is scattered with monuments to the military men of this period. In the uniforms of hussars and dragoons, with buff breeches and clover-shaped epaulettes, these men fought off the British and gained their independence from Spain. "All that delirium of the brave," as Yeats would later call it. And now, splendidly poised on granite pedestals, they sternly survey the busiest intersections of the modern city, or rise up on rearing steeds in the centers of its plazas and parks.

Modern Argentina begins in 1806 with the first British invasion of Buenos Aires. This assault would set in motion the process by which, ten years later, a new nation was born, the United Provinces of the Rio de la Plata, with Buenos Aires as its capital. But the process by which Argentine independence was won proved to be very different from that same process of liberation in the United States: Among the Spanish colonies, however, and especially among the Porteños, eminent orators and thinkers arose only after the fact, in response to circumstances they had never actively promoted. There had been but few true intellectuals in colonial Buenos Aires. Newspapers like the *Gaceta de Buenos Aires* and the *Telégrafo Mercantil* covered the shipping news and developments in Europe, but most men of learning, aside from lawyers, were affiliated with the Catholic Church, and the church was committed to the monarchy. Porteño merchants might grumble at Spanish meddling in their livelihoods, but there was no Boston Tea Party in Buenos Aires, no outcry of anger, no fervor for independence, until suddenly the possibility of it rose up, unbidden, before them.

The push for independence was inspired by far-off events in Europe. In the first decade of the nineteenth century, England had been eyeing the Rio de la Plata estuary and had long considered planting a colony there, or taking over the preexistent Spanish colonies. Indeed, for nearly a century before its invasion of Buenos Aires, England had been interested in settling South America and had been one of the main trading partners of the criollo merchants at least since 1713, when it received the asiento, or commission, to sell slaves in the Plaza de Retiro. But several events now impelled the British to take more drastic action. The loss of their North American colonies, pursuant to the 1783 Treaty of Paris, was a devastating blow to their economy; but the resulting hardships worsened considerably after Napoleon's Continental System effectively blocked England from all European markets. Thereupon, Spain entered into an alliance with France, which, in addition to declaring war on England, invaded Portugal, a British ally. It was this combination of military and economic necessities, together with what seemed like a great and unforeseen opportunity, that moved England to invade Buenos Aires.

In the two centuries and more since Juan de Garay founded the second Buenos Aires, the city had never seen an enemy force like the one that now sailed into the Rio de La Plata. Almost every able-bodied man in the city would soon be pressed into its defense, as were slaves and criollos from other parts of the viceroyalty.

On the morning of June 27, 1806, 2,500 British troops, led by Sir Home Riggs Popham, invested the city. The viceroy, Sobremonte, had feared just such a threat and repeatedly petitioned Madrid to send reinforcements. But he received only arms, not the troops he desperately needed. And so, by the time the British appeared, he had already fled with the entire treasury to the town of Lujan, forty-two miles northwest of the capital. The laws of the viceroyalty required that he do this, but the locals, who greatly mistrusted the Spanish in any case, interpreted his flight as an act of craven, even treasonous desertion. The fact that most of the viceroy's Spanish functionaries, together with the wealthiest of the Spanish merchants, followed him into exile did nothing to mollify the criollos' antagonism toward Spain.

The British were familiar with such entrenched resentments through their long and profitable experience in Buenos Aires, and so they assumed that they would be greeted as liberators. At first those expectations seemed to be borne out. Though there had been some initial resistance, the British 71st Regiment, led by General William

Beresford, marched essentially unopposed and to the sound of bagpipes from the Riachuelo up the Calle Larga (now Montes de Oca) to the Plaza Mayor. For forty-six days they occupied the fort and ruled the largest city in South America. "A salute was fired from the Fortress in honor of His Britannic Majesty's colors being hoisted in South America," the historian Ian Fletcher writes. "At a cost of just one man killed and twelve wounded, Beresford's force had captured a city of around forty thousand."

The reaction of the Porteños initially recalled that of the citizens of New Amsterdam—later New York—when the British expelled the Dutch in 1664: as long as the merchant class could sell their wares, they did not care greatly who claimed possession of the colony. As for the often burdensome viceroyalty, its thirty years in existence were hardly enough to burnish it with the sanction of tradition. Throughout the period of British rule in Buenos Aires, most of the officers, as well as the rank and file, were quartered in the homes of the Porteños, and, under the circumstances, their intercourse with the citizens was remarkably civil. There were balls at which they danced together and, even as the wealth of the viceroyalty—which a British foray had brought back from Lujan—was being carried with great ceremony through the streets of London to the Royal Treasury, British merchants jubilantly loaded ships with their wares and set sail for the Rio de la Plata.

Soon, however, some of the Porteños regrouped and prepared to fight back. Part of the British success had resulted from their martial reputation and from a stratagem by which they contrived to appear more numerous than they really were. But the Porteños began to doubt these first impressions. One Briton, William Gavin, wrote in his diary that "I was accosted one day by an inhabitant who enquired as to our numbers, which I exaggerated some hundreds, when he very impertinently asked 'how they were fed, as rations were only issued for such a number.' I accounted for it as men in hospital, servants, etc, but it would not do, they knew to a man our strength."

Armed opposition first took the form of a skirmish between the British and Juan Martín de Pueyrredón, he of the broad avenue that runs through Recoleta. They met on the field of Perdriel, about fourteen miles west of the Plaza Mayor, just beyond the modern boundaries of the city. In this encounter, Pueyrredón, the son of a Frenchman from the Basque country and a Porteña of Irish ancestry, was roundly defeated.

But the reverse was only temporary, for presently a native Frenchman, the fifty-three-year-old Santiago de Liniers, arrived in the city with a force of several thousand men recruited and trained in Montevideo. These troops, many of African or mixed criollo-Indian descent, were the famed Patricios, so named because they came from the fatherland, *la patria,* rather than because they could boast of any exalted birth. On August 7, they made landfall at the bañado of what is now Plaza San Martín and began to stream south along Florida, San Martín and Reconquista to the Plaza Mayor (now de Mayo), where, before their ultimate victory, they sustained important casualties from the British, who fired at them from the roofs of the Recova, the Cabildo and the cathedral.

But then the tide of battle began to turn. The British took refuge in the fort, and several hours later, Beresford raised the white flag. The Porteños, however, appeared to be unfamiliar with this convention and became increasingly rowdy. One of the members of the 71st Regiment, Robert Fernyhough, recalled, "Never shall I forget the scene which followed the hoisting of the flag of truce . . . 4000 raggamuffins rushed into the square, brandishing their knives, threatening us with destruction. The savages paid no regard to our flag of truce, and were firing in all directions."

Only when Liniers himself appeared was order finally restored. Beresford offered his sword, but Liniers chivalrously refused. Indeed, his comportment in victory was so exemplary as almost to defy belief. He "embraced [Beresford] and apologized for the behavior of his men owing to their ignorance of the rules of war." The two officers then fixed the terms of surrender, and so ended la Reconquista, the reconquest of the city, that would enter the lore and mythology of Buenos Aires and Argentina. And despite the anger of the Porteño populace in the moment of victory, thereafter the British, although prisoners, were treated with the greatest respect before being sent home.

But the British still could not shake the belief that the Porteños really favored them over the Spanish. And so they returned one year later, this time under General Whitelocke, for a decisive battle at the point where the Plaza San Martín slopes downward toward what was the waters of the river, now Avenida Libertador. Again the British suffered a humiliating defeat, and Lieutenant General Whittingham offered this rueful assessment: "History will record, and posterity with difficulty will believe that such an army as ours capitulated with the rabble of a South American town. . . . Would to God the waters of Oblivion were as near at hand as are those of La Plata."

This subsequent conflict is known as la Defensa. And two Porteño streets, Reconquista and Defensa, each a continuation of the other, commemorate these victories as they run from the northernmost part of the city all the way to the Parque Lezama in the south.

The foremost consequence of the two attempted invasions was the development of what Jonathan C. Brown has called "criollo consciousness." The criollos were well aware that they were the ones who had stayed to fight, while the Spanish fled to safety in the hinterland. Having been thus steeled in the heat of battle, the Porteños felt an esprit de corps that would have been unimaginable before this time. And so, once the British had left and the Spanish attempted to regain their previous influence in the city, they were blocked by the ruling council of the Cabildo. This body was now dominated by the criollos and had the full support of the militias, who remained in the city, fully armed and mobilized. To make matters worse, the Cabildo confiscated money that the Spanish tried to send to Spain and kept it to benefit the city of Buenos Aires. In the boldest display of their new powers, the criollos replaced Viceroy Sobremonte, the Spaniard who had fled before the British, with Santiago de Liniers, the hero of la Reconquista. This was the first time in the Rio de la Plata, or perhaps anywhere else in the Spanish Empire, that a local population replaced a royal appointee with someone of their own choosing.

Even though the British had been defeated in battle, they had, according to Maxine Hanon, "sown the seeds for a pacific invasion of British interests, which dominated the city for more than a century." As remarkable as anything about the conflict was the speed with which, in a matter of months after their second defeat, the British were back in

Buenos Aires, trading as eagerly as ever and being received by the locals without the slightest hint of rancor over the recent bit of unpleasantness. Indeed, the exuberance of the Porteños toward the British was little short of Anglophilia. Two tea salons soon sprang up in competition with one another, la Fonda Britannica and the Esmeralda Tea Garden. And one of the newest hotels of the period, the Hotel de Londres, stood out among the neighboring buildings by soaring to two full stories and by being one of the first structures in the city to boast a balcony.

And it was from two British ships that sailed into the port, in 1808, that the citizens received the momentous news that Napoleon had invaded Spain, imprisoned the king, Phillip VII, and replaced him with Joseph Bonaparte, his older brother. In Spain itself, what remained of the Bourbon monarchy fled to Seville in the south and formed a junta, or committee, to rule in the name of the king, all the while demanding that the Porteños swear loyalty to them. Although the citizens of Buenos Aires had been in a position to declare independence after their triumph over the British invaders, at the time that would have seemed too radical a move. Indeed, it may serve as an indication of their general docility that, before 1810, few if any of them even considered declaring their independence from Spain. Now, however, they began to wonder aloud what possible allegiance they could owe either to this upstart Frenchman or to the junta that presumed to rule in the king's name. And so, for the time being, they hit upon an ingenious evasion. They declared, at least to their own satisfaction, that they were still loyal to the deposed king by rejecting the usurper Bonaparte, without, however, admitting the legitimacy of the Seville junta. In the words of Martín de Álzaga, a merchant and one of the more outspoken patriots of the day, "Either the king or no one!" This, in essence, was a declaration of independence.

The citizens clamored for a *cabildo abierto,* an extraordinary meeting of the town hall in which all the citizens, rather than only the anointed oligarchs, could participate and be heard. The meeting began on May 22, 1810, as the militias took up their positions around the Cabildo (which still stands, somewhat truncated, on the western edge of the Plaza de Mayo). This move was plainly intended to intimidate any Spaniards in attendance—though most of them knew better than to show up in the first place. As sometimes happens in May on the Rio de la Plata, shortly before the onset of winter, the weather was miserable throughout the entire week of the *cabildo abierto*. But then, in the afternoon of May 25, the final day of the Cabildo, as these deliberations were ending and independence was declared, the sun appeared suddenly out of the west, flooding the Recova and the Plaza Mayor with its light. This, of course, was seen as a clear sign of divine favor. That same sun, *El Sol de Mayo,* appears on the flag of Argentina.

The new and sovereign state would now be ruled by something called *la Primera Junta,* the First Junta, whose president was Cornelio Saavedra. Its members included, among others, Manuel Belgrano, Manuel Alberti, Miguel de Azcuénaga and Juan Larrea, all of whom live on in the names of the streets and avenues of the capital.

Declaring independence, of course, was the easy part. The former subjects of the Viceroyalty of the Rio de la Plata would have to battle the remaining royalists until victory was finally achieved on July 9, 1816. But henceforth, and for the duration of the war, the theater of Argentine history shifts from the streets around the Plaza de Mayo to the open fields, rivers and mountains of the hinterland.

Inside the city, the next six years would see incessant disorder as the citizens, hopelessly divided, formed and then discarded one government after another. The *Primera Junta* was disbanded in the name of the *Junta Grande,* which in turn gave way to the First Triumvirate, the Second Triumvirate and finally a series of short-lived "Supreme Directors"—Viamonte, Rondeau, Álvarez Thomas, Balcarce—all of whom, once again, live on today as Porteño streets.

Even after independence was won, another ten years of violence convulsed the entire continent as it sought to free itself of the Spanish yoke. And just as the provinces of the Rio de la Plata had been liberated from Spain, now it occurred to these same provinces to win their freedom from Buenos Aires. The port city, as we have seen, had been the capital of a vast territory that included modern Bolivia, Paraguay, Uruguay and part of Chile. But although it made perfect sense to the Porteños to break free from Spain, it seemed far less apparent to them that any of the outer provinces should likewise seek to liberate themselves from the hegemony of Buenos Aires. Ultimately, most of these rebellious provinces remained in the union, but the ensuing conflict between the Federales of the provinces and the centralizing Unitarios of the capital would dominate Argentine politics for another three generations. One could argue that, even today, this conflict has not been fully resolved.

❊

IN THIS STRUGGLE for independence, the citizenry of Buenos Aires underwent a subtle transformation. The commotion of independence and the growth of the city to nearly 50,000 souls imbued the Porteños, for the first time, with the sense that they were indeed a city, in fact, the largest city in South America. Soon they began to take on fancier manners, even benignly urbane pretensions, that would have felt senseless only one or two decades earlier. For the first time, a hierarchy developed of fashionable, as opposed to less fashionable, forms of entertainment, restaurants and shops.

In 1812 a theater known as El Coliseo Provisional, which could seat up to 1,600 spectators, opened its doors at the corner of Perón and Reconquista, opposite the Iglesia de la Merced. Five years later, Juan Martín de Pueyrredón established the Sociedad de Buen Gusto del Teatro, the Society for Good Taste in Theater, which determined which plays were suitable for performance. This society elevated the locals with such tasteful—if dull, but in any case irreproachably European—fare as the plays of Voltaire and Alfieri, as well as one work, by a local dramatist, titled *El 25 de Mayo* that addressed the city's recently won independence from Spain. As of 1824, the Coliseo also presented operas and concerts featuring the music of Hayden, Mozart and Rossini. For those who sought less edifying entertainment, El Vauxhall offered circuses and musical-hall varieties near the modern Plaza Lavalle.

Bullfights were forbidden as of 1816 and the bullring in Retiro, that vestige of the viceroys, was razed to the ground. But cockfights, handball and billiards remained popular forms of entertainment, and each Tuesday, at one in the afternoon, there was a drawing of the lottery in front of the Cabildo, with the winner taking home up to 300 pesos. In the summer, during the February Carnival—in what was surely a holdover from colonial days—Porteños of the lower classes would douse pedestrians with water and occasionally pelt them with eggs if they were found walking through the streets during the siesta. Among the many newspapers that rose up at this time, the *Gaceta de Buenos Aires* and *El Tribuno,* as well as *l'Echo Français* and the *British Packet,* in French and English respectively, were full of reports of injuries thus sustained.

Little of importance was built in Buenos Aires during this period. But if one style predominated, it was neoclassicism. It arrived in Buenos Aires as two intermingled strains: from England, where it retained traces of Palladianism, and from France, where it was associated with Napoleon and his empire. It was a style that aspired to find unaging nobility in the pared-down classical language of ancient Greece and Rome. But its aesthetic concerns went beyond the look of cities to the ways in which men and women dressed and spoke and acted.

Not the least monument of this style is a poem, "El Triunfo Argentino" (1807), by the then twenty-year-old Vicente López y Planes, who would later become an eminent statesmen as well as the author of the Argentine national anthem. This is the man whose statue rises up before the lovely Plaza Vicente López on a street that also bears his name. His poem, one of the earliest attempts at what could be called literature to emerge from Buenos Aires, commemorates the second Porteño victory over the British. A few lines, honoring the heroic locals who fought off the foreign invaders, will suffice to give an idea of both the poem and the neoclassical mood in general:

Oh, ínclito Señor . . .
Buenos Aires os muestra allí sus hijos:
Allí está el labrador, allí el letrado,
El comerciante, el artesano, el niño
El moreno y el pardo; aquestos solo
Ese ejército forman tan lucido.
Todo es obra, Señor, de un sacro fuego,
Que del trémulo anciano al parvulillo

Corriendo en torno vuestro pueblo todo
Lo ha en ejército heroico convertido.

(Oh, Lord, . . . Buenos Aires shows you here its sons, the laborer and the
learned man, the merchant, the artisan and the mere boy, the Negro
and the son of mixed parentage. These alone have formed so splendid
an army. It was all, Oh Lord, the work of a sacred flame that, from the
trembling old man to the child, ran through all the populace, transform-
ing it into a heroic army.)

❋

MOST OF THE SPARSE BUILDING ACTIVITY of this period
was superseded by later, more ambitious projects, and thus very little of
it has survived. But the foremost monument from the period of Argentine independence, and the most emphatically neoclassical, has survived
fully intact. This is the massive twelve-columned facade of the Metropolitan Cathedral on the Plaza de Mayo, the former domain of Archbishop Bergoglio, now Pope Francis. (The interior, however, dates to the
1770s, and a church, in one form or another, has occupied the site since
the early 1600s.) Once again, one cannot make any great claims for the
cathedral according to the universal standards of architecture. Erected
in 1822 and designed by a naturalized Frenchman, Prosper Catelin, it is
a mediocre, if remarkably faithful, imitation of the facade of the Palais
Bourbon, the seat of the Chambre des Députés, on Paris's Left Bank.

But for all that, how striking this new facade must have seemed to
the Porteños, most of whom had never traveled beyond the city limits,
much less to France. This was the first example of *modern* architecture
that most of the Porteños would ever have seen. The city's churches and
the Recova were more or less traditional, but the Cathedral's facade,
with its austerely white Corinthian columns supporting a pristinely geometric triangular pediment, was as up-to-date as any building in the
world. As such, it was both the first self-consciously European building
ever to rise in the city and its first example of modern architecture. The
recently expanded Cabildo and the similarly conceived Recova Nueva,

Cathedral of Buenos Aires (Prosper Catelin, 1822) and the Pirámide de Mayo (Francisco Cañete, 1811). (Archivo General de la Nación)

built in 1818, looked exactly like what one had seen before, exactly like the architecture that covered much of the Spanish Empire. The cathedral, by contrast, seemed like something new under the sun.

The second grandly neoclassical structure in Buenos Aires was not a building at all but a monument, the Pirámide de Mayo, erected in 1811 to commemorate the events of the May Revolution of the previous year. For more than a century, until the completion in 1936 of the far larger Obelisco at the intersection of Avenues 9 de Julio and Corrientes, this was the defining national monument in Buenos Aires, the center of the city's and the nation's focus, a source and record of its pride. Despite its name, however, the relatively diminutive Pirámide de Mayo, scarcely forty feet tall, is more an obelisk than a pyramid. Its pristine whiteness, rivaling that of the nearby cathedral, must surely have stood out amid the brown mud that continued to cover the Plaza de Mayo at the time. Although it has been moved several times during its two centuries of existence, it now stands exactly in the center of the plaza, at the point once occupied by the Arco de los Virreyes, the great central arch of the

Recova. As we see it today, it is different from its original conception. There is a trace of Victorian fussiness in the details, an edge of prim, mid-nineteenth-century moralism to its decor, the work of Prelidiano Pueyrredón, one of the leading Porteño artists of that later age. But the original monument, designed by a Frenchman, Joseph Deburdieu, was far more chaste and neoclassical, a simple and almost unadorned object rising on an equally unadorned base, and crowned with a modest urn. Now it is crowned by a sculpted female figure incarnating either Liberty or the Republic. This was taken from the facade of the old Teatro Colón, which stood directly to the southeast, where the Bank of Argentina, in its second incarnation, now fronts the Plaza de Mayo.

Even bigger changes were conceived for the city at this time, but they came to nothing. They were the dream of Bernardino Rivadavia, who is often considered by the Argentines to have been their first president and who governed the country between 1826 and 1827. Technically, however, he was the president of the United Provinces of the Rio de la Plata rather than of Argentina, a slightly different entity that would come into existence only in 1860.

The best-known portrait of Rivadavia, painted in London, depicts him in the manner of Ingres. You sense an air of stolidity in the great man's ruddy complexion, his chubby fingers and expansive girth. But beneath the precise arc of his broad brows, we find in his large, dark eyes the stirrings of loftier ambitions. Rivadavia was, in South America at least, the most modern man of his age. With the possible exception of Tupac Amaru II, the mestizo leader of a revolt in Alto Peru in 1781, no one before him in South America had been so thoroughly imbued with the ideals of the European Enlightenment. Even though his eminent contemporaries, Bolívar and San Martín, had spent time, like him, in Europe, they were inspired to liberate their countries politically, more than spiritually or intellectually.

A native of Buenos Aires, Rivadavia was the first to dream the defining dream of Porteño history, that of re-creating Europe, with all its immemorial culture and intellectual nobility, on the western bank of the Rio de la Plata. He is thus the prototype of those men of later generations—Juan Domingo Sarmiento, Esteban Echeverría, Torcuato de

Bernardino Rivadavia. (Archivo General de la Nación)

Alvear and all the rest—who labored and fought to turn Buenos Aires into the Paris of South America. His great goal, he once said, was to liberate Buenos Aires from its Spanish past. Spain, of course, was also part of Europe, but not the Europe that counted.

Most of what Rivadavia accomplished in this respect he achieved before he became president. In one sense, his ambassadorial stint in Paris and London in 1820 and 1821 failed to accomplish anything that it set out to achieve. His attempts to win crucial financing for the newly independent nation came to nothing. Nor did he have great success in his truly visionary goal of persuading French and British thinkers, scientists and artists to emigrate en masse to Buenos Aires in order to educate and refine the population. But he did persuade the biologist Aimé Bompland, the architect Prosper Catelin and the painter Charles Pellegrini to take up residence in the capital.

On his return from his European sojourn, Rivadavia was appointed minister under Martín Rodriguez, the governor of the province of Buenos Aires. With fantastic energy, he set about creating the University of Buenos Aires, to this day one of the great academies of South America, as well as schools for theater, geology and medicine. The wondrous, if underfunded, Museo Argentino de Ciencias Naturales that stands today, as it has for the past eighty years, beside the Parque Centenario, would never have existed without his passionate advocacy. Throughout the city he founded schools and greatly expanded the famed Biblioteca Nacional over which, more than a century later, Jorge Luis Borges would preside as director.

But perhaps his greatest goal had to do with the city itself. During his presidency, he passed a law, on May 9, 1827, to reform the grid, to purge it of its uniformity and tedium by creating a hierarchy of streets and avenues. To this end he ordered, among other changes, that "from the Calle de la Plata in the north four streets will open, each 30 varas wide . . . the first in the direction of Calle Corrientes, the second that of Córdoba, the third that of Santa Fe, and the fourth three blocks from the plaza and, not having another name, will be called Calle Juncal." For the south were planned the Avenidas Belgrano, Independencia and San Juan. In addition each of these avenues was to be paved with stone rather than covered with the dirt and mud of the day. All of this was indeed brought to pass, but only some eighty years later, after Rivadavia was long gone.

For he, like many dreamers, was entirely lacking in the pragmatic ability to realize his visions, or the political skill to persuade a population that would eventually see his point, but only half a century or more after he made it. As evidence of his poor executive skills, he succeeded in talking the legislature into authorizing a 1 million pound loan for public works, but none of these works was ever undertaken. In true Porteño fashion—of which more recent administrations afford numerous instances—that vast sum evaporated into graft, while the loan itself would not be fully paid off until 1904.

It may well be that no elected official could have ridden the tiger of independence. Or perhaps it required a despot, like Rosas, whom we will meet in the next chapter. But few men were less suited to the task than Rivadavia, who lasted hardly a year in office before fleeing into European exile two years later in 1829. After an unsuccessful attempt, in 1834, to return to the city of his birth, he was exiled anew, and he died in Spain in 1845. Like so many of the patriots of his generation, he died in bitterness against the country he had fought so hard to raise up. He even stipulated in his will that his body never be returned to Buenos Aires. In this too he failed. Go today to the Plaza Miserere, in the shadow of the Once train station, and you will see his massive sepulchre. Though one of the most imposing monuments in a city of monuments, it is a shambles. Surrounded by a menacing gate meant to ward off vandals, its reflecting pools are dry and rust covers parts of the fountains. In this, one of the dreariest parts of the capital, it is hard to find, amid the transients and addicts who haunt the plaza, a single person who knows for whom the monument has been raised, or even that a man's ashes lie within it.

SIX

JUAN MANUEL DE ROSAS

(1829–1852)

HISTORY IS FILLED WITH DESPOTS WHO, WHATEVER their other moral failings, were great builders: in their passage to ultimate perdition, they left in their wake a trail of palaces and stadiums and even entire cities with shimmering vistas and sunlit avenues. But there is another kind of despot who is entirely indifferent, if not openly hostile, to even this degree of culture, and under such a man little is built beyond prisons and barracks.

Juan Manuel de Rosas was decidedly a despot of the latter sort. He ruled the city and province of Buenos Aires—and so, in effect, the entire Argentine nation—for almost a quarter of a century, from 1829 to 1852 (with a gap between 1832 and 1835). In this time, almost nothing of consequence was built in Buenos Aires. Little music remains from this period. Few poems or novels were written, and few works of visual art were produced. And although it is true that Buenos Aires remained a functioning port throughout the period of his rule, with merchants and diplomats pouring in from England and France, nothing of that cosmopolitanism is reflected in the culture of the time. The two great works of Argentine literature from these years, Sarmiento's *Facundo* and

Juan Manuel de Rosas. (Archivo General de la Nación)

Esteban Echeverría's *El Matadero,* were written in exile by the mortal enemies of Rosas, and they read as hymns to their authors' implacable hatred of the man.

But if Rosas built little, it would not be too great an exaggeration to say that, in the hearts and minds of the Porteños, he erected vast infrastructures of fear, cathedrals of fear, that continued to operate in them even after he was gone. In this he may be seen as a progenitor of all those murderous tyrants of the next century in his ambitions to subdue an unruly human race to his will. Just as a newly paved or lighted street materially influences the behavior of the citizens, even so did these metaphorical walls of fear influence when the citizens chose to set out and when to stay indoors and draw the curtains. The entire city became a theater of violence carried out for the instruction and intimidation of the citizens of Buenos Aires. When Rosas apprehended the assassins of Facundo Quiroga, an ally of his from the province of La Rioja, he left their lifeless bodies dangling for days from the arches of the Cabildo, for all to see and learn from.

Rosas stands in the full light of history as an insoluble enigma. He was seen as a champion of the poor, even though he held the poor in contempt and was himself the richest man in the country. Unlike many tyrants, however, Rosas managed to earn or inherit his wealth before becoming ruler and to do so approximately honorably. And yet he never exhibited a great love of money, except as it enhanced his hold on power. And even as regards his hold on power, he seemed genuinely reluctant to accept it in the first place, and on several occasions he wanted to be rid of it. For the first of many times in Argentine history, he was happy to play the card of economic nationalism against France and Britain, and yet, even when he was in a state of open war against those nations in the summer of 1845, he conducted himself with conspicuous, even perverse courtesy toward their ambassadors. Finally, despite his aversion to building, the mansion he commissioned in Palermo de San Benito was perhaps the only important structure completed in Buenos Aires during the quarter-century of his rule.

It would be difficult to imagine a man who was more different from Bernardino Rivadavia than Rosas. If Rivadavia was an idealist, the vessel of all the hopes and strivings of the European Enlightenment, Rosas was, by instinct and conviction, a man of the profoundest conservatism. He loathed with all his heart the aspirations of men like Rivadavia. Most of all he hated anarchy, and he believed, with some justice, that the anarchy that the nation had witnessed in 1828, just before it turned to him for salvation, was the consequence of men like Rivadavia, who lacked the competence, the mother wit, to see the world as the murderous Hobbesian slaughterhouse that it really was. By contrast, Rosas was a man of awe-inspiring competence who seemed—at least for most of the quarter-century in which he ruled Argentina—intuitively to understand how to acquire, maintain and use power. Rosas, in short, presents us with the striking instance of a man—rare but by no means unique in the world—who believed in absolutely nothing.

———— ❊ ————

AS A RULER, Rosas understood that he must appear to believe in something, and it was in this spirit that he accommodated, as he saw it, the stupidity of others. The closest he ever came to a credo—and this would seem to have been expressed with some sincerity—was in a letter to a friend, from late in his life: "When even the lower classes increasingly lose respect for law and order, and no longer fear divine punishment, only absolute powers are capable of imposing the laws of God and man, and respect for capital and its owners."

Rosas must be understood in the context of the struggle between the Unitarios and the Federales (the Unitarians and the Federalists). This conflict dominated the political life of Buenos Aires and of Argentina until 1862, when the city was assimilated into the newly formed Argentine state, and long after that as well. In many ways this conflict is remarkably similar to the one between the Federalists and the followers of Jefferson in the early years of the United States. On the one hand there were the proponents of a highly centralized and progressive government, and on the other, the advocates of a confederation of quasi-autonomous agrarian states. The Argentine Federales would thus have been the ideological adversaries of the American Federalists.

As so often is the case in these conflicts, there was an aesthetic or stylistic dimension to the two sides. The Unitarios read Byron and Chateaubriand and wrote poetry and prose in imitation of them. They were technocrats who favored learning and culture. They wore European clothes, and even their beards, which swept down under the chin from one temple to the other, were thought to form a U-shape, for Unitario. The Federales, by contrast, were nativists who favored the varied and immemorial traditions of the heartland and professed to look with grave suspicion on any doctrines imported from abroad. In their mistrust of political institutions, they inspired the rise of the *caudillo* or local strongman in each of the provinces of the confederation. Among these men were Juan Facundo Quiroga in La Rioja, Estanislao López in Santa Fe, José de Urquiza in Entre Rios and Rosas in Buenos Aires. Instead of the frock coat, they favored the poncho, their beards extended from the chin and they sported mustaches that no Unitario would ever dream of wearing.

The conflict between these two factions, combined with the limited competence of both sides when in power, brought the confederation to the verge of anarchy. The occasion for this anarchy was the conclusion of a war fought with Brazil over the east bank of the Rio de la Plata. Although it had been part of the Viceroyalty of the Rio de la Plata, the Portuguese (now Brazilians) had been eager to claim it since the seventeenth century and now undertook to do so. By 1827, however, this very unpopular war had turned into a protracted stalemate. Rivadavia submitted his resignation and was replaced by the Federalist Manuel Dorrego. One year later the British-brokered Treaty of Montevideo ended the war, with neither Argentina nor Brazil winning possession of the disputed territory. In a compromise that displeased both sides, the new and independent state of Uruguay came into being. To the Argentines this felt like a defeat, and in short order, the entire federation collapsed, with each province having to shift for itself. The Unitarios seized the opportunity to have Dorrego arrested and put to death, among the first of a sequence of murders that, in generations to come, would degrade the political realm of Argentina. Dorrego's successor as governor, and one of those responsible for his fate, was Juan Lavalle, who won election by somewhat questionable means. He too came to a bad end a decade later, in a way that illustrates the tenor of the times: well into Rosas's regime, Lavalle was gunned down while prosecuting a campaign against Rosas in the far north. His followers, fearing that his body would be desecrated if buried in those parts, bore it away to Alto Peru. En route, however, it began to decompose and so was boiled down to the bare bones. Many years later, in a more propitious political climate, these bones found their way back to Buenos Aires, where they now lie entombed in the Cemetery of Recoleta.

But that lay in the future. Presently, Lavalle himself was ousted by the Federalist Juan José Viamonte who, as governor, facilitated the accession of Rosas. The rise of Rosas was due to his having fought with distinction against the indigenous tribes and to his defense of the capital. Just as the Argentine people, a century and a half later in 1976, initially would welcome a military coup after several years of mostly left-wing anarchy, they now looked to a *caudillo* to save them from themselves. According to the terms of the confederation, Rosas was nothing more or less than the governor of one province, Buenos Aires. But in virtue of his ruling the largest, wealthiest and most populous province of the entire confederation, he became de facto ruler of what already was, in essence, Argentina. José de San Martín, the greatest of the Argentine generals, is universally honored in the country as *El Libertador,* the Liberator, for having defeated the Spanish and their allies in the region and so winning the liberty and independence of the nation. In the same spirit, Rosas was known—at least among his allies—as *El Restaurador,* the Restorer, for having brought peace to a nation convulsed by years of anarchy.

In the context of the Unitarios and Federales, Rosas is seen as the preeminent representative of the latter, but that was only partially true. The Unitarios, as we have seen, were philosophically inclined, and they offered richly articulated arguments for their position. The Federales, by contrast, differed from their Jeffersonian counterparts in not generally framing their convictions in philosophical terms, other than an innate conservatism and a desire to protect their turf against a centralized government in far-off Buenos Aires. It is somewhat ironic, however, that in Buenos Aires itself, the warring parties coincided in one great goal: ensuring the primacy of their province.

❉

UNDER ROSAS, Buenos Aires may well have obtained a lugubrious distinction in the history of the world, that of being the birthplace of totalitarianism. If Rosas did not impose a truly totalitarian regime, that is mainly because, of course, the means of one-directional mass communication had not yet been invented. Repressive and authoritarian regimes, to be sure, were nothing new. Nor was the pervasive deployment of visual propaganda. But there is something different about the regime of Rosas, a quality that is without precedent in earlier history, but that, in the light of the twentieth century and beyond, feels unnervingly familiar. For Rosas not only undertook to suppress rebellious thoughts in a subject population and to engender thoughts favorable to himself, something that most rulers aspired to do: he also tried, through the relentlessness of his propaganda, to dominate the thoughts of his citizens to the point where it would be impossible to see the world in any other way than his. Throughout the city, the slogans and battle cries of his regime were inescapable: "Long live the Argentine Confederation!" and, far more sinister, "Death to the savage Unitarians!"

Rosas's desire to control the Porteños even extended to their dress. Women were to adorn their hair with red ribbons, the color of the confederation, while men had to wear badges inscribed with the two slogans quoted above. And it goes without saying that they were obliged not only to grow beards, but to do so in the manner prescribed by the Federales. This went on for nearly twenty-five years. When Rosas's wife, Encarnación, died, an elaborate funeral cortege—a presentiment of the reaction, more than a century later, to the death of Eva Perón—bore her body from the fort to the nearby Church of San Francisco. The entire city was draped in mourning and remained that way for fully two years. Unrelated to these obsequies, Rosas went so far as to place his portrait on the altar of every church in the province of Buenos Aires.

As so often happens, not only in totalitarian regimes, but even in simply authoritarian ones, it was necessary to remove the checks and balances that the Unitarios—in conscious imitation of the United States—had imposed upon the workings of government. For the first time, but by no means the last in Argentine history, Rosas contrived to subvert and suborn the judiciary and the legislature.

But where slogans, banners, portraits, beards and processions ended, the work of the Mazorca began. This was Rosas's secret police, charged with the duty of intimidating into submission (and if that failed, murdering) all those upon whom Rosas's thought control proved unsuccessful. An armed wing of the Sociedad Popular Restauradora, the Mazorca should be seen as a forerunner of the Stasi in East Germany and the

Savak under the Shah of Iran, among many other such entities down to the present day. The name *mazorca* refers to a head of corn and was originally intended to suggest strength through unity or confederation or something of the sort. But in Spanish it sounds nearly indistinguishable from *mas horca,* "more hangings," a train of association that the regime was only too happy to foster in the minds of the Porteños.

In due course, prisons arose throughout the city: the Cuartel de Serenos, the Cuartel de Cuitino in Chacobuco, the Cuartel de los Restauradores at the corner of Mexico and Defensa, and, worst of all by far, Santos Lugares, the military headquarters of the regime, which stood about ten miles west of the Plaza de Mayo, just beyond the boundaries of contemporary Buenos Aires. Many of the murders carried out by the regime, however, were not hidden from sight behind prison walls but occurred in broad daylight, as the terrified citizens averted their gaze and pretended to see nothing. And the manner of death was as richly symbolic as the act itself. The victim's throat was cut in a single swift, clean sweep, from one side to the other. The verb for this was *degollar,* and the perpetrator of the act was a *degollador.* Although it has been claimed that this method had been used against the Federales by the Unitarios when they were last in power, it was a technique first employed by the gauchos on the pampas to slay cattle. "Execution by cutting the throat with a knife instead of by shooting," Sarmiento wrote, "is the result of the butcher's instinct which Rosas has exploited to give executions a more gaucho-like form, and more pleasure to the assassins." Once the deed had been done, it was not uncommon for the victims' heads to be impaled on long poles and displayed in the main public squares.

Despite the secretiveness of many of their operations, the names and deeds of the Mazorca were proudly published in the *Gaceta Mercantil,* the unofficial organ of the Federales. And when their death squads were not going house to house, they would show up in force to intimidate the legislature, even though that body had long since been reduced to a rubber stamp of the regime. The leader of the Mazorca was Julián González Salomón, formerly the owner of a corner dry-goods store. The *mazorqueros* themselves, the rank and file, came mostly from the lower classes, whether police officers and night watchmen or career criminals and delinquents.

Nevertheless, as might be expected of a man as self-controlled as Rosas, the terror that his regime unleashed was never wanton or indiscriminate, but tactical and premeditated. It was mostly limited to the period from 1839 to 1842, with the height of the terror falling between September 23 and October 27, 1840, when a French blockade of the city threatened to undermine the entire regime. For much of this period, the streets of Buenos Aires were eerily deserted. On such occasions, only the Mazorca was abroad in the capital. Unmistakable in their red ponchos and peaked caps, they brandished guns, knives and clubs as they moved from house to house, searching for anyone they suspected of being an enemy of Rosas. The British ambassador Mandeville, though generally on good terms with the governor, felt compelled to denounce the "wild mob rampaging in [the] immediate vicinity" of his house. When similar violence flared up two years later, Mandeville protested so forcefully that the murders stopped.

In reviewing the bloodletting of the Rosas regime, in trying to understand it, one must acknowledge its discipline. The violence that has been seen at other points in the history of Buenos Aires—under Perón in the 1950s, under the leftist Montoneros in the early 1970s, under the dictatorship from 1976 to 1983—was a very different thing, greater in scale and, more crucially, entirely lacking in control. Such later violence was, so to speak, the homage of anarchy to disciplined repression. In the name of control, its authors had lost control. With Rosas and his dismal crew, that, at least, never happened.

The exact number of deaths under Rosas will never be known. At the lower end, the *Gaceta Mercantil* calculated 500 in the years between 1829 and 1843, of which 250 took place in the provinces, 100 were executions of refractory indigenous peoples, and another 150 were citizens of Buenos Aires. Opposition writers like Rivera Indurate put the number at nearly 6,000 victims of terror. But that number, according to John Lynch, is "probably too high." Political executions, he concludes, were "perhaps in the region of 2,000 for the whole period 1829–1853. These were not mass murders. The targets were precisely chosen and carefully identified. It can be assumed that Rosas calculated the amount of terror needed to produce results in wider circles beyond the victims. If ever a state ruled by the principle of fear, it was his."

Rosas never apologized for the violence he unleashed on his own population: "When I was given this hateful extraordinary power, I was given it not on condition that I always had to be right, but to act with complete freedom, according to my judgment, and to act without restrictions, for the sole object of saving the dying country." Such dispassion and candor, together with an admission of fallibility, are not admirable, but they seem, at the very least, fundamentally different from the brittle, evasive vanity of those subsequent and equally murderous regimes that have stained the streets of Buenos Aires with blood.

❋

ROSAS, BOTH IN HIS OWN DAY and subsequently, was so closely associated with the heartland of Argentina, with those provinces farthest from its glittering, Europhile capital, that one almost forgets that he was a native of Buenos Aires and that, until he escaped into exile in 1852, his entire life was spent there. He was born on March 30, 1793, in a small house at 94 Coy Street, in what is now the Microcentro, or Financial District. With exquisite if unintentional irony, this street would later be renamed Sarmiento, after his most committed enemy, the man who contributed to his defeat on the day of Caseros. After his marriage to Encarnación, Rosas moved into her house at the corner of Bolívar and Moreno in the barrio of Monserrat. From its turreted roof, it is said, he enjoyed looking out at the river and watching the coming and going of ships in the harbor of the Riachuelo.

But the place with which Rosas will always be associated is Palermo de San Benito, in what is now the barrio of Palermo. It received this name in the 1690s from the original settler, a trader from Sicily. Now the biggest and most complex barrio in the city, Palermo was little more than a wetlands in the 1830s, when Rosas began to buy up property here. It stands over three miles northwest of the Plaza de Mayo and at the time there were no good roads between them, due to frequent

The Caseron of Juan Manuel de Rosas, completed in 1838; designed by Felipe Senillosa. (Archivo General de la Nación)

rains and the constant inundations of the Rio de la Plata. The area now known as Palermo, in any case, was very much on the outskirts of the city until nearly the end of the nineteenth century. It was mostly a place of summer retreats, farms and brick factories that, due to their acrid smell, were kept far from the center of the city.

It was here that Rosas chose to construct his great house, or *caseron*. Fortunately the building lived on in various functions for nearly half a century after he had been driven into exile, and so we have excellent photographs of it. Built on lands extending for nearly two and a half square miles, the house itself was surprisingly ambitious for its day: in its typology it resembled other contemporary country houses and *estancias*, but it was constructed out of whitewashed brick, not out of wood, as they tended to be. Conceived in something like the neoclassical style by the architect Felipe Senillosa and completed in 1838, it was a one-story structure with a flat roof, and it consisted of a large central block with smaller square pavilions at the four corners. These, like the central block, were surrounded by arcades that were surprisingly elegant, even advanced, for the time.

With over three hundred functionaries milling about, this vast structure served not only as Rosas's home but also as the seat of government for the province of Buenos Aires (and so, in a sense, for the entire country). Students of the topography of ancient Rome will find something almost Neronian in its extravagance, with its private menagerie of rare birds and beasts, and no fewer than three jesters on hand to divert the governor with jibes at his enemies. But Rosas spent his own money and opened his *caseron* to all Porteños, whom he fed and encouraged to stroll through the elegantly landscaped grounds. When Rosas himself could not be present, his daughter, Manuelita, for whom even his worst enemies never had a unkind word, would take his place. And so, already in the 1840s, his home served almost as a public park, the first in the city. Indeed, after his overthrow in 1852, the grounds were transformed into the Parque Tres de Febrero, to this day the finest park in the capital.

A visitor to the area now can easily form some idea of what the grounds looked like in Rosas's day, since one of the bodies of water, the small lake where he rode around in his steamboat, still exists and remains a popular place for picnics. For nearly half a century after his fall, the house continued to serve a number of municipal functions before it was dynamited out of existence in 1899. Nothing remains beyond a pile of six or seven red bricks preserved a few meters from the Avenida Libertador. And in what certainly seems like a cruel jest, Rodin's statue of Sarmiento stands on the very spot that is rumored to have been Rosas's bedroom.

As I have said, Rosas's contributions to the city of Buenos Aires were restricted almost entirely to infrastructure. It is true that he extended the Paseo de la Alameda, which had been initiated under Viceroy Vértiz in 1780 and which ran beside the waters of the Rio de la Plata at the eastern limit of the city. Originally it had been only three blocks long and could be traversed in about six minutes. Rosas, however, extended it all the way north to his villa in Palermo, roughly three and a half miles away, and south, about a mile, to Avenida San Juan. Not only was the

Alameda the only tree-lined avenue in the city at the time, but it also represented the first major incursion of landscaping and engineering into the semiwild farms, summer homes and mudflats of what would come to be called the Barrio Norte. This new walkway, then, was the direct antecedent of one of the most important avenues in modern Buenos Aires, the Avenida Libertador.

A far more important development, however, and the immediate pretext for extending the Paseo de la Alameda in the first place, was Rosas's decision in 1845 to embank the Rio de la Plata within the city. A recurring theme in the development of Buenos Aires has been its odd, even adversarial relation to the river. Before Rosas's embankment, nothing separated the citizens from the water. For two and a half centuries and more they thought nothing of descending into the Rio de la Plata to wash their clothes or to splash around on warm summer nights. It may be that in effecting this infrastructural modification, Rosas was driven by a motive no more sinister than efficiency. But it is also easy to imagine that an ineradicable habit of control induced him to subdue the wayward forces of nature to his will and also to regulate the behavior of his citizens. A photograph from 1865, twenty years after the embankment was begun, reveals these primly admirable modifications. For the first time a sense of order, even of civilization, confronts the anarchic misrule of the waters. Where the barrancas that surround the city once descended to the water's edge, one now found a perfectly flattened esplanade formed from earth transported from the river. With a wrought-iron fence and rows of sullen bollards, it rose around twenty feet above the sandbars and the waters of Rio de la Plata.

❋

THE END OF ROSAS'S REGIME was long in coming. The summit of his glory, in the eyes of the Porteños, the Argentines and the world, was reached in 1845, when he led his nation in resisting a blockade of British and French ships and defeated them at the Battle of Vuelta de Obligado. By 1846, the Mazorca had been disbanded, its work having been carried out all too efficiently.

Ironically, it was a violent act, but one less violent than many others committed by Rosas, that began to turn the Porteños against the regime. It had to do with the 1847 elopement of Ladislao Gutierrez, a twenty-four-year-old Jesuit priest, and Camila O'Gorman, a well-born woman of twenty-three and the granddaughter of the viceroy Santiago de Liniers, hero of the Reconquista. She was also a friend of Rosas's daughter, Manuelita, and had been a frequent visitor to the house in Palermo. Gutierrez was a parish priest in the church of Nuestra Señora del Socoro, which still stands at the corner of Suipacha and Juncal, not far from the Plaza San Martín. The young couple eloped to the distant town of Goya in the province of Corrientes, where, under assumed names, they established a small school and passed themselves off as a married couple. Eventually, however, they were discovered and brought back, amid great scandal, to Buenos Aires, where they were imprisoned in the notorious Santos Lugares. Meanwhile, the opposition press in Montevideo and Santiago de Chile, and Sarmiento most of all, exulted in this evidence of Rosas's moral corruption. According to Lynch, "Rosas now suffered loss of face as well as an affront to his authority." Manuelita tried in vain to intervene on the couple's behalf and even provided Camila, in her prison cell, with books and a piano. But Rosas would not be moved to clemency, claiming that the scandal required "a show of my undisputed power, as the moral values and sacred religious norms of the entire society are at stake." And so Gutierrez and O'Gorman, eight months pregnant, died by firing squad on August 18 of that year. The Porteños did not dare express publicly their sympathy for the couple and their revulsion at their fate. But they began to look differently at Rosas, and they feared most of all a recrudescence of the violence that appeared to have abated a few years before.

As it turned out, Rosas's day of reckoning arrived three and a half years later during a conflict known as the Platine War. Once again the Argentine confederation that he led was fighting against an expansionist Brazil, allied to Uruguay and the breakaway Argentine provinces of Entre Rios and Corrientes. But before Entre Rios broke away, Rosas made the strategic blunder—surely the greatest in his career—of providing its leader, José de Urquiza, with a standing army that Urquiza now turned against him. More than that, Rosas had armed his new enemy with far better ordnance than he himself possessed. As for Urquiza, he had finally grasped the essential truth that eluded all the other provincial rulers: that Rosas was cynically using the rhetoric of Federalism to assert Porteño control over the rest of the country. And so, on February 3, 1852, at the small town of Caseros—a few miles beyond today's Avenida General Paz, the western limit of Buenos Aires—the two armies met and Rosas was soundly defeated. With the enemy closing in on Palermo de San Benito, Rosas slipped quietly away—with British assistance—to a life of exile in Southampton, England.

For the next quarter-century, until his death in 1877 at age eighty-four, Rosas eked out a straitened existence in that town. Since all of his Argentine property had been confiscated, he had to subsist on whatever he received from friends and from his own modest efforts as an English farmer. Throughout this time, he repeatedly contrived to return to Buenos Aires, but nothing ever came of his schemes. His devoted daughter married against his will, and he effectively disowned her. She too lived in England until her death in 1897 at eighty-one.

Rosas remains one of the most controversial figures in the history of Argentina, and so of Buenos Aires. His removal from power after the Battle of Caseros spelled the complete victory of the Unitarios, a victory that would endure for nearly a century until the accession of Juan Perón in 1946. In that time, the history of Rosas's regime was written almost exclusively by his enemies, who did such a thorough job that, to this day, the man is still reflexively reviled.

In the past generation, it is true, the Left has tried to rehabilitate Rosas, perhaps the most conservative ruler in the nation's bloody history. And so, in 1999, an equestrian statue of El Restaurador was set up near the former site of his house in Palermo. But even this presumes to celebrate not so much his regime as his victory over the French and British at the Battle of Vuelta de Obligado, a victory that even the most committed Unitarian would have applauded. Furthermore, it stands on Avenida Sarmiento, directly facing Rodin's statue of Sarmiento. And though the final stop on the C line of the Subte (or subway) has recently been named for Rosas, it comes immediately after Estación Esteban

Echeverría, named for the only man in Argentina who hated Rosas more than Sarmiento did.

It is the supreme irony of recent Argentine politics that self-styled progressives, and especially those associated with Perónism and its Kirchnerite wing, should choose to honor the most conservative figure in their nation's history; that in pursuit of La Patria Grande (a pan–South American movement that supports indigenous populations) they extol the man whose life's work was to impose the hegemony of Buenos Aires on the rest of the country; and that, for the sake of economic redistribution, they pay homage to a man who violently defended an oligarchy of which he was the richest member. One can only imagine what Rosas would have thought of them.

SEVEN

BUENOS AIRES, THE BIG VILLAGE

(1852–1880)

THE CITY OF BUENOS AIRES RESEMBLES A MAN WHO, in adulthood, betrays no trace, either physical or spiritual, of the child he once was. Indeed, he has forgotten that younger self to such a degree that the events of his early years, if he even remembers them, seem to have occurred in another lifetime and to another person. Beyond the persistence of Juan de Garay's grid and the enduring centrality of the Plaza de Mayo, the physical essence of Buenos Aires, its building stock, bears little or no relation to its earlier state. The Cabildo remains, although greatly modified and reduced, as do a few eighteenth-century churches that were atypical of the city even when they were built.

But if we cannot feel our way back to the Buenos Aires of Rosas's regime, we begin to witness, in the years and even the months following his fall, the awakening of the great city that we know today. It is not an exaggeration to say that, with the emergence of the new Unitarian regime, the history of Buenos Aires, the true Buenos Aires, can finally begin in earnest, and that everything that has preceded this point was but a prologue.

The Battle of Caseros, which forced the defeated Rosas into exile, spelled the end of rule by *caudillos,* or local strongmen, and the emergence of the unified and largely modern state of Argentina. But Caseros stands even more emphatically as a watershed for Buenos Aires itself. The year 1852 divides the city's urban history into two parts: from 1580 to 1852 and from 1852 to the present. Only with the inception of this latter period do we finally begin to see, albeit in inchoate form, the modern city of Buenos Aires.

After the fall of Rosas, it was quite obvious to everyone that there would be at best an uneasy peace. The factions that had defeated him were Unitarios like Sarmiento, who hated him for all the usual Unitarian reasons, and Federales like Urquiza, who felt that Rosas had sold out the confederation in the interests of Buenos Aires. Between these two groups there could be only tension. For the space of two years Urquiza, the victor of Caseros, was provisional director of the Argentine Confederation and he performed the duties of his office more or less responsibly. But pursuant to the premises of federalism, he proceeded to distribute the wealth of the nation more equitably among its sundry provinces. In consequence, Buenos Aires received a smaller share than in the past, which meant, in essence, that some of its own wealth was now being given away to distant, almost alien provinces like La Rioja and Jujuy. That, of course, did not sit well with the citizens of the port. And so, on September 11, 1852, while Urquiza was away in the province of Entre Rios, the Porteños rejected the federalist pact that they had signed only a few months earlier and, declaring their independence, chose Valentín Alsina as their new governor. And thus the federalist constitution was enthusiastically ratified by every province in the nation except Buenos Aires, the largest and wealthiest of them all. Soon thereafter, from December 6, 1852, to July 12, 1853, Urquiza laid siege to the city. Ultimately, however, the siege was lifted on terms favorable to the Porteños, who preserved their independence and their control over the revenues of the port.

For a period of six years, from June 1853 through October 1859, the entire province of Buenos Aires would become a sovereign and independent state, El Estado de Buenos Aires, even though it continued to perform all of its former functions relative to the economy of Argentina as a whole. The new nation claimed dominion over much of the pampas and even over the Falkland Islands, or the Islas Malvinas as they are known to the Argentines. While Urquiza ruled in the city, Porteño anger against the remnants of Rosas's regime was largely contained. But now with his removal it was finally unleashed, the more furiously for having been held in check. In one day, on October 17, 1854, several members of Rosas's secret police, the Mazorca, were hanged from the central arch of the Recova in Plaza de la Victoria, and two others died by firing squad in the Plaza de la Independencia.

Perhaps the leading local political figure of this period, in both the city and province of Buenos Aires, was its governor, Pastor Obligado, a lawyer by training and for a time a committed ally of Rosas. It may seem paradoxical that a follower of Rosas should cooperate in the Unitarian hegemony of Buenos Aires over Argentina, but this paradox is more apparent than real. As mentioned in the previous chapter, the Federales in Buenos Aires differed from the Unitarios in ideology and style, but they shared the goal of ensuring that the port retain control of its revenues. They wanted to continue to dominate the country in the future as they had in the past and to ensure that Buenos Aires would never fall under the rule of the other provinces. In all of these ambitions Obligado fully shared, and no one ever promoted them more energetically than he did. Obligado proved to be a major force for progress in the city, as Rosas had never been. He reopened a number of schools, preeminently the Colegio Nacional de Buenos Aires, that had been all but shut down under Rosas, and he was responsible for providing the city with its first gas lamps and indoor plumbing, among many other important infrastructural improvements. The significance of these latter advances, although in one sense lowly and pedestrian, can hardly be overstated, since they fundamentally altered how the citizens of Buenos Aires inhabited their homes and the city itself.

The Estado de Buenos Aires came to an end after six years, at the Battle of Cepeda, in 1859, when Urquiza successfully vanquished the Porteños and retook control of the city. With the Pact of San Juan de Flores, the Porteños reaffirmed their compliance with the Federal Constitution of 1853, even though they were not yet technically integrated into the confederation. But Urquiza's triumph proved to be short-lived.

Only two years later, in 1861, he decisively lost the Battle of Pavón to Bartolomé Mitre, who, in a national election held shortly thereafter, was elected the first president of the Republic of Argentina, which now included Buenos Aires as well.

———— ❋ ————

ALTHOUGH BARTOLOMÉ MITRE'S ROOTS were Greek (his family name was shortened from Mitropoulos), his ancestors had lived in Buenos Aires for centuries, and he felt Porteño to the core. He was born on June 26, 1821, at the corner of Suipacha and Lavalle, in that hyperactive section of the Microcentro that today abounds in multiplexes and steakhouses. Over the site of the very church in which he was baptized, San Nicolás de Bari, now rises the famed Obelisco, the universal symbol of Buenos Aires.

From his earliest youth Mitre had exhibited a gift for letters and ideas. As such he was almost certain to become an object of suspicion to Rosas and his followers. And so, scarcely twenty years old, he fled across the Rio de la Plata to Montevideo, one of the centers of the Unitarian opposition. There he gained a knowledge of artillery that would stand him in good stead, twenty years later, at the Battle of Pavón. But it was also in Uruguay that he published his first poems and essays. As a poet, he was entirely of his age, the age of Romanticism, whose influence was just beginning to blow in from France. There is, to be sure, a certain callowness to his early verse, but it also contains a forceful expression of his patriotism and the pains of exile. In the entire corpus of earlier Argentine writing, no one had expressed so forcefully or so personally a love of the city of Buenos Aires itself:

> *Oh patria! Oh Buenos Aires! Oh sueño de mi vida!*
> *Como inmortal recuerdo reinas en mi memoria,*
> *Recorriendo los días de dicha promisoria*
> *Que en tu seno amoroso, Buenos Aires, pasé.*
> *Recuerdo la ribera do a meditar yo iba*

Bartolomé Mitre. (Archivo General de la Nación)

Y el árbol perfumado que sombra me prestaba,
Recuerdo los momentos en que se deslizaba
Mi vida por un lago sereno de placer.

[Oh fatherland! Oh Buenos Aires! Oh dream of my life! You reign in
my recollection like an undying memory, bringing back those days of
promised happiness that I passed, Buenos Aires, in your loving embrace.
I remember the river where I went to enjoy quiet reflection and the per-
fumed tree that gave me shade; I remember those moments in which my
life slipped away in an untroubled sea of delight.]

❋

ONLY A GENERATION EARLIER, in 1800, it would have been unimaginable for anyone to feel that way, let alone to write that way, about Buenos Aires.

For many years, Mitre led a nomadic existence, passing through Bolivia and Peru before finding in Chile a safe haven for himself, his wife and his six children. Along the way, he studied the languages of the indigenous peoples he encountered. In Santiago de Chile he met the great Sarmiento, who hired him to work on his Unitario newspaper, *El Progreso*. Twenty years later, on becoming president of Argentina, Mitre returned the favor by appointing Sarmiento ambassador to the United States. Sarmiento would succeed Mitre as president in 1868.

Soon after the Battle of Caseros, Mitre returned to Buenos Aires and quickly became one of its leading citizens. He defended the city against Urquiza's siege in 1853, even sustaining a head wound that caused him to wear a hat in public for the rest of his life. But Mitre was at most a citizen soldier, primarily interested in cultivating his mind. The very breadth of his interests makes him one of the most admirable men of the nineteenth century. In addition to studying indigenous languages amid the hardships of his exile, he found time to translate the *Divine Comedy* and the *Odes* of Horace. His six-volume biography of José de San Martín, the Liberator of Argentina, is still read by students of Argentine history, as is his four-volume biography of San Martín's lieutenant, Manuel Belgrano. All the while he continued to write an abundance of poetry and one novel. But perhaps his most lasting contribution to Argentine letters was his founding of the newspaper *La Nación* in 1870: one and a half centuries later, it remains the most respected daily in Argentina.

All of this he did from his home at 336 San Martín, a few minutes' walk from where he was born. It is now a museum devoted to his presidency, and well worth a visit, not only for what it tells us about Mitre himself, but also for the light it sheds on the houses of the Porteño haute bourgeoisie in the latter half of the nineteenth century. At the Museo

Mitre one sees the gilded mirrors and marble fireplaces, the canopied beds and Gallic privies of the time, as well as the sturdy oak desks and pool table that the age required. This was one of the more sumptuous houses of its time, and so a good indication of what the merchant and professional elite valued. But as a home—whatever its other qualities—it lacks a certain charm and grace. The bare, wooden floors do not go with the overly fussy refinement of its midcentury furnishings. Its style stands in stark contrast to what would emerge at the end of the century, during the city's gilded age. Surely there was something overwrought, perhaps even decadent and gaudy about that later style, but it was real style. In the case of Mitre's house, one senses that it occupies a transitional point between the largely Spartan homes of colonial days and the Gallic palaces that would soon arise. Far more impressive than the decor is the president's astonishing private library, which contains fully sixty thousand volumes.

Mitre is also the beneficiary of one of the finest monuments in Buenos Aires. Among the best of many equestrian statues in the city, it towers over the grassy landscape of the Plaza Mitre. Of all the many felicities of urban stagecraft that abound in Buenos Aires, few have been carried off with such tact as this Mitre monument. Cast in bronze by Eduardo Rubino and David Calandra and completed in 1927, the horse and rider stand atop a twenty-foot-tall pedestal of gleaming marble that rises over the steep barranca that overlooked the river and now descends toward Avenida Libertador. Seen from forty feet below, horse and rider look as though they might come charging down upon the sunbathers sprawled out, in fair weather, halfway between the Museo de Bellas Artes and the Biblioteca Nacional.

✳

A COMMITTED UNITARIO, Mitre promptly reasserted Porteño control over the rest of the country. But, as so often throughout the city's history, its relation to the nation as a whole was complicated and ambiguous. From the beginning of Mitre's presidency, through the presidencies of his successors Sarmiento (1868–1874) and Nicolas

Avellaneda (1874–1880), Buenos Aires was not technically the capital of the nation, even though it was the seat of all three branches of the national government. In law and protocol, the president, the legislators and the judicial branch were merely guests in the city of Buenos Aires, which was still ruled by the governor of the province.

The architecture of Buenos Aires—between the fall of Rosas in 1852 and the city's official selection as the nation's capital in 1880—is a direct consequence of this ambiguity regarding its ultimate status. Many of the buildings constructed during this period were replaced a generation later, when the city's role as capital was assured. The former buildings are apt to seem like humbler, plainer versions of the latter. Even when these buildings served a national function before 1880, they were really municipal buildings in spirit and form. Consider the now demolished Congreso designed by Jonás Larguía in 1865. Fronting the Plaza de Mayo at an oblique angle, it was a surprisingly good piece of work. It consisted of a central temple front whose three arches were crowned by triangular pediments and flanked by wings of two arches each to create a powerful and harmonious facade. The form of the central arches was especially well done and represented a rare instance in which the academic tradition, whether in Buenos Aires or anywhere else, broke through to real architecture.

Under Obligado, Mitre and his two successors, new and ambitious architecture, for the first time in the history of Buenos Aires, became almost plentiful. It was not yet good architecture, with some exceptions like the Congreso, but at least it had the virtue of being pretentious. After nearly three centuries in which it would not have occurred to anyone to go beyond the entrenched habits of one's forebears—the neoclassical facade of the cathedral being, perhaps, the unique exception—it is pleasant indeed to encounter buildings with real architectural ambitions, that proudly make their statements and do so with self-conscious, if still imperfect, art. One can easily believe that this relative outpouring of architecture responded to an impulse that had been repressed under Rosas and that now, with his overthrow, was finally given free rein.

From the perspective of architectural history, it is convenient, if a little arbitrary, to call this period Victorian more than Beaux Arts. It was in many respects a pan-Western style, in the sense that its effects—with regional variants—pervade the Western world from Saint Petersburg to Dublin and from Boston to Buenos Aires. The true Beaux Arts style that would dominate European architecture in the Belle Époque was being invented at that moment in Paris, but it did not yet reach much beyond the French capital. In Buenos Aires after the overthrow of Rosas, architecture had a prim, tentative fussiness to it that is different from the imperious volumes and maximalist ambitions of the true Beaux Arts style that reached Buenos Aires only in the 1890s. Instead, the earlier taste, especially in its Porteño variants, favored surface decor over structure and an Italian Renaissance vocabulary over the French Baroque idiom that was yet to come.

In one sense, the architectural conditions of Buenos Aires at this time were the opposite of those in the United States. In the middle years of the nineteenth century, no American architect—with the unique exception of Richard Morris Hunt—had studied abroad, let alone graduated from the École des Beaux-Arts. Nor were many foreign architects lured to North America to deploy their rare and coveted skills. For better or worse, American architecture was almost entirely homegrown, and despite some fine results, it betrayed the provincialism of amateurs who had improvised their way through pattern books and secondhand accounts of practice on the Continent.

In Buenos Aires, by contrast, almost every important building, deep into the twentieth century, was the work of a foreigner or, failing that, a first-generation Argentine with enduring ties to the country of his ancestors. This had been the case almost from the first moment when the Porteños resolved to build something more than single-story dwellings of mud and straw. The three main architects in eighteenth-century Buenos Aires were Johannes Krauss, Giovanni Battista Primoli and Andrea Blanqui: a German and two Italians. The most important architects of the earlier nineteenth century were the Frenchmen Prosper Catelin and Pierre Benoit. Now, with the removal of Rosas, a generation

of pent-up architectural ambition came to the fore, and architects from
every corner of the Old World poured into the city. Their very names
tell the story: Henrik Åberg, Giovanni Arnaldi, Otto von Arnim, Jean
Leon Pallière, Edward Taylor and hundreds more.

And yet, perhaps the most stunning revision of the city at this time
was not the creation of a building, but rather its destruction. One of
the first acts of Pastor Obligado was to begin the demolition of the
fortress on the Plaza de Mayo, which—in its sundry forms—had dominated and defined Buenos Aires from its very foundation. As long as
the fortress stood, there was something ugly at the heart of the city. It
was virtually the first thing one saw on approaching by boat. With its
removal, the Porteños must have felt that a great weight had been lifted
from their city, the weight of their Iberian past.

Consequent upon the commencement of this demolition, the most
dramatic changes to the cityscape, over the next two decades, would
occur in the general vicinity of the Plaza de Mayo. Among the earliest
initiatives of the new regime was the construction, in 1855, of the city's

*First Teatro Colón, completed by Carlos (Charles Henri) Pellegrini in 1855. (Archivo
General de la Nación)*

first real opera house. Although the Teatro Colón, that refined building that opened on the Plaza Lavalle in 1908, is renowned among music lovers throughout the world, few people, even the locals, know that it is in fact the second structure of that name, that it was preceded by an earlier version, as large if not as sumptuous. This earlier building stood beside the Plaza de Mayo just north of the Casa Rosada, on what had once been the farmland of Juan de Garay and is now the site of the second Banco de la Nación Argentina, completed by Alejandro Bustillo in 1938. The first Teatro Colón was designed by the French architect Charles Pellegrini, who had arrived in Buenos Aires thirty years before and, like a number of other architects in Buenos Aires, had survived the interminable Rosas regime by selling such paintings as he could. His son, incidentally, was Carlos Pellegrini, who much later would become president of Argentina and whose grandiose statue stands in the center of Plaza Carlos Pellegrini in Retiro.

To judge from the surviving photographs, this theater was a singularly weak piece of work, at least as regards its exterior. But it was weak in a way that sheds light on much of the Porteño architecture of the time. Essentially it formed a brutally simple, even insipid three-story box that occupied an entire block. To its dull rows of windows with rounded tops were added, in almost arbitrary fashion, pilasters and blind niches over a rusticated base. The role of ornament in Buenos Aires was as yet a subject of some ambivalence. In no sense did it seem to penetrate the surface of the structure. The building itself was reconceived on two occasions, in the 1870s and again around 1910, when it became the headquarters of the Banco de la Nación Argentina. The transition from the first version to the third powerfully illustrates the growing confidence and refinement of the city's architects: the ornamentation becomes progressively better and the facade acquires a volumetric substance and interest that are entirely lacking in the earliest version.

In regard to ornament and mass, however, the Casa Rosada is only a little better than the first Teatro Colón. The official seat of the federal government's executive branch, it is surely the preeminent surviving monument from the years around 1880. It is also one of the oddest presidential palaces in all the world. With its curious color, a kind of

Central Arch of the Casa Rosada, F. Tamburini,
1886–1898. (Archivo General de la Nación)

bubble-gum pink mixed with ox-blood red, it is a composite of two
preexisting buildings: to the north is the Casa del Gobierno, begun in
1873, and to the south the Correo Nacional, or General Post Office
Building, begun in 1882. They were designed, respectively, by Henrik
Åberg and Carl August Kihlberg, Swedish partners in the same architectural firm. Examples of the palace typology, these two buildings are
nearly identical in size, shape and conception. The central portion of
each has a mansard roof and is flanked by a pavilion on either side.
Like much of the architecture built in Buenos Aires in this period, their
style is largely Italianate, with extensive use of Florentine windows in
both. And although each of these buildings by itself was an advance
over the first Teatro Colón, the federal government that took over in
1880 felt that neither structure was sufficiently functional or monumental. And so, in 1886, Juan Antonio Buschiazzo was hired to shear
off the entire southern wing and pavilion of the post office and to unite
what remained, through a kind of triumphal arch, to the Casa del Gobierno. This strange gestation explains the unified building's present

asymmetry. Nevertheless, one has to admire Buschiazzo: faced with a thankless task, he managed to unite the two preexistent structures so skillfully that few visitors notice anything amiss.

Among the first of the new buildings to rise in Buenos Aires after the removal of Rosas was the vast Aduana Nueva, or Customs House. At the time of its construction, it was, together with the first Teatro Colón, the largest building in the country, although both would soon be superseded by the still larger Penitenciaría Nacional. Whatever the sins of Rosas, trade had greatly increased in Buenos Aires during his regime. The port had long since outgrown the one-story brick and adobe residence of Domingo Basavilbaso that served as the customs house for the entire nation from the beginnings of the viceroyalty in 1778 all the way to 1857. Acutely aware of this deficiency, Pastor Obligado held a contest to design a customs house that would stand directly east of the now partially demolished fort.

Edward Taylor, a Londoner who had been living in Buenos Aires since 1824, won the competition. Like Pellegrini, he had experienced thirty lean years during the Rosas regime, in which period he supported himself by designing smaller country houses for the growing British community in today's Retiro and Recoleta. But now, at the age of fifty-four,

Aduana Taylor, inaugurated in 1857. (Archivo General de la Nación)

he would be yanked out of anonymity to build one of the most ambitious structures ever seen in Argentina. The Aduana Taylor, as it came to be called, was a marvel, a massive piece of infrastructure. Indeed, it can almost be seen as infrastructure more than architecture since it was essentially free of all ornament, at a time when any self-respecting public building was expected to be covered, like the first Teatro Colón, in all the frilly swags and furbelows of the classical tradition.

The Aduana Taylor formed a massive semicircle whose dimensions—nearly a century and a quarter after its demolition—are still clearly visible in the contours of Parque Colón, which fills the site where the Aduana once stood (although it is slightly larger and not quite centered on the same axis). To judge from the surviving images of the exterior of the building—which was demolished to create the Puerto Madero forty years later—it possessed the charm, interest and beauty of the best utilitarian architecture of ancient Rome: Trajan's Market, for instance, or the Aurelian Wall. There is, at the same time, a strikingly improvised quality to the entire thing: the hundred arched vaults that wrapped around the building's three-story semicircular drum resembled a giant dovecote and were unprecedented in earlier architecture. Its one concession to the contemporary taste for ornament was the lighthouse that rose up an additional two stories in an impressive mannerist arch at the Aduana's easternmost point. The interest of the structure was enhanced by a jetty, El Muelle de la Aduana, that extended from the lighthouse nearly a thousand feet into the river. This pier was soon joined by a second pier, El Muelle de Pasajeros, about half a mile to the north, and by a third pier, El Muelle de Santa Catalina, roughly half a mile north of that.

Together with the three piers, the Aduana represents the city's first physical incursion into the river. The Aduana stood on landfill, the first step in a process that, over the next century, would push the river ever farther from the center of the city, with the construction of the Puerto Madero at the end of the nineteenth century, the Puerto Nuevo in 1926 and the nature preserve in the Dársena Sur in the 1970s. Ultimately, from Belgrano to La Boca, from the city's northwestern limit to its southern limit, the entire coastal region of Buenos Aires forms a buffer, two kilometers thick in parts, that separates the citizens of Buenos Aires from the water that had once been central to their existence and their identity.

Time has not dealt kindly with the works of Edward Taylor. Most have been demolished. Directly south and west of the Aduana rose the Administración de Rentas Nacionales (roughly the Internal Revenue Service). This flat-roofed, two-story brick pile, which became three stories as it descended toward the river, was as utilitarian as the Aduana, but couched in the more conventional terms of classical architecture, thanks to a few half-hearted flourishes like rusticated giant-order pilasters and lintelled windows that opened onto narrow balconies. Completed in 1860, it has no distinction other than that it must surely have seemed shockingly big. Only one work by Taylor survives in Buenos Aires, at the corner of Yrigoyen and Chacabuco, just west of the Plaza de Mayo. Its exterior treatment recalls that of the Rentas Nacionales. But between the recent two-tone paint job and an illuminated sign proclaiming the real estate offices of Vinelli Inmobiliaria, it has suffered as unenviable a fate as if it had been demolished altogether.

———— ❋ ————

ONE OF THE LARGER and better parks in the Barrio Norte is Parque Las Heras, which extends from Avenida Las Heras to Juncal and from Coronel Diaz to Salguero. Midway in size between Washington Square Park in New York and Green Park in London, it is the site, on summer weekends, of the usual countercultural markers of many big cities in the West: didgeridoos and jugglers, amorous couples and marijuana fumes hanging thick in the humid air. But few visitors to this fashionable stretch of Palermo have any notion of what once stood here. From its completion in 1876 to its demolition in 1962, this was the dread Penitenciaría Nacional, the largest prison in the country and, at its completion, quite possibly the largest man-made structure as well. At that time it stood far to the north and west of central Buenos Aires, in an area largely uninhabited except for farms and the summer houses of the Porteño elite, whose main homes lay within a few blocks of the Plaza

Penetenciaría Nacional, designed by Ernesto Bunge, inaugurated in 1877 and demolished in 1962. (Archivo General de la Nación)

de Mayo. By 1877, the area was only just beginning to be colonized by the wealthier citizens of the south.

This massive, almost pharaonic building was inspired by the penal reforms advocated by the early nineteenth-century British philosopher Jeremy Bentham. As with Bentham's prototype, the Penitenciaría Nacional was dominated by a central watchtower, known as a Panopticon, from which wardens could see every activity in each of the structure's five irradiating arms or pavilions. More specifically, it was modeled on the influential Eastern State Penitentiary, built in Philadelphia in 1836. The tennis courts of Parque Las Heras rise over the point where the central tower once stood. The sandlot and merry-go-round occupy what was once the triangular garden between Pavilions 2 and 3. The Penitenciaría Nacional was designed by Ernesto Bunge, an Argentine of German descent—his family is still distinguished in the intellectual life of the nation—who, like many Porteño architects of this period, had studied abroad, in Paris and Berlin, before beginning his practice in Buenos Aires.

Today's contemporary taste is apt to find a stark, functionalist elegance in these unadorned stone walls, with their meager, unadorned windows and equally unadorned interiors. Such elegance, obviously, was not at all the intention of the state or the architect. Indeed, the free, law-abiding Porteños who passed along Avenida Las Heras would never see, and possibly never imagine, the central tower and five pavilions that stood concealed behind high walls, impenetrable to the gaze of outsiders. But in keeping with the overwhelming thrust of contemporary architectural taste, any surface that could be seen—at least by *la gente decente,* the proper and upstanding citizens—must have ornament. And so, a primly medieval line of machicolations ran along the top of the section facing Avenida Las Heras, with a diminutive turret at each corner. But few Porteños passed this way in any case, since it was still the ragged edge of the city, the point where it began to fritter away into the infinite expanse of the pampas.

In due course, more Porteños colonized this part of the city, which explains the decision in 1962 to remove the penitentiary from what had become by then one of the most desirable upper-middle-class neighborhoods in Buenos Aires.

Time has dealt more kindly with Ernesto Bunge than with Edward Taylor. The penitentiary is gone, but two of his other works still stand in the capital: the Escuela Normal, or Normal School, on Avenida Córdoba, from 1885, and the lovely church of Santa Felicitas in Barracas, from 1876. This latter building was completed in the same year—a remarkably good year for the thirty-seven-year-old architect—as the Penitenciaría, but at the opposite end of the city. Architecturally it seems even further away. Though the Penitenciaría aspired to nothing more than the strictest functionalism, the ambition of Santa Felicitas was to be a thing of beauty, an ornament of the barrio in which it was built. It is conceived in the neo-Gothic style that was in favor throughout the Western world in the 1870s, but it is a willfully idiosyncratic, even macaronic, version of that style. Generally based on the Italian version of Gothic architecture, its narthex or principal facade consists of a central entrance flanked by two bell towers that are structurally disengaged from it. Like most neo-Gothic architecture, Santa Felicitas is so concerned with conjuring the spirit of the past that its details have completely forgotten or ignored the formal integrity of their sources: these details are charming, often very charming, but nothing more. As so often in the architecture of Buenos Aires, however, the overall structure manages to attain to a presence and a formal power that can surprise the unsuspecting pedestrian. In this case, the clarity with which, externally, the narthex is distinguished from the nave and the nave from the transept is masterful.

The church was built as a memorial to a young woman, Felicitas Guerrero, who was considered to be the wealthiest and most beautiful Porteña of her time. When she became a widow at age twenty-five, many of the most eligible bachelors in Buenos Aires came to court her. What happened next is not entirely clear, but it seems as though she finally decided on a suitor, at which point one of his disappointed rivals—Enrique Ocampo, the great uncle of the well-known writers Silvina and Victoria Ocampo—shot her dead and then killed himself. Just in case the reader is interested in such details, her ghost is said to walk at night amid the aisles and choir of the church that was raised in her memory.

❄

MANY OF THE CHANGES that Buenos Aires experienced in this period were driven by the steady increase in its population, although that increase was nothing like what would start to occur in the 1880s. The growth of Buenos Aires at this time distinguishes it from other Latin American cities, Rio de Janeiro, Caracas and Mexico City, whose population surges would come only much later. In the two decades following Rosas's overthrow, between 1850 and 1870, the population of Buenos Aires more than doubled from 81,400 souls to 178,100, four times what it had been at the time of independence. The direct cause of this transformation was the first wave of European immigrants who, propelled by revolutions, famines and economic hardship back home, would become the preeminent force in Argentine history over the next half century. But the ultimate cause of that immigration was a dramatic shift in the economy of Argentina itself from smaller-scale farming and herding to an increasingly industrialized production of commodities. Even when the locals sought work in this sector—and most did not— the nation's insatiable appetite for labor demanded more of it than the local population would ever have been able to supply.

Although the population of Buenos Aires had more than doubled in less than twenty years, the Porteños continued to occupy the constricted terrain that lay within walking distance of the Plaza de Mayo. As yet, there was no great movement to the west or to the north. Nor was there any great impetus to build up: one-story houses, expanding almost languorously across their generous lots, continued to dominate the strikingly flat cityscape. The result was a housing crisis, and the answer to it, the so-called conventillo, was surely one of the worst solutions to a housing crisis ever conceived.

These conventillos responded to demographic patterns that were largely unique to Buenos Aires. Thousands of dockworkers and farmhands arrived in the city, mostly from Italy or Spain, in the knowledge that a few months in the shipyards of the capital or the farmlands of the interior would enable them to return home with enough money to feed their family for an entire year. Others, however, brought their families and intended to settle in the capital. In either case, they ended up in the conventillos of San Telmo and La Boca. The word *conventillo,* which can be translated as "a small convent," does not refer to any architectural style or typology, but rather to the use to which preexistent buildings were put. The admirable home of Bartolomé Mitre, already described, could have been a conventillo if, instead of housing the president and his family, it contained as many as a hundred men, sometimes fifteen in a single room.

❋

TRADITIONALLY A RENTED DWELLING, whether a house or part of a house, contains rooms with varying functions. In a conventillo, by contrast, tenants rented a single room (like a convent cell, hence the name) that was meant exclusively for sleeping. All other functions, from cooking to personal hygiene, were carried out in the shared public spaces. It was not unusual for a single toilet to serve over a hundred tenants, many of whom were sickened by the ammoniated stench.

The conditions in which these immigrants lived were laid bare during the great yellow fever epidemic of 1871. There had been similar outbreaks of the disease in 1852 and again in 1858, but the outbreak of 1871 was more virulent than any other epidemic in the city's history. To this day, neither the British invasions of 1806–7 nor the Guerra Sucia, or Dirty War, of the 1970s and 1980s proved as lethal to the population of Buenos Aires as this one epidemic: over 8 percent of the population, some fourteen thousand men, women and children, were carried off in the space of three months.

At the height of the Argentine summer, on January 27, 1871, the first three cases of the disease were reported in San Telmo, one of the most densely populated sections of the city, on Calle Bolivar 392. The disease spread steadily throughout February until it manifested itself at last as a full-blown epidemic. By this point it had traveled beyond the conventillos of San Telmo to the wealthier dwellings on the northern side of the Plaza de Mayo. Those who could fled to the relative safety of Recoleta and Palermo, leaving behind mostly immigrants and blacks.

By the beginning of March more than a hundred people were dying of the disease each day. By April that number had become 300, with 563 people dying on April 10 alone. The authorities offered free train rides out of the city into the countryside. Schools and government services were suspended, as were garbage disposal and police patrols. By this point, a city of 178,000, one of the largest in the Western Hemisphere at the time, had been reduced by some estimates to fewer than 30,000 inhabitants.

While the epidemic was raging, it was thought best to remove the people from their dwellings. But this plan came up against the resistance of often illiterate immigrants, who harbored a deep mistrust of the authorities. Frequently the police had to be called in. A report from the Commission on Health of the Parish of El Socorro vividly describes one of these scenes and, incidentally, provides a fair sense of the circumstances in which these immigrants lived:

Commissar Sequi . . . accompanied by 12 gendarmes and the inspector Salvadores, presented himself at the aforementioned conventillo. The Italian immigrants asylumed there surely understood what was about to happen. They had positioned themselves strategically. The men had occupied the upper part of the building while the women, almost all of them with children in their arms, stood in the courtyard and at the doors of the building. The former stood threateningly, armed with ropes, bottles and stones, proffering uncivil words that expressed the anger that dominated them. The women, many of them weeping, came and went continually, inciting the men to more decisive action.

Soon, however, the removal of tenants ceased to be an option. A quarantine was imposed and whole sections of the city were under police lockdown. The army was called in to prohibit movement from the southern sections of the city into the now wealthier sections of the Barrio Norte. The doctors, who had numbered roughly one for every thousand Porteños before the epidemic, chose to stay away. Only priests continued to minister to the sick and poor, and fully a quarter of them died as a result. Thousands of victims were thrown into mass graves in the empty dirt fields that much later became the Parque de los Andes. In time, however, this area proved insufficient and an even larger space was found nearby: this would become the Cementerio de Chacaritas, which remains the largest cemetery in the city.

One of the most valuable records of the epidemic is a diary kept by the businessman Mardoqueo Navarro. His daily entries, though rarely more than twenty words, possess the eloquence of their brevity. On February 7 he wrote, "The panic begins." One month later, on March 16, we hear of how a man "alive, but mistaken for dead, climbed out of his casket." On March 22: "*La muerte. El espanto. La soledad.* (Death. Terror. Desolation.)" On April 4: "The living are dying even as they hope to inherit or rob from the dead."

Only in May 1871, after nearly four months of devastation and the death of over fourteen thousand citizens, did the first cool winds of the Argentine autumn begin to blow, and people were finally able to return to the city. To this day, even though Porteños tend to know little of their city's history before 1900, the yellow fever epidemic of 1871 remains embedded in their collective memory. On the facade of the Church of San Telmo, which was ground zero for the epidemic, appears the following inscription, placed there exactly one century later: "To the victims of the yellow fever outbreak of 1871 and to those heroic neighbors of San Telmo who fought the Dantesque dimensions of this epidemic."

At the time of the epidemic no one knew what caused yellow fever. Only in 1881 did a Cuban doctor, Carlos Finlay, divine the true cause of the disease, the mosquito *Aedes aegypti*. This insect was abundant in the rainforests of Paraguay, but occasionally it spread south into the Rio de la Plata. Nevertheless, to this day, several myths persist in Buenos Aires concerning the outbreak. One often hears that the crowded conditions in the conventillos increased the virulence of the epidemic or that soldiers returning from the War of the Triple Alliance, which was fought in Paraguay from 1864 to 1870, brought it home with them and infected others. For either of those explanations to be true, however, the disease would have to be contagious, susceptible to transmission from one person to another. In fact, it can be caught only from the bite of a specific kind of mosquito that tends to gather in standing water, of which there was a great deal amid the exposed drainage systems of San Telmo and La Boca. One newspaper report came very close to divining the real cause when it noted that "the spread of yellow fever seems to follow the drainage courses."

Relative to the subsequent history of Buenos Aires, the yellow fever epidemic had two material results. The first was the decision of some of the wealthier citizens to leave the southern and central parts of the city and move to the northern section known informally as Barrio Norte, which comprises the actual barrios of Retiro, Recoleta, Palermo and Belgrano. Before that time, this area was all farmland, empty fields and the sandy shallows between the river and the tableland of the pampas. It was largely unpopulated except for a few religious orders, like the Monastery of the Recollect Fathers, who gave their name to the barrio of Recoleta, as well as some farms and factories and the dumping grounds for the bones of livestock. With few roads leading in that direction, and those rather poor, the only people likely to venture that far beyond the city limits were wealthy citizens eager to escape the heat of summer by retreating to their country villas. But after the yellow fever epidemic, Porteños began to reconsider the overpopulation of the area around the Plaza de Mayo, and many moved to the northern parts of the city. In time this area would become, as it remains today, the most residential section of Buenos Aires. As for the area around the Plaza de Mayo, also known as the Microcentro, it is now the city's central business district and has relatively few permanent residents.

But it would be a mistake to think that, after the epidemic, San Telmo was more or less abandoned by the wealthy and became one of the city's poorer areas. Almost every building one now sees in San Telmo or in neighboring Monserrat was built in the half century after the epidemic, and some of these buildings were clearly intended for the well-to-do. Only much later, in the 1930s and 1940s, did the area's fortunes decline, to such a degree that they are only now, perhaps, beginning to recover.

The second important response to the epidemic was an increased sense of urgency in improving and modernizing the city's infrastructure. Before the fall of Rosas in 1852, Buenos Aires, like most premodern cities, was what met the eye and nothing more than that. Its buildings lay flat upon the earth, rarely having so much as a basement. Such drainage as there was lay open to the sky, as rushing brooks after sustained rains and as dried-out gullies much of the rest of the time. There were no pipes to convey water or gas, and, of course, no electric cables or telephone wires hung overhead, and the use of steam had only just been introduced. The nineteenth century would be drawing to its close before Buenos Aires received a proper sewer system. And despite some infrastructural enhancements under Pastor Obligado, things like garbage collection and the ready availability of drinking water had improved little since the days of Juan de Garay. Throughout the intervening three centuries this insufficiency had been bothersome, even unpleasant, but rarely worse than that. Now, however, through overpopulation and the yellow fever epidemic, the problems inherent in the infrastructure had become catastrophically clear. The epidemic was not, of course, related to overpopulation, but Porteños thought it was, and that belief now drove them to act with greater urgency.

The need for infrastructural improvements had already been felt in the decade before the epidemic, and steps were already being taken, though as yet hesitant and insufficient. In 1859 the Irish engineer John Coghlan (for whom the western barrio of Coghlan is named) devised a unified system to address the provisioning of potable water and the construction of sewers. It was not really put into effect, however, until 1871, when a 1,000-cubic-meter water tower, rising over 130 feet above the city and fashioned from iron lattices, presented to the bewildered pedestrians in Plaza Lorea a spectacle such as they had never seen before. Three years later, the British engineer J. B. Bateman created a system that, on its completion in 1880, provided water and efficient sewage to fully a quarter of the population. Thus when cholera struck the city in 1884, the Porteños found themselves in far better condition to endure it than they had been during the yellow fever outbreak thirteen years before. At this time as well, the first incinerators were built for the disposal of garbage, and in 1875 the first systematic garbage collection was established—as opposed to the older system of throwing it into the river or the street.

One of the most dramatic changes to befall Buenos Aires at this time was the introduction of the railroad. On August 29, 1857, the first train in Argentina, *La Porteña*, pushed out of a brand new station on the Plaza Lavalle that would later become the site of the second Teatro Colón. It proceeded along the curve of the Pasaje Discepolo—as that bend is now called—at six miles an hour in the direction of Flores, an independent town at the time, seven miles to the west. Within thirty years, those seven miles of track would grow to more than four thousand. Soon a spur of the train line was brought down beside the river where the Estación Central was built. Like so much of the infrastructure of Buenos Aires, this station and the train it served were a British venture installed with British capital. Indeed, the station, designed by the English architect William Wheelwright, was actually built in London and only assembled in Buenos Aires. It was a thing of striking ugliness, a two-tone Victorian shed formed of wrought iron, wood and

Paseo de Julio (now Avenida Leandro N. Alem), c. 1880, with the Estación Central on the right. (Archivo General de la Nación)

galvanized sheet metal. Where once the Porteños looked out and saw the shimmering river, they now saw this, and they would continue to do so for another forty years until finally, mercifully, it burned to the ground in 1897. If the very existence of the Aduana was the first violence done to the Rio de la Plata, the railway was the second step in a process that would thoroughly alienate the Porteños from their port. Within a generation one would no longer hear the *lavanderas* singing in the shallows of the river as they washed their clothes, or children splashing around in the water on warm summer days.

Trains, of course, were introduced for travel not within the city but away from it. In answer to the former need, the first tramways appeared in 1870. Within three years, six different companies were operating in Buenos Aires, the two most successful being those of Federico Lacroze and Mariano Billinghurst, each of whom has an important street named in his honor. By 1887 over 100 miles of tramway tracks crisscrossed the city. These trams changed the city even more than the trains had done. For the first time workers could live farther from their places of employment than they could conveniently walk. Tramways also made it possible to consolidate the far-flung towns of Belgrano, Flores and Barracas into the vastly expanded Buenos Aires that came into being after 1887. And it was the tramway that, in due course, filled out the interstitial spaces between those towns, giving rise to such entirely new communities as Villa Urquiza, Parque Patricios and Almagro. Originally trams were horse-drawn and relatively expensive. It was only when they began to run on electricity in 1905 that they became cheap enough for the common laborer. And it was then that the settlement of the more distant areas of the city began in earnest.

By virtue of these infrastructural changes in the second half of the nineteenth century, Buenos Aires, like all the major cities of the West, began to undergo a transformation from a preindustrial to an industrial state, powered by steam and gas and electricity. The period covered in this chapter is often referred to as *la gran aldea,* the big village, a phrase that comes from the title of a popular 1882 novel by Lucio Vicente López. The phrase suggested that, despite the city's growth and

Newly laid train tracks divide the city from the river, looking south from the Administración de Rentas Nacionales, c. 1870. (Archivo General de la Nación)

infrastructural advances, it still contained unassimilated traces of its earlier condition. That is because, for some time, the new technology was only imperfectly integrated into the existing cityscape. Fenced-off train tracks and exchanges now cut clear across the former *bañado*, or shallows, of the Rio de la Plata. And together with these trains arose an entire infrastructure of stations, train yards and hangars. Meanwhile, that ugly water tower, rising to the height of a thirteen-story building, continued to stand in crude isolation in the middle of Plaza Lorea. For much of this period, through a lack of parks and greenery, the city was a monotone of gray walls and brown earth. In unnumbered photographs from the period, the exposed soil is a constant presence, caked, clotted and muddied by the rains, from the new Parque Tres de Febrero to the parade grounds of the Plaza San Martín and the cart depots of Plaza Constitución and Plaza Miserere.

In a word, Buenos Aires was not a beautiful city at this time; indeed, it never had been. It was functional at best and not always even that. But this condition was about to change. Within the space of a single determined generation, Buenos Aires would be well on its way to becoming one of the loveliest, and largest, cities in the world. For now, the architecture that came into being in the aftermath of the Rosas regime felt like a dress rehearsal for what was to emerge in the next generation. Many of the municipal and federal projects of this period would be demolished only to be replaced—often in other parts of the city— by larger, more grandiose and far more beautiful versions of the same. The Congreso, the Government House, the Central Post Office, the Aduana, the Teatro Colón—these and a dozen other structures would be torn down and rebuilt to accommodate a later, more populous and architecturally more demanding generation.

EIGHT

THE PARIS OF
SOUTH AMERICA

(1880–1920)

ON CHRISTMAS DAY 1876, A STEAMER FROM FRANCE arrived in Buenos Aires with twenty tons of frozen meat and vegetables, which, when sampled, were found to be edible.

Consequent upon this seemingly insignificant item of shipping news, several things occurred: over the ensuing generation, three and a half million immigrants descended on Buenos Aires; a Parisian-style avenue tore through two kilometers of the city's densest urban space; a brand-new legislative palace arose at the western end of that avenue; Lucia Crestani sang the role of Aida, to universal praise, at the inauguration of the second Teatro Colón; and dozens of private mansions, tricked out in profane opulence, heralded the dawn of Argentina's gilded age.

The voyage of *Le Frigorifique,* for such was the steamer's name, was a triumph of commercial refrigeration, the first to demonstrate that meat could be shipped across the Atlantic and arrive at its destination in palatable form. This specific voyage was an experiment, almost a stunt, to prove the viability of the refrigerating processes developed by the French inventor Charles Tellier. Obviously, the last thing that Argentina needed, then as now, was to import meat. What the shipment showed was exactly the reverse, that the meat of the numberless herds that roamed the pampas could be successfully shipped to Europe. This development, combined with the dogged exploitation of other commodities, revolutionized the entire economy of Argentina. In time the nation would need so many foreign workers that its magistrates nearly bribed them to immigrate. And with their help, in little more than two decades, Argentina would take its place as the eighth-richest nation in the world.

The province of Buenos Aires had been cow country for centuries. The export value of cattle, however, had been limited to its hide and fat and to salted beef, which was cheap and insipid and used primarily to feed slaves and sailors on long voyages. But due to the success of Tellier's refrigeration, the whole cow could finally be monetized, acquiring a vastly greater value than ever before. In due course other commodities—such as wheat, barley and most recently soy—would be harvested to the ever greater enhancement of Argentina's fortunes. The role of silver in the colonial economy was now taken over by livestock and agriculture, as remains the case today. From that time on, Argentina would not generally manufacture things—certainly not for export—but rather would import everything that it needed, and that it could now easily afford, from trains and train stations to grain elevators, shoes and even El Grecos.

The implications of this sudden influx of wealth were twofold. On the one hand, the magistrates now had the means to reorder the city in accordance with their most extravagant visions of European progress and gentility. On the other, the waves of immigrants who came to Buenos Aires from across the Old World fundamentally altered the dimensions of the city and in time would revolutionize its spirit and its culture.

Nearly half a century after Charles Tellier's ship reached the port of Buenos Aires, another Frenchman, the Parisian landscape architect Jean-Claude Forestier, arrived in 1923 and assessed the impact of his countryman's inventions. He informed one of the local dailies that "in this city, I feel as if I were in Paris. If there are any differences, they are only with regard to details." Then, fearing that this might sound too measured, he added, "There is no boulevard in Paris that can compare with your winter gardens or the Rosedal [part of the largest park in Buenos Aires]." Forestier was, of course, soliciting a commission, so his equating Buenos Aires with Paris may or may not reflect his true feelings. But in a sense that hardly matters, since, in either case, his words bespeak a far more interesting truth. In 1923, after several tumultuous decades in which Buenos Aires was transformed from a relatively large but nondescript South American city into a rival of Paris itself, nothing so delighted the Porteño, nothing so pleasantly confirmed what he already hoped and suspected, as the suggestion that he inhabited "the Paris of South America." To this day, the term is often heard, and it seems apt. As for Forestier, the grand avenue of the Costanera Sur, which he designed, eloquently attests to the success of his solicitations.

Rare if not unprecedented is this dream of the Porteños to create, to the extent of their abilities and abounding resources, a simulacrum of Paris in the New World. Perhaps Peter the Great's founding of Saint Petersburg offers a parallel of sorts. The Argentine writer Beatriz Sarlo,

Turn-of-the-century residential development on Avenida Caseros. (Photograph by the Author)

however, disputes this association of Paris and Buenos Aires. "Paris was not the only model," she writes. "For the most part, public buildings did not present the imprint of a dominant French style: their facades showed the aesthetic consequences of neoclassicism, Italian style, art deco, and even expressionism and modernism." Sarlo is correct that much of Buenos Aires revels in a plurality of styles—but then, Paris does as well. And in any case, such an argument misses the more important point, that the wealth of a nation was expended not to re-create Paris but to approximate it, by conjuring up the scenographic grandeur of Haussmann's city and by doing so in a style that closely resembled that of the French capital. In the latter half of the nineteenth century, many world capitals went to school on Haussmann's Paris, but none of them came as close as Buenos Aires to the spirit of the source. And so there are many parts of Buenos Aires—the Avenida de Mayo, Plaza San Martín, a stretch of buildings on Avenida Caseros in San Telmo—that do indeed look Parisian, if not exactly like a specific place in Paris.

More exactly, the goal of the oligarchs and of Rivadavia before them was to create the first thoroughly modern city in Latin America, the first European city, the first "First World" city, as we would say today. And Paris was the undisputed model for all of those ambitions. Anyone who arrives in Buenos Aires after seeing the great cities of Europe will experience a shock of recognition. Buenos Aires looks like some great Old World city that one cannot quite name or place, at once tantalizingly familiar and entirely new. With elements of Paris, Madrid and Milan, it seems constantly to affirm and then to belie that curious mirage of familiarity. Indeed, even if Buenos Aires does not look exactly like any of those capitals, it feels invincibly, proudly, even polemically European. No other city in North, South or Central America comes as close to the mood and rhythms of the Old World. Visit South America's other major cities—Lima and Santiago, Rio de Janeiro and Asunción—and you will grasp at once the essential difference. Those cities were formed through the convergence of Spanish or Portuguese colonialism and the pre-Columbian past. In Buenos Aires, by contrast, the indigenous peoples have left no trace, while the marks of Spanish colonial dominion have been almost entirely eradicated.

Many architectural styles have competed for preeminence on the streets of the Argentine capital. In addition to the *estilo frances,* or French style, that has already been mentioned, we find the influence of the Italian Renaissance in the Teatro Colón and the Casa Rosada, both designed in part by Francesco Tamburini. There is the Barcelonese art nouveau, or Modernisme, of the Casal de Catalunya, designed by Julián García Núñez, as well as the magnificent Galería Güemes of Francesco Gianotti. Reacting against the Frenchified tastes of the oligarchs, some patrons chose to invoke the Plateresque style of seventeenth-century Spain in the Teatro Nacional Cervantes by Arias and Repetto and the Banco de Boston, conceived, oddly, by a pair of architects sitting in New England. You can even find British influence in Constitución train station and the Christopher Wren–inspired Torre de los Ingleses, opposite the Plaza San Martín. Still, even when subsequent generations produced an abundance of buildings inspired by Art Deco and the International Style, by postmodernism and Deconstructivism, when we shut our eyes and think of Buenos Aires, the blurred composite of images that we see is apt to be dominated by monuments inspired by the French Baroque and the École des Beaux-Arts.

❋

THIS REINVENTION OF BUENOS AIRES, however, did not come easily. For all the splendor of this chapter of the city's history, it began in bloodshed and tumult. Although Buenos Aires is the capital of Argentina, the exact status of the city relative to the rest of the nation, and the process by which it became the capital, were perplexing in the extreme. Usually, when there is any question of which city will become the capital of a nation, it involves the competing claims of two or more cities, each of them eager to claim that status and to deny it to its rivals: such was the case with New York and Philadelphia, Sydney and Melbourne, Rio de Janeiro and São Paolo. In Buenos Aires, however, the quarrel was entirely different. Thirteen out of fourteen Argentine provinces wanted Buenos Aires to be their capital. The one exception was Buenos Aires itself. And the reason was the same as under Rivadavia in 1827 and Urquiza in 1852. In any federation with a unified system of taxation and revenue sharing, some areas receive more from the central government than they pay into it, and others, of necessity, receive less. In Argentina in 1880, the great preponderance of the nation's wealth, and a large part of its population, were in the city and province of Buenos Aires. Thus it was fully in the interests of the other provinces to federalize the city and of Buenos Aires itself to resist that assimilation.

In the presidential election of 1880, Carlos Tejedor, the governor of the province of Buenos Aires and an opponent of nationalizing the city, ran against General Julio Argentino Roca. The latter had just completed his famed Conquest of the Desert, which consisted in ridding the provinces of Buenos Aires and La Pampa of their indigenous populations. Never again would the descendants of the Mapuche and the Araucanians harass the criollo farmers and herdsmen in those parts. To this day, Roca's campaign is the primary reason that Argentina is so "white" and that there are far fewer people of indigenous descent on the banks of the Rio de la Plata than anywhere else in Latin America. Despite the extreme violence of Roca's attacks, they were a precondition for the agricultural exploitation of the pampas, upon which, then as now, the nation's prosperity depended.

Roca won the election, but in a way that revealed the deep divisions between Buenos Aires and the rest of Argentina. Tejedor won only the city and province of Buenos Aires (as well as the province of Corrientes), while the rest of the country went with Roca. In anticipation of conflict, Tejedor had established El Tiro Nacional, a militia that promptly secured the allegiance of some two thousand young men from the highest echelons of Porteño society, eager to carry a rifle around in what promised to be a brief and diverting *promenade militaire.* The immediate cause of the conflict was Tejedor's attempt to smuggle rifles into the city in order to arm his militia. The national congress, which resided in Buenos Aires, tried to prohibit this action, but the local officials refused to intervene against it. Thereupon, the congress retreated six miles northwest to Belgrano, which is now one of the lovelier parts of Buenos Aires, but which at the time was an independent town. The senate, the Chamber of Deputies and the supreme court all moved into

a classicizing temple of a building, designed by Juan Antonio Buschiazzo, that still stands on the corner of Juramento and Cuba and is now
the Museo Sarmiento.

At the same time, the national army under Roca laid siege to Buenos Aires. The fighting, though fierce, took place entirely outside of
what were then the city limits, in Barracas and Parque Patricios (like
Belgrano and Flores, they too would become part of Buenos Aires only
in 1887). In fairly short order, Tejedor was routed, and on September
21, 1880, the congress in Belgrano officially approved the *Ley Nacional
1029,* which federalized the city of Buenos Aires and removed it from
the jurisdiction of Buenos Aires province. Thus the congress finally
settled the thorny question of the city's relation to the rest of Argentina.
Long the dominant city of Argentina, Buenos Aires now became its official capital.

For the city itself, the consequences of this law were immediate and
far-reaching. If, in the previous chapter, the ambiguities concerning its
status had imparted a timid, anxious, almost stunted and provincial
quality to the buildings that went up in the 1860s and 1870s, now the
new assurance of Buenos Aires's rank engendered a very different style
of architecture. In many cases buildings completed only a few years
earlier had to be modified, like the Casa Rosada, or entirely replaced,
like the Congreso.

An analogy suggests itself between the Argentine capital and the
humble goldfish, *Carassius auratus.* This creature usually inhabits a two-
gallon bowl and grows to be about an inch and a half in length. But if
you place it in a lake, the same fish will grow to almost a foot and a half
in length, and every part of it, from its gills to its tail, from the speed of
its movements to its capacity for consumption, will grow accordingly.

As long as Buenos Aires was officially the capital of a province and
nothing more, its leading citizens, elected officials and developers would
not commit their time, wealth or energy to building more imposing
structures. Even if they had tried, their efforts would have come to
nothing, since the city would have lacked the vital energy to sustain
such ventures. Surely the oligarchs could have afforded big buildings,
but there would have been nothing to fill them with, and they would

have been little more than frigid, lifeless showpieces. Everything about Buenos Aires before 1880, everything in Buenos Aires, from the size and style of its buildings to the caliber of singers in its opera house, was commensurately small—perhaps the largest in Argentina, perhaps even the largest in South America, but still small by the standards of Europe, the standards that mattered most to the oligarchs in the Barrio Norte. But with the *Ley Nacional 1029,* the city underwent a crucial shift in degree and in kind. There settled upon the city, almost as though it were a condition of the climate, an air of imperious self-importance that no other South American city—not even Potosí and Lima in all their glory—had ever possessed.

But the *Ley Nacional 1029* of 1880 was only part of the legal framework that had to be in place in order for Buenos Aires to undergo the fundamental transformation from a provincial South American city to a world capital. At the time, and for seven years to come, the city extended scarcely two miles west of the Rio de la Plata and scarcely three miles along its north-south axis. Beyond these narrow dimensions lay the seemingly infinite pampas, but not exactly the state of nature. For several of the roads that traversed the city (Rivadavia, Santa Fe, Las Heras) along its east-west axis penetrated deep into the surrounding countryside. This was populated, though sparsely, by farms and the occasional church, brick factory or slaughterhouse. More materially, several independent towns in the jurisdiction of Buenos Aires Province lay five or six miles beyond the western limit of the city: Belgrano, Flores, Barracas, parts of San Miguel. Each was an oasis of settlement separated by miles of farmland or undeveloped pampas.

After protracted debate, the federal government resolved that the city would now fan out, about eight miles west, northwest and southwest of its earlier limits, so as to engulf these townships. But that proved to be more easily said than done. For those towns were part of Buenos Aires Province, which was still smarting from the loss of the city of Buenos Aires, and so was in no mood to part with an additional sixty square miles of its territory. The brand-new city of La Plata, with its fastidious grid and gleaming Beaux Arts palaces, was founded in 1882 to serve as the new capital of Buenos Aires Province and as a sort of consolation prize for the loss of the city of Buenos Aires. But it was hardly enough to mollify the provincial government. In the event, the federal government won out yet again, and now the capital extends about ten miles beyond the Plaza de Mayo. Its western limit is defined by the Avenida General Paz, a massive highway of polygonal rather than parabolic shape that was not actually completed until 1941.

❋

THIS TRANSFORMATION OF THE CITY of Buenos Aires was largely due to a national Unitarian government that had emerged from, and was intimately allied to, the landed oligarchy of Buenos Aires Province. These were the owners of the estancias that blanketed the pampas, cattlemen and wheat producers. If the overthrow of the Spanish in 1810 had brought the criollo merchants to power, and if the Battle of Caseros in 1852 had ensured the primacy of the Unitarian party, the revolution of 1880 signaled the consolidation of power and prestige in these landowning grandees, known as *la Generacion del '80*. The Anchorenas and Azcuénegas, the Ortúzars and Unzués: to this day they are names to conjure with in the capital, and they adorn its streets and even entire barrios. Obviously, these oligarchs did not spend much time on their estancias. They were urbanites whose gaze was fixed on Europe. Ideologically and emotionally, they were Francophile and Anglophile to their core, but they were feverishly patriotic as well: they could simply have moved to Paris, but they preferred to reinvent the city of Buenos Aires in accordance with their newfound tastes.

The spirit in which they now proceeded to transform Buenos Aires recalls the mood in Manhattan a few decades later that Rem Koolhaas describes in his book *Delirious New York*. The developers and architects of America's largest city, Koolhaas argues, were motivated less by hard-headed practicality than by showmanship and a kind of aesthetic one-upmanship to construct the Empire State Building, the Chrysler Building and Rockefeller Center. But although the architects and developers in Buenos Aires shared, to some degree, this later taste for Art Deco, it was the Beaux Arts style of a generation earlier, *la Generacion del '80,* that produced most of the boldest structures in the city. Both at street level and in the popular imagination, these are the buildings that define the capital. Such besottedness with the swags, acroteria and acanthus leaves of classical architecture, with its porte-cochères and its fluted pilasters, took on an almost ludic quality, if not a life of its own, among the oligarchs of Buenos Aires.

Like the Beaux Arts tradition itself, the resulting architecture was not entirely Gallic in taste, but it was entirely historicist, even when it invoked the Italian Renaissance, Tudor, Spanish colonial or Gothic styles. Everything about the architecture of Buenos Aires at this time is surplus and concealment. Form never follows function in the architecture of Buenos Aires's Belle Époque. Likewise, those principles of rational design—the utilitarian rather than ornamental disposition of space—that were fundamental to nineteenth-century Beaux Arts architecture were not uppermost in the minds of the Porteño architects or their patrons in this gilded age. The thing to which they all aspired, whatever the cost or inconvenience, was Europe and especially Paris. What was supremely important to them was pure appearance, the look of things, the power of built structures to evoke grandiose and exotic dreams far beyond their strict formal dimensions.

It was an age when even brothels, or at least the better sort, must be done up in the best Parisian style of the Second Empire and the Third Republic. As Adolfo Batiz, the subcommissioner of the municipal police force, wrote in 1908, "Prostitutes occupied houses of greatest luxury, where one found floors covered in rugs of excellent taste, elegant borders of pale blue, red and purple brocade; in short, a decent comfort, a piano, proper rooms, everything needed to receive people of means."

The obsession with Beaux Arts taste and its sundry historicist variants can be seen everywhere in the capital, not least in the great Buenos Aires zoo, founded by President Sarmiento in 1874 on land that had once belonged to Juan Manuel de Rosas. Most of the architecture that we see there today, however, was commissioned by Clemente Onelli, who served as the zoo's director from 1904 until his death in 1924. A native of Rome, he commissioned the so-called Temple of Vesta, now the zoo's library, as well as a nearby simulacrum of the Arch of Titus

One of the pavilions of the Jardin Zoologico, c. 1904. (Archivo General de la Nación)

in the Roman Forum and the so-called Byzantine Ruins that stand on an artificial island in the zoo's lake. A similar mood inspired the elephant house, designed by Virgilio Cestari as a Hindu temple, as well as the Moroccan-style zebra house and the Venetian-Gothic pavilion that houses a subtropical forest display.

But this historicist longing is nowhere more exuberant than in the Cemetery of Recoleta, perhaps the premier tourist attraction of the capital. As any number of writers have remarked, its rigid grid and the abundance of monuments from the early years of the last century have almost transformed the cemetery into a parody of the imperious city that surrounds it. It is also one of the foremost ornaments of the capital.

Originally called the Cementerio del Norte because, when it was founded in 1821, it lay on the northern outskirts of the city, it was built on lands that had belonged to the monks of the Order of the Recoletos, who were attached to the adjoining church of Nuestra Señora del Pilar. After Spanish rule ended in 1810, the land was seized by the state, and the staunchly anticlerical Rivadavia ordered that it be turned into a cemetery. Its general design was the work of Prosper Catelin, the same architect who conceived the neoclassical facade of the Cathedral of

Tombs in Recoleta Cemetery. (Photograph by the Author)

Buenos Aires, and it was redesigned about sixty years later by Juan Antonio Buschiazzo. Said to be based on Père Lachaise cemetery in Paris, it
contains nearly five thousand vaults crowded into a fourteen-acre square
footprint and is the last resting place of some of the most famous names
in Argentine history, from Sarmiento and Mitre to Rosas and Eva Perón
(her husband is buried in the far larger and more populist Cementerio
de Chacaritas about three miles to the west).

Anyone who has seen Piranesi's fanciful eighteenth-century depic-
tions of funerary monuments along Rome's Appian Way will appreciate the almost shocking density of tombs in Recoleta. Every sort of
architectural style, from Beaux Arts to Bauhaus, is represented along
the streets and avenues in this city of the dead. But here, as in Buenos
Aires itself, it is the Beaux Arts style that predominates, with a strong
dose of Hellenism, in row upon row of domed and columned aedicules,
adorned with weeping Victorian angels and brass tablets that fulsomely
eulogize the departed.

Nothing is more peculiar about this place, however, or about Buenos Aires itself, than the seamlessness with which the cemetery has been integrated into the city, and the fact that—perhaps uniquely among the world's necropolises—it is a vibrant, even happy place. At least fifteen outdoor bars and restaurants face its eastern and southern walls. These are interspersed with hotels that offer, for a premium, first-rate views down into the cemetery. But some of the finest views of all are those from the outdoor terrace of the McDonald's on the fourth floor of the neighboring Village Recoleta Cineplex.

This passion for Beaux Arts historicism, but especially for Parisian style, filtered into every aspect of Porteño life, from the cafes, restaurants and billiard parlors along the new Avenida de Mayo to the vast department stores, like Gath & Chaves, that opened on Calle Florida. It would not be an overstatement to say that the oligarchs of Buenos Aires at this time collectively rebuilt the city as each of them individually commissioned his own *hotel particulier,* whether the Palacio Errazuriz, the Palacio Paz or the Palacio Grimoldi, all of which began to appear at this time. In understanding how these oligarchs now set about transforming the capital, therefore, it helps to examine the houses they built for themselves. Not the least of their ambitions was to impress the public and especially other oligarchs with their wealth, splendor and taste. But one must not rule out a certain civic-mindedness as well. To adorn the city with these Frenchified baubles not only would delight the pedestrian but would also afford him some measure of pride, perhaps for the first time, in the beauty and stature of the city and the country. The first order of business was to import some architect from France or, failing that, Italy or, failing that, England. The palace itself must have a *piano nobile* or main floor—the first floor by European counting, the second by American—with public rooms whose twenty-foot ceilings would overawe all who entered. In addition to a grand dining room, it must have a ballroom, a reception room and antechambers, a bowling alley perhaps, a billiards room surely. Likewise, the premises must have a grand piano. Meanwhile the private chambers must include suites of magnificent bedrooms, as well as servants' quarters and a mechanical

Palacio Ortiz-Basualdo (now demolished) and, in the background, Palacio San Martín, c. 1910. (Archivo General de la Nación)

core that included elevators, electric wiring, telephones and hot running water, all the most up-to-date amenities of Paris, London and New York.

During the Belle Époque, such designs were repeated literally a hundred times and more among the privileged enclaves of the very rich in Buenos Aires. In Retiro their palaces collected around the Plaza San Martín, where one can still see two of the best, the Palacio San Martín and the Palacio Paz, directly across the plaza. In Recoleta one mansion after another, to this day, aligns Avenida Alvear from Cerrito all the way to Callao; in Palermo they arose, and many survive, on Avenida Libertador and Barrio Parque, and in Belgrano they collected near Avenida Juramento.

The grandest of these palaces, though not the largest, is the aforementioned Palacio San Martín at the corner of Arenales and Esmeralda. It was completed in 1905 for Mercedes Castellanos de Anchorena, according to designs by Alejandro Christophersen, one of the busiest and best architects of Buenos Aires's gilded age. Decked out with paired

Pool Room of the now demolished Palacio Ortiz-Basualdo, completed in 1909 on the Plaza San Martín. (Archivo General de la Nación)

giant-order pilasters and oculus windows under a mansard roof, the pavilions of the Palacio San Martín project outward from a corps de logis to form a courtyard whose grandiose wrought-iron entrance has become one of the signatures of the Argentine capital. It now houses the Ministry of Foreign Affairs.

It was to be expected that the opulent taste of the oligarchs would soon influence the residential architecture of the middle class. And it is this latter architecture, the most common and widespread in the city, that causes Buenos Aires to seem as Parisian as it does. Many of these residential developments follow French precedent, but rarely to the letter. In Buenos Aires, the external articulation of Baron Haussmann's residential buildings was largely preserved, but not the hierarchy of floors that diminished in value as they rose. This is because the Parisian buildings date to the 1860s—when elevators were rare and very costly—whereas most of the Porteño buildings are from half a century later, when elevators were fairly common. (One of the glories of these

buildings, by the way, is their open-cage elevators, which, unfortu-
nately, have been replaced in other countries as a potential fire hazard.)
Furthermore, there is no distinction in height between the first floor
(second by American counting) and the others, and there are balconies
on every floor. This latter fact accounts for the stunning abundance of
fer forgé, or wrought iron, throughout Buenos Aires, even in its poorer
neighborhoods, to such a degree that it too has become one of the signatures of the city.

There is another important difference between Parisian residential
developments and those of Buenos Aires. In Paris, entire blocks were
often developed in a uniform style by a single entrepreneur working
with a single architect. Such large-scale developments were very rare in
Buenos Aires, although an elegant and noteworthy example stands at
the intersection of Defensa and Caseros in San Telmo. In Buenos Aires,
by contrast, most of these residential buildings arose piecemeal, each
the project of a different developer working with a different architect.

Ultimately, both cities have the defects of their qualities. Paris, in
consequence of the consolidated development of its domestic architecture, is one of the most harmonious cities in the world. But at times
it can suffer from a certain tedious sameness due to its uniformity of
style and height across entire blocks and even neighborhoods. In Buenos
Aires, by contrast, there is considerable variety within a single block, as
many styles compete among themselves. But the resulting diversity can
feel clamorous and unlovely, especially when a two-story Beaux Arts
dwelling is flanked and overmastered by some twenty-story rationalist
towers from the 1970s. At the same time, these mismatched juxtaposi-
tions result in a great many exposed sidewalls, vast windowless expanses
of white or gray. These are so prevalent that the locals even have a name
for them, *medianeras,* which was also the title of a 2011 film that sought
to capture the urban angst of young Porteños. They too are an architectural signature of the capital.

Perhaps the grandest single example of Parisian residential architecture in Buenos Aires is the Estrugamou, which rises over the corner
of Juncal and Esmeralda in Retiro, its massive length extending all the
way to Calle Basavilbaso. Completed in 1929 according to the designs

of Eduardo Sauze and August Huguier, it was named for its developer, Alejandro Estrugamou, a Frenchman of Basque descent. The Estrugamou is at one and the same time the supreme Parisian apartment building in Buenos Aires and a building unlike any other in the city. Most Parisian-style apartment buildings in the capital are relatively small, rarely occupying more than one or two lots or rising more than six stories. The Estrugamou, however, rises nine stories if one counts the *chambres de bonne* on the top floor, and it takes up almost its entire block. Only the Palacio de los Patos, at Ugarteche 3050 in Palermo, rivals it in size, if not in the extravagant sumptuosity of its details. Built atop the barranca that once reached to the sandbars of the Rio de la Plata, the Estrugamou strives to achieve an impressive overall effect through ad hoc classical references more than through any systematic use of the classical orders: above a rusticated base, giant-order pilasters vie with Corinthian columns, while at three different points an irregularly triangular pediment arises out of nowhere and disappears into nothing. The Estrugamou invokes the palace typology that, as we shall see, was almost an *idée fixe* of the regnant oligarchs. And its most palatial element of all is the grand entrance on Esmeralda, at the intersection of Arroyo: this tremendous, twenty-foot wrought-iron gate vies with that of the nearby Palacio San Martín as one of the sites of the city.

───── ❊ ─────

IF THE BUENOS AIRES OLIGARCHS collectively recast the city as each of them individually commissioned his private mansion, what, in their view, must a proper city have? Obviously it should have all of the newest infrastructural enhancements that modernity—as of 1900—could provide: a system for water distribution, railways for travel beyond the city, and tramways and subways for travel within it, paved and well-lit streets, and an efficient police force and sanitation system. These things were necessities, but they would not suffice by any means for a proper city. Here the criterion was not necessity but luxury, not utility but leisure. And the solutions were self-evident to the oligarchs who, in general, governed the city in the Belle Époque with prudence, altruism and even patriotism. For them the city must have plazas and at least one great park to rival Central Park, Hyde Park and the Bois de Boulogne. And it must have an opera house and hippodrome where the quality can gather *en galas* in their carriages and imported finery. It must also have a zoo and a botanical garden, a tree-lined walkway along the river, a museum of fine arts and a natural history museum. Surely it must have grander, wider avenues that any yet seen in the city, and some of these must form diagonals, primarily because Paris had diagonal avenues and so, therefore, must they.

Such, then, were the views of the oligarchs. But behind many a great urban center stands a solitary figure, a magistrate or a potentate, who is hell-bent on imposing his will until the city conforms to his views of how it should function and look. In Rome that man was Sixtus V. In Paris it was Baron Haussmann. In New York it was Robert Moses. And in Buenos Aires it was Torcuato de Alvear who laid the foundations for the city as we know it and, perhaps more importantly, as we imagine

Torcuato de Alvear. (Archivo General de la Nación)

it today. And although he acted entirely according to his own judgment and counsel, he was so much a creature of the oligarchy that he could be trusted to understand their interests and needs and to carry them to completion. Alvear was handpicked by the new president, Roca, to serve in the new magistracy of intendente, except that he was appointed by the executive rather than elected by the people. He would hold the office from 1883 to 1887.

When people speak today of Torcuato de Alvear, assuming that they remember him at all, they are apt to refer to him as "the aristocrat." It was not for nothing that he was widely known to his fellow citizens by the archaic title of Don Torcuato. Among the wealthier men of his time, he commissioned Juan Antonio Buschiazzo in 1884 to design one of the finest private homes in the city, an impeccable Parisian house that for nearly half a century dominated the intersection of Cerrito and Juncal.

———— ✳ ————

IN PHOTOGRAPHS FROM THE PERIOD of his mayoralty, Alvear (or Torcuato Antonio de Alvear y Saenz de la Quintanilla) appears as a rich, powerful and eminently respectable man in his early sixties. With his starched collar and flowing mustache, he seems the very epitome of prim, humorless Victorian rectitude. This impression is only strengthened by his gaunt expression and the focused intensity of his small, dark eyes. By all accounts he was respected, even feared, more than he was loved. Stories abound of how he personally oversaw the laborers at their varied tasks around the city, how he worked them day and night, directing their shifts and goading the mules with a long baton that he carried with him at all times.

Don Torcuato was the scion of wealthy landowners and wine importers, as well as the son of General Carlos Maria de Alvear, the hero of Ituzaingo and one of the *próceres,* or leading men, of the early Argentine Republic. This fact explains why, as one of his first acts as intendente, he renamed the city's most beautiful avenue—the tree-lined Paseo de Mayo that Rosas had extended from the port all the way to Palermo—as Avenida Alvear, in honor of his father. Because this avenue

Artificial Grotto in the Paseo de la Recoleta, c. 1890. (Archivo General de la Nación)

was ultimately renamed Avenida Libertador, the present Avenida Alvear lies two blocks to the south: it was cut by Don Torcuato through the residual farmland that occupied this territory into the late nineteenth century. Today it is one of the most elegant avenues in the city, with some of its finest hotels—the Alvear Palace and the Park Hyatt—as well as some of its most distinguished fin de siècle palaces and several more recent apartment blocks.

Before he was appointed intendente, Alvear had not shown any great interest in public life. But few Porteños of his time knew more, or had thought harder, about urban issues. Alvear had visited the capitals of Europe and witnessed firsthand the convulsive reforms of Baron Haussmann. And these impressed him to such a degree that, when Roca appointed him in 1883, he leapt into action, setting in motion transformations of almost pharaonic dimensions that would be completed only long after his death.

In the real world, especially in a free and democratic state like Argentina, a public figure cannot simply impose his will upon a pliant and disengaged population. Alvear could never have realized his grand Parisian vision of Buenos Aires if that vision had not answered to the pressing exigencies of the oligarchy and an expanding middle class, as well as to some powerful yearning, as yet only partially awakened, in the population as a whole.

In one sense, Alvear had an easier time of it than Haussmann or Moses: he did not have, for the most part, to ride roughshod over a densely inhabited cityscape. Surely there were disruptions and grousings from some of the citizens. At one point the city council tried to oust him, only to be overridden by President Roca. But his opponents were never numerous or unified, and ultimately they did little to stand in his way. In another sense, however, one could argue that his achievement was perhaps greater than Haussmann's because he could not count, as Haussmann could, on a dowry of beautiful and imposing monuments from the Middle Ages, the Renaissance and the Baroque. Just as Augustus had boasted of transforming Rome from a city of brick into one of marble, so Alvear could justly claim that he had turned what had been a provincial South American city into a grand European capital.

One of Alvear's first undertakings was to begin refining the Porteño grid, a process that would take several generations. In this he did nothing more or less than to act upon the goal that Rivadavia had articulated as long ago as 1827. That consisted in the strategic broadening or *ensanchamiento* of certain key streets, and thus the hierarchical subordination of most of the Porteño grid to a few mighty avenues. Along the east-west axis this resulted in such thoroughfares as Santa Fe, Córdoba and Corrientes and along the north-south axis in the expansion of Callao and Pueyrredón, which continue to dominate and structure the lives of Porteños to this day. Alvear even conceived of what would eventually become the Avenida 9 de Julio, that vast boulevard—possibly the broadest in the world—that was not actually undertaken until the 1930s and not ultimately completed until 1980. He also insisted on greening the city by planting trees and by creating or remodeling public squares and parks, among them the Plaza San Martín, Plaza Lavalle and Sarmiento's Parque Tres de Febrero. As a result, although the Porteño grid has been scrupulously preserved, it no longer seems as monotonous as Charles

Darwin found it in 1832, when he described Buenos Aires—and not by way of a compliment—as "the most regular [town] in the world."

Another early initiative of Alvear was to tear down the Recova, the massive one-story arcade that cut across the center of the Plaza de Mayo, the symbolic heart and soul of the city. Invoking a procedure later mastered by Robert Moses, Alvear struck in the dead of night—on May 25, 1883, as it happened, the anniversary of the Porteños' declaration of independence from Spain—and so presented the city, the next morning, with a fait accompli: before any serious objections could be raised, enough of the structure had been destroyed that it was essentially beyond repair. In a similar spirit, the nearby Cabildo, one of the few colonial structures that have survived into the present, saw its northern half unceremoniously sheared off to accommodate the new Avenida de Mayo.

The reasons for la Recova's demolition were as symbolic as they were practical. But for Alvear its removal felt like a matter of utmost urgency: Buenos Aires was now the capital of Argentina and it must conduct itself accordingly. It must shed even the appearance of its colonial past, something that the previous generation had hardly succeeded in doing. True, Charles Pellegrini had built the first Teatro Colón on the Plaza de Mayo, and Åberg, Kihlberg and Tamburini were now completing what would become the Casa Rosada. But amid such fastidiously European piles stood this temple of base commerce where tradesmen continued to hawk their lowly wares. Worse still, the Recova had been designed in the vernacular style of the Spanish crown, that backward and oppressive regime. By removing the Recova and opening up the Plaza de Mayo, Alvear endowed Buenos Aires with a public space to rival in size, if not quite in splendor, the Place de la Concorde, the Piazza San Marco and the Plaza Mayor in Madrid.

But this demolition and the corresponding redefinition of the Plaza de Mayo were relatively small tactical interventions in a far larger urban strategy. By removing the Recova, Alvear set the stage for what was to become one of the most spectacular vistas in Buenos Aires. This would consist of building a massive legislative palace, modeled on the United States Capitol, as well as an avenue two kilometers in length, the

Avenida de Mayo at the turn of the century; notice the absence of women and the bourgeois attire favored even by the working classes. (Archivo General de la Nación)

Avenida de Mayo, to link the legislature to the executive branch in the Casa Rosada.

The Avenida de Mayo, the grand coup de théâtre of Alvear's urbanism, represented a major innovation in the layout of the Argentine capital. It was the first new street created within the traditional boundaries of the city since Juan de Garay had established his grid three hundred years before. But it consisted, uniquely, in piercing the preexistent block bordered by Rivadavia and Yrigoyen. Also, by placing the Congreso, the national legislature, at the western end of the avenue two kilometers away, Alvear boldly extended the institutional dimensions of the city far beyond their traditional center in the Plaza de Mayo: in a daring physical and geographic manifestation of the new power structure, the legislative and executive branches each presided over a large public square, as they faced one another at either end of the Avenida de Mayo. (The third branch of government, the judiciary, housed in the Palacio de Tribunales that was designed by Norbert Maillart for the Plaza Lavalle, stands in a similar relation to the Casa Rosada at the other end of the Diagonal Norte—a somewhat later undertaking—about a mile away.)

During the period when it was being built, between 1885 and 1894, the Avenida de Mayo was sarcastically called the Avenida de los Pleitos, the Avenue of Law Suits, because many owners of the properties through which it plowed were angry at the damage and dissatisfied with the compensation. But all of that is easily forgotten today as we walk along the avenue. This tree-lined boulevard was designed by Buschiazzo, the very architect Alvear had chosen to design his own mansion. No Parisian thoroughfare, neither the Avenue des Champs-Élysées nor the Avenue de l'Opera, neither the Boulevard Haussmann nor the Rue Royal, surpasses it in dignity and beauty. Thirty meters wide, it was, at the time of its completion, the broadest thoroughfare in the city. That width was noteworthy, since it matched to the centimeter the width of the newest and grandest boulevards in Paris. Also in accordance with Parisian precedent, its buildings were all of the same height, none rising more than eighty feet. Because of this strict uniformity (despite a few variances granted in subsequent decades) the Avenida de Mayo offers a prospect of breathtaking harmony that is highly unusual in today's Buenos Aires.

Alvear would likewise initiate, though he would not live to see, the Palacio de Tribunales and, facing it on Plaza Lavalle, the grand Teatro Colón that replaced the original on the Plaza de Mayo. Along what is now the Avenida Leandro N. Alem, Alvear began constructing the new and vastly enlarged central post office, and northeast of the Congreso, he drew up plans for the city's main water supplier, the Aguas Corrientes. He even studied the expansion of the port, which at the time was the key to the city's and the nation's expanding wealth and which largely bankrolled Alvear's urban visions. Perhaps even more important, the changes he implemented were not restricted to landmarks and grand avenues. By planting trees throughout Buenos Aires, by paving over the streets and improving the lighting, he brought about a transformation whose effects directly touched and improved the lives of all its citizens.

After he had fulfilled his four-year mandate in 1887, Alvear rested from his labors by revisiting the European capitals that had inspired him in the first place. On his return to Buenos Aires, he agreed to serve a second term as intendente, but he died suddenly on December

8, 1890. Despite the incalculable influence that this one man had on the Argentine capital, he has been almost entirely forgotten by the very citizens whose lives he did so much to improve. One of his ten children, Carlos, would follow in his footsteps as *intendente,* while another, Marcelo, would serve as president of Argentina from 1922 to 1928. But even if their father has been honored with an important plaza near the Cemetery of Recoleta and a fine monument in the middle of it, still he deserves to be far better known. One could fairly invoke in his behalf the inscription on the tomb of Sir Christopher Wren in Saint Paul's he designed: *si monumentum requiris, circumspice:* If you seek a monument, look around you. And if you do, you will find wonders everywhere. For even where they are not the direct consequence of Alvear's stewardship, they nevertheless continue the great work that he began.

❋

A GOOD EXAMPLE of the urbanistic enhancements undertaken by Alvear is found at the western end of the Avenida de Mayo. The Palacio del Congreso stands between Rivadavia and Yrigoyen, at the point where Avenida Callao becomes Entre Rios (Rivadavia being the dividing line between the northern and southern parts of central Buenos Aires and the point where each north-south street undergoes a name change). Like the United States Capitol that inspired it, the new Congreso had a protracted gestation. Conceived as early as 1882, its actual construction did not begin until 1896 (six years after Alvear's death), and even at its official inauguration nine years later, the structure was far from complete. Many architects competed for the Congreso commission, which was finally won by the Italian-born Vittorio Meano.

The Congreso, of course, was conceived roughly half a century after the Capitol and in response to a very different cultural context. If the Capitol achieves its incomparable presence through the purity of its classical balance, the Congreso projects a somewhat eccentric air, an attitude, that is rare among the official architecture of the age. Like the Capitol, it is a cross between a palace and a domed Roman temple, rising on a pedestal and flanked by pavilions that are joined

Palacio del Congreso, designed by Vittorio Meano and completed in 1906. (Archivo General de la Nación)

with the core via colonnaded wings. But the stately proportions of the Capitol have been replaced by an almost mannered elongation, most notably in the dome. Such distortions provoke a sense of unrest that is heightened by the spiky detailing of the roof, as well as by the quadriga of sculpted horses that serve as the transition between the temple front and the dome, and by the sculptural groups that crown each of the pavilions.

The Congreso is but one of a fairly large number of buildings constructed around this time in accordance with the palace typology, which tends, especially in Buenos Aires, to stress bilateral symmetry, its central structure flanked by identical pavilions to which it is joined by identical wings. Schools were especially susceptible to this treatment: the Escuela Normal Nº 9 "Domingo Faustino Sarmiento" on Avenida Callao, designed by Carlo Morra; La Facultad de Ciencias Económicas at the Corner of Córdoba and Junin, designed by Gino Aloisi, and, just down the street, the Escuela Normal 1, designed by Ernesto Bunge, the architect of the Penitenciaría Nacional. *Palacios sín reyes*—palaces without kings—is the phrase that was applied to this particularly Porteño and peculiarly republican besottedness with the palace typology.

Some of the grandest of these palaces were the stations for the city's three main train lines: the Western or Sarmiento line that left from Once; the Southern or Roca line out of Constitución; and the Northern or Mitre line that departed from Retiro. Their typology is a fairly standard one: like the Gare du Nord and Gare de l'Est in Paris, or Paddington and Waterloo stations in London, these are imposing Beaux Arts wedding cakes that dominate a major public square and are inspired, at least in part, by the Roman baths of Caracalla and Diocletian. Behind their public structures, invisible from the street, lie the tracks themselves, housed in towering glass sheds constructed out of iron lattices.

The best and most harmonious of the three buildings, from a purely architectural perspective, is the Retiro station in the north. The gallant *porte-cochère* of its noble facade curves gently toward the slopes of Plaza San Martín. Begun in 1909 and completed in 1915, it is noteworthy in that, despite its Gallic verve, it was designed by British architects Eustace L. Conder, Roger Conder and Sydney G. Follet. Indeed, it was fabricated in Britain and shipped piecemeal across the Atlantic. Thus the pervasive rustication of its facade, its mansard roofs enlivened by ribbons of balustrades and its rows of single or paired Doric columns belong as much to British architecture as to Argentine, specifically to the period of Sir Edwin Luytens's neoclassical work in New Delhi and Sir Reginald Blomfield's redesign of Regent Street.

Everything about the Retiro station is opulent. Even in its present state of decay, with Porteños in their tens of thousands entering and leaving the structure without paying the slightest heed to its faded beauty, it retains many traces of its former majesty: the century-old bronze sconces and the overwrought chandeliers, the turquoise majolica of the ticket windows, with their battered wooden counters and barriers of tarnished brass. This is public architecture of the highest and most idealistic order. As magnificent as were the private mansions and clubhouses that the oligarchy was building at precisely this moment, they were no match for the opulence of the Retiro station, whose curved entrance seems to embrace all Porteños who enter, irrespective

Grand Hall of the Constitución train station, begun in 1925. (Photograph by the Author)

of class, income or even sanity. Consider, too, the sumptuous restaurant that once occupied the southern pavilion: it still exists, though a mere shadow of what it was. Gone are the potted palms and the white linen tablecloths, and the clientele is not, perhaps, as exalted as it once was. But given how charming this brilliant white space remains today, with its Corinthian columns supporting a lofty atrium, it is easy to imagine how splendid it was in its day.

All the way at the southern end of the city stands Estación Constitución. Surely the interplay of its parts—the result of several building campaigns—makes for a less harmonious whole than that of the Retiro station. The most public face of it, the northern facade, was completed in 1887 by the London firm of Parr, Strong & Parr. Although it is said to be based on the French Baroque palace of Maisons-Laffitte, its sturdy, slightly ponderous treatment feels more like the sort of late Victorian building that arose in such English cities as York and Manchester. Far better is its unforgettable and somewhat later interior, dominated by a single barrel vault, sixty feet high and covered in coffering, that extends

Palacio de Aguas Corrientes at Córdoba 1950, designed by Karl Nyströmer in 1894. (Photograph by the Author)

across the entire expanse of the building for a length of four hundred feet. The vaulted ceiling of New York's Grand Central Terminal may be more refined in its details, but it cannot match the sublime force of this structure, whose very pertinacity evokes the architectural fever dreams of the eighteenth-century masters Claude-Nicolas Ledoux and Étienne-Louis Boullée.

But perhaps the oddest and most delightful of Buenos Aires's palaces is the Palacio de Aguas Corrientes, designed by the Swedish architect Karl Nyströmer. Like so many of the city's large infrastructural projects of the time, this was paid for by British capital, specifically that of the Buenos Aires Water Supply and Drainage Company Limited. Completed in 1894, it was intended to replace the tall, ugly water tower that rose over the Plaza Larrea near the Congreso. A perfect square, its four equilateral facades occupy the entire block from Córdoba to Viamonte and from Ayacucho to Riobamba. Nearly every inch of its facade bristles with brilliant polychrome tiles from the Royal Doulton factories in Lambeth, and they look as fresh today as the minute they were made. They are arranged in a mannerist style that recalls the Château de Fontainebleau in its massing, rustication, mansard gables and countless details. As befitted the patriotism of the time, its terra-cotta adornments form an intricate iconographic program in which the heraldic shields and representative flowers of each of the nation's provinces were dutifully depicted.

At the same time, there is something almost comical in the disparity between the structure's shimmering surface and its lowly function as a pumping station, a palace of plumbing. That glorious facade is little more than a screen for twelve colossal water tanks that soon proved inadequate to the growing city's needs, both in their operation and in their capacity. Today only a small part of the Palacio de Aguas Corrientes is used as offices for the local utilities agency, and it contains what is probably the best museum of plumbing in the world.

One thing that, strangely, Buenos Aires never acquired was an impressive network of museums, although it could easily have afforded them in the years around 1900. True, there are many small to mid-sized museums around the capital, but none of them equals the size or prestige of the Victoria and Albert Museum and the Natural History Museum, which sit side by side on London's Cromwell Road, or New York's Metropolitan Museum of Art and its American Museum of Natural History, which face one another across Central Park. In Buenos Aires, something of the sort was considered at one time or another, but nothing came of the proposals. The Museo de Bellas Artes, opposite Plaza Mitre, is a worthy institution and an impressive one if you come to it with sufficiently modest expectations. But its collection is not a hundredth the size of the Metropolitan Museum or the National Galleries of Washington and London. Its plain structure is a former water purification center from the 1860s that Alejandro Bustillo adapted as a museum in the 1930s. Likewise the city's natural history museum, the Museo Argentino de Ciencias Naturales, at the northern rim of Parque Centenario, is in many ways a charming and whimsical building. But purely from the perspective of its architecture, it is less prepossessing than several of the city's high schools.

———— ❋ ————

THERE IS ONE ESSENTIAL ELEMENT of the Porteño streetscape that has been almost universally overlooked. It is, in its subtle way, a thing of rare beauty: every corner of every block of Buenos Aires is chamfered or blunted. The word for this in Spanish is *chaflan,* but the locals call it an *ochava,* possibly derived from *octava,* since the part lopped off was thought to account for about an eighth of the corner lot. This one refinement of the grid fundamentally altered the cityscape of Buenos Aires, as well as how the locals have inhabited and used it for more than a century.

Throughout the world, wherever cities are laid out as a grid, their streets intersect at sharp right angles. There is no great disadvantage to this other than a certain tedium. But in Buenos Aires each corner becomes a theater for four separate urban events, whether a shop, a restaurant or a residence, each clamoring in some colorful and emphatic way for the attention of the pedestrian. The intersection becomes a destination in its own right, one charged with interest and meaning. And the cumulative effect of thousands upon thousands of these intersections across Buenos Aires has few exact parallels anywhere else in the world, not even in Paris and Barcelona, where, in some neighborhoods, chamfered corners are seen frequently, but not consistently.

The origins of this motif are unclear. Some historians refer to the little shops that, in colonial days, were carved out of the corners of buildings. More likely was a law passed by Rivadavia in 1821 requiring such chamfered corners for the protection of pedestrians: apparently, before street lights were widely installed, one of the perils of the Porteño grid was muggers who lurked around corners, ready to pounce on unsuspecting pedestrians. But here, too, the law seems to have been applied in a very partial way, since many buildings into the 1880s did not account for it. Today only twenty or so corners without ochavas survive in the entire city, mainly in the barrios of San Telmo and Monserrat and mainly from the 1860s and 1870s.

———— ❋ ————

EVERY ITEM OF ARCHITECTURE that has been described to this point in the present chapter has had a kind of aristocratic aspiration to it. In a more jaundiced reading, one could see it as nouveau riche or parvenu, or any other term in the arsenal of snobbery. One could, but one would be wrong. First of all, the Porteño elite that commissioned these architectural follies—which is what they occasionally were—was neither more nor less "authentic" than their Parisian counterparts, the progenitors of the style. The terms *nouveau riche* and *parvenu* could almost have been invented to describe the entire official culture of France's Second Empire, not to mention all those European cities, including London, New York and Washington, D.C., that sought to learn from its example. Second, one is almost compelled to admire the sincerity and conviction with which the Porteño oligarchs pursued their goals, a sincerity and conviction of such force that it finally broke through to a kind of cultural integrity. Some of this striving among the cattlemen of Avenida Alvear can be seen as well in the apartment buildings of the Porteño middle class. Indeed, for years to come this mood would touch all levels of Porteño society. "Except for those actually performing the rudest or dirtiest of manual labor," James Scobie writes, "the universal uniform of the Porteño man was a white shirt with celluloid or starched collar, a dark tie, a hat, and a suit of somber colors." Workers would don their actual work clothes at the place of their employment and remove them at the end of the day. In this way, a pedestrian on the streets of Buenos Aires was hard put "to distinguish a shopgirl from the granddaughter of the President . . . [or a bank clerk from] the son of the Minister of War."

In a matter of only a few years, this working class would grow many times over as the first and second waves of immigrants arrived from Europe. From a demographic perspective, this was the most important single event in the history of Argentina—and, even more so of Buenos Aires, through which all of these immigrants passed and where many chose to remain.

The oligarchs, however, did not want just any immigrants, but Europeans, and not just any Europeans, but, ideally, those from northern Europe. "We want colonists who can work, who can build houses, clear virgin territory and fence off a desert," Alejo Payret, a transplanted Frenchman and fervent promoter of immigration to Argentina, wrote in a letter to Sarmiento in 1870. "And that is not something that you will get from the immigrants from Naples who sell oranges on the streets of Buenos Aires. . . . Not even France can provide the Republic of Argentina with the population it needs. For that it is necessary to look to the people of the North." In this ambition they were to be disappointed, since most of the immigrants came from the less desirable south.

It was during the administration of Intendente Alvear, as the pace of immigration picked up, that the magistrates of Buenos Aires began to think big. Beyond the beautiful palaces and tree-lined avenues, these magistrates were conceiving a far vaster city than most of them had ever seen, the sort of metropolis of millions whose only precedents in human history were contemporary London and Paris. When Alvear took office, it would almost have required clairvoyance to foresee that such growth was even possible.

Argentina, like the United States, can fairly claim to be a nation of immigrants. Open any Porteño newspaper or any local telephone directory and the names are as likely to be Italian, German, French or English as Spanish and Basque. As a port city, Buenos Aires had always had a large number of foreigners clamoring about its streets. But that was nothing like the waves of immigrants who began to appear in the 1880s. Only the United States, with fully 20 million immigrants, would receive more of them in this period. But one could argue that the 3.5 million who now arrived in Buenos Aires represented an even more impressive number relative to the size of the country and its population at the time. Indeed, these immigrants would soon surpass the native population, mostly the sons of the initial Spanish settlers, who numbered some 2.5 million souls in 1880. By the mid-1940s, when large-scale immigration had largely ceased, 1.5 million Spanish immigrants, and 1.4 million Italians, as well as 600,000 people of other nationalities, had settled in Argentina, all of them hoping to *hacer America* in the idiom of the day, to achieve what, in the United States, was called "the American dream."

As late as the 1880s, the population of Buenos Aires had been fairly homogeneous. It is true that slaves—who were not fully emancipated until 1860—and their descendants made up nearly a third of the population at one point. But the Porteños were overwhelmingly white and criollo, the descendants of the Spanish, even though a fair number of other nationalities achieved wealth and eminence as well. In consequence, you did not see before the 1880s that most Porteño of urban units, the barrio, a subdivision of the city distinguished by character, food, attire and language. But now, the newly arrived Spanish immigrants began to gravitate to Monserrat and San Nicolás, while the Italians, greatly in the majority, preferred San Juan Evangelista and Balvanera Sud. Russian Jews turned to Balvanera Este, Sud and Norte where, to the extent to which they have not assimilated, they remain to this day as a large Hasidic community. Buenos Aires, by the way, now has the seventh-largest Jewish community in the world.

These barrios, though indeed a new occurrence in Porteño life, had one precedent. A community of freed slaves had gathered around the Plaza de la Independencía in the final years of the eighteenth century, beside the bullring that occupied that site for about ten years. But their descendants, whose numbers dwindled over the course of the nineteenth century, would not be welcomed in the new Buenos Aires that was coming into being after 1880. Why or how this happened is unclear. "The decline and disappearance of the black population of Buenos Aires," writes George Reid Andrews, "is one of the most striking events of Argentine history. It even qualifies as one of the more curious footnotes to world demographic history." Although they were never systematically persecuted, as were the indigenous peoples in Roca's Conquest of the Desert, it is also true that they were not made to feel especially welcome in the capital or most anywhere else in the country. What is certain is that their disappearance must have altered the entire look of Buenos Aires. Far into the first half of the nineteenth century blacks were as common a sight in Buenos Aires as they are now in Rio de Janeiro. Today, however, most people of African descent in the capital are tourists from the United States or Brazil.

For nearly a generation after the first large waves of immigrants arrived, they tended to settle within walking distance of the port or the Plaza de Mayo, where their work was located. The tramway system became affordable for the average worker only after 1905, when it began to run on electricity, and it was this one technological advance, as much as any other urbanistic or political development, that made possible the city's westward expansion beyond Avenida Pueyrredón. Before that time, most of the immigrants lived amid the squalor of the conventillos, as many as fifteen inhabitants to a room. Most of these conventillos were in San Telmo and some were in San Nicolás, but the liveliest of the new immigrant communities was La Boca, near the port.

La Boca represents a kind of proletarian retort to the Parisian reveries of the rest of the city. Today it is made up primarily of recent arrivals from the interior of the country, as well as from neighboring Paraguay and Bolivia. But a century ago it was overwhelmingly Italian, specifically Genoese. In 1882, in response to a protracted general strike, the new inhabitants of La Boca officially seceded from Argentina, declared an independent republic, and hoisted the Genoese flag. The conflict ended quickly, however, when Roca, as president of the republic, arrived and personally tore down the flag.

Today La Boca is a major tourist attraction, alive at all hours of the day and night with tango dancers, souvenir shops and overpriced *parrillas* or steakhouses. But it does succeed in preserving that air of proletarian marginality that it had a century ago, especially along the so-called Caminito, or little path. This was once the bed of a small stream that dried up and was replaced by train tracks. They are still visible, even though no train has been seen in these parts since 1954. The most idiosyncratic element of La Boca, however, is its building stock, which remains largely as it was in 1900. In general, you have to head very far out of the center of the city to see wooden houses, but here they are found in abundance. Slapped together with wood and corrugated iron, each of them looks as if it were the first house ever built by whoever built it. Upper stories seem to have landed at an inconceivable angle to the ones below, receding or protruding in perilous cantilevers where one would least expect them. But the most striking thing about these houses is their brilliant patchwork of primary and secondary colors, as many as five on a single wall. The origin of this practice, apparently, dates to the nineteenth century, when the local houses were slathered with whatever pigment was left over by the sailors who painted the ships in the nearby docks of the Riachuelo. Since there was rarely enough of any one color to cover an entire wall, let alone an entire house, this astonishing expedient was hit upon.

❋

THE VAST INFLUX OF IMMIGRANTS to Buenos Aires resulted in a tenfold increase in the city's population in the space of less than two generations. This convulsive growth, combined with the city's territorial expansion after 1887, demanded massive investments in infrastructure. Two of the most ambitious of these projects were the enlargement of the port and the creation of the city's subway system, or Subte, as it is called locally.

And yet, in an odd way, and despite the considerable costs and travails of opening the first subway line on December 1, 1913, it is not clear that the system was really needed in the first place. The subway as it exists today is an important and efficient means of moving around the city, despite its inadequacies, namely that the system so emphatically affirms the centrality of the Plaza de Mayo, from which the four main lines fan out along the east-west axis, that movement from north to south is unusually difficult. For more than sixteen years, however, until the Linea B was completed in 1930, the entire system consisted of trains moving between the Plaza de Mayo and the Congreso and a bit beyond, a distance of little more than one and a half miles. Construction of the Linea A may have been in part a response to the overtaxed tramway system, if indeed that system was overtaxed, but one strongly suspects that there was an aspirational element to the whole thing, the feeling that Paris, London and New York had their subway systems and so, too, must Buenos Aires.

Like so much infrastructure in the city, the Linea A was built with British capital, specifically that of the Anglo-Argentine Tramways Company. The Buenos Aires Subte is not one of the beautiful subway systems of the world. You will find here neither the rococo chandeliers and stucco cartouches of the Moscow underground, nor the radiant postmodernity of London's Jubilee Line Extension, nor the operatic modernism of Ligne 14 of the Paris Metro. Most of the six lines that form the Buenos Aires Subte were constructed between the 1950s and 1970s in what, even for the time, was a stale and unimaginative idiom. The exception, however, is the first, the Linea A, the only one built during the Belle Époque. In its demure and decent way, this is one of the finest subway routes in the entire world. Whereas each of the other lines in the Buenos Aires Subte is a hodgepodge of accidents and halfhearted design ideas, the Linea A is gloriously uniform throughout its length and preserves, almost without alteration, the original designs of a century ago. Its decor is the soul of simplicity: smooth, cream-colored tiles tastefully enlivened by either a dark blue or magenta trim. The purity of this conceit puts one in mind of a calling card or engraved invitation from 1913.

But the best thing about the Linea A was the subway cars themselves, which, before their retirement in 2013, served with distinction for exactly a century. At the time when they were taken out of service, they were the oldest functioning subway cars anywhere in the world. In recent years the trains seemed to clank, rattle and lurch from one station to the next, but their record of efficiency was admirable to the end: nineteen mechanical failures for every 100,000 km, one of the lowest rates in the system. The car itself was officially known as *La Brugeoise,* because it was designed and fabricated in the Belgian city of Bruges. Over the decades, the metal exteriors of the cars were repainted several times, and many were awash in graffiti. But the interiors, with wooden accents and slatted wooden seats, remained largely untouched, even as they sank deeper into decrepitude. The ceilings and sideboards were of galvanized steel. The arched windows were raised or lowered along wooden sashes by means of a worn leather strap—a nice Argentine touch. There was little actual ornament, however, beyond acanthus-leaf light fixtures and demure rosettes crowning the pale metal poles in the center of each car. Nothing, however, suggested the passage of a century more than the mirrors near each entrance: they survived as little more than a sequence of mottled and abstract patches, most of their quicksilver having vanished decades ago.

Far more urgent, however, than building this rather diminutive stretch of subway was addressing the issue of the port, upon which the wealth of the city and the nation depended. Today Buenos Aires has three ports, only two of which are functioning: one all the way to the south in La Boca and Barracas; the Puerto Madero, the best known of the three, which stands, useless, to the east of the Plaza de Mayo and extends along the entire north-south axis of the traditional city from Retiro to La Boca; and finally the Puerto Nuevo, to the north beyond Retiro. Although the southernmost port continues to see some activity, the one all the way to the north is essentially the port of modern Buenos Aires. But what most citizens and tourists think of as the city's main port, the Puerto Madero, has not functioned as such in nearly half a century and has been more recently transformed, with some success, into the city's forty-eighth official barrio, a fashionable zone of high-end restaurants and luxury high-rises.

To most Porteños, the Puerto Madero seems like an unalterable fact of life. As James Scobie has written, "Few Porteños know that their city might have developed in any other way than with its waterfront and port located directly in front of the Plaza de Mayo." In fact, one of the battles royal of the last third of the nineteenth century involved precisely this issue of where to place the new port that, everyone admitted, was urgently needed. This necessity was the direct consequence of steam-powered ships that were far larger, and therefore drew far more water, than ships of earlier generations. Until the middle of the nineteenth century, the sandbars that stood between the city and the Rio de la Plata were a nuisance, but they were manageable for the craft of the day. By the end of the century, however, when ships had doubled in size, they were essentially barred from approaching the city itself. Many solutions were considered, the two most important of which were those of Luis A. Huergo and Eduardo Madero. Huergo wanted to build the new port in La Boca at the mouth of the Riachuelo, all the way to the south, while Madero wanted it to lie parallel to the eastern face of the city. Obviously Madero carried the day—hence Puerto Madero—but not before Huergo had made considerable progress in improving and enlarging the lesser port of La Boca.

But as is always the case in Buenos Aires, there was a political dimension to the issue. More traditional elements of Porteño society—still orientated to the south—favored Huergo's choice of La Boca, while the Europhile oligarchs, and especially the London banks who would have to provide backing, favored Madero's placing the port parallel to the city's north-south axis, which thus reinforced the centrality of the Plaza de Mayo. For much of a generation this debate continued but was ultimately decided by Madero's ability to procure the backing of the London bankers, specifically Baring Brothers, as well as by the simple fact that the oligarchs wanted the port to sit east of the Casa Rosada and that they held more power than their opponents. And so it is that four massive basins were excavated from the sandbars that had stood for several hundred thousand years between the barrancas of the city and the waters of the river, with harbors added in the north and the south.

In short order the entire shape and appearance of the city's eastern side was altered forever. No longer did one look out from the Plaza de Mayo or the Paseo Colón to see the waters of the Rio de la Plata gleaming in the midday sun. Instead one saw rows of four-story red-brick warehouses that looked curiously like something in London, precisely because they had been designed and built by the London firm of Hawkwood and Sons. Beyond them phalanxes of grain elevators rose up like dumb giants for nearly a mile. The actual construction of the port began in 1889 and was completed nine years later, by which time Madero had already died. In part because of its inherent design, in part because its success doubled the number of ships that entered it, the port soon proved inadequate, and after a protracted decline, it was officially closed in the early 1960s. But even if more recent attempts to resurrect the area have met with some success, it is quite clear that by blocking the citizens' access to the river, the massive and costly Puerto Madero was a mistake, perhaps the greatest single mistake in the city's history. In the competition for that dismal honor, it has only one real rival, the Avenida 9 de Julio, the subject of a later chapter.

Around 1917, the decision was made to embellish the landfill at the eastern end of the port, and so to turn it into a destination for the middle class. The first element to be completed was a fine little park, done up in the Beaux Arts style and known as the Espigón Plus Ultra. For more than sixty years it jutted out, an isolated peninsula, into the waters of the estuary. Several years after its construction it was attached to a landscaped boulevard known as the Costanera Sur, designed by Jean-Claude Forestier, the French landscapist whom we have already met. Rising improbably between the river and the grimy, hardscrabble port, the Costanera Sur was completed in 1924.

It extended along the banks of the river for two miles, an impeccable stretch of rusticated limestone with twelve steps leading down into the water. Along the way were columned pergolas and swerving balustrades, as well as sculptural interludes like Lola Mora's *Fountain of the*

Swimming on the Costanera Sur, c. 1945. (Archivo General de la Nación)

Sirens, which still stands there today. The Costanera Sur stood fully a kilometer farther out into the Rio de la Plata than the sand pools, mud pits and rocky shoals in which the original settlers had bathed three centuries before. The three great *muelles,* or piers, that, for much of the nineteenth century, had jutted out from the Paseo Colón, never reached this far.

But the citizens did not come, in their tens of thousands, only to stroll along the landscaped boulevard. Amid its rusticated details and classical urns, people from all classes and from all barrios would swim here on warm summer days, and they continued to do so into the 1970s. In time an entire infrastructure of leisure, even fun, arose around the walkway, from changing stalls and stands selling panchos and chori-panes (local equivalents of a hot dog) to fairly elaborate *cervecerias* or beer halls, most of them designed in the Art Deco style by the Croatian-born architect Andrés Kálnay. The most famous of these, the Cerveceria Munich, still stands along the along the Costanera Sur. But it has been transformed into an art museum with few visitors, alas, since these days few people visit this part of the city. Why that is so will also be the subject of a later chapter.

❋

THE DEVELOPMENT OF THE COSTANERA SUR was but one small part of a revolution in the way in which the Porteños inhabited their city and humans inhabited cities in general. Until the middle years of the nineteenth century, the presumption of fun, pleasure or amusement was not integrated into urban structure. Le Notre's redesign of the gardens of Les Tuileries, around the year 1670, was one of the first interventions designed specifically to delight the locals and to serve as the context of their leisure. But such interventions remained fairly rare into the second half of the nineteenth century, when, for the first time, a growing middle and working class began to enjoy greater leisure than ever before.

The oligarchs of Buenos Aires had seen the advances that Haussmann had made in this respect, and they were determined to reproduce that infrastructure of leisure, even fun. And when they turned to consider the amenities with which they might enrich the city, it was quite clear that they would have to create parks, a zoo, a botanical garden, carrousels and a racetrack, in addition to the bathing facilities of the Costanera Sur.

To this day, and in spite of all the lean and difficult years that have intervened, Buenos Aires remains a city of great and abundant parks, most of them dating to the period around 1900. This prodigious development of the city's park system is the more remarkable in that, until the middle years of the nineteenth century, the city remained without any parks, not counting the narrow band of greenery that was the Paseo Colón. That space stood on the outskirts of the city and, in any case, was intended for strolling and nothing more.

Today Buenos Aires, like most major cities, has all manner of parks. Smaller parks like the Plaza San Martín and Plaza Vicente López are fully integrated into their neighborhoods. They are meant for sitting and lying on the grass. Larger parks, like Parque Centenario, Parque de los Andes and Parque las Heras are destinations in themselves and invite the citizens not only to sit, but to exercise, hear live music or visit an artisan fair.

But really large parks, like Parque Sarmiento, Parque Almirante Brown and especially Parque Tres de Febrero are of an entirely different order: they are worlds unto themselves. They enable the visitor to get lost in them, as in nature itself, and they invite him to believe—at least while he remains within their enchanted precinct—that he is at some infinite remove from the city that surrounds him. Such parks seem, to the receptive soul, to be—as Wordsworth said of nature itself—All in All.

The man responsible for most of the parks in Buenos Aires was Carlos Thays. Indeed, four men shared this name: from Jules Charles Thays, a naturalized Frenchman, to his son, grandson and finally great-grandson, all of them have distinguished themselves in the creation of parks or, in the case of the last, the related field of agronomy. But it is primarily the first two who concern us here. Between them, they oversaw the park system of Buenos Aires for more than half a century, from the arrival of Jules Charles Thays in 1889 to the retirement of his son, Carlos León Thays, in 1946. Intendente Alvear and his expert on landscaping, Eugene Courtis, had already taken steps to enhance the greenery of the city, but that was nothing compared to the work of Thays, father and son. The father, who was appointed director of parks and walkways for the city of Buenos Aires in 1891, was responsible for more than eighty projects in Buenos Aires, from parks and parkways to public and private gardens. He was the Porteño equivalent of Frederick Law Olmsted, the main designer of Central Park and much else, as well as of Jean-Charles Alphand, who designed most of the parks in Paris that were created under Baron Haussmann. Alphand was, in fact, something of a mentor to the elder Thays. The Parques Avellaneda, Centenario, Chacabuco, Lezama and de los Andes, just to proceed in alphabetical order, were his creations. But he also planted trees by the hundreds of thousands. He was the force behind the lovely Jardin Botanico, or botanical garden, between the Avenues Las Heras and Santa Fe, on whose grounds he lived with his family for decades and where important plant research continues to be carried out to this day. It was there that he could often be found in overalls, with a hoe in his hand, as he carried out his sundry experiments in horticulture.

His masterpiece is indisputably the Parque Tres de Febrero, more popularly known as *Los Bosques de Palermo,* the Woods of Palermo. This park is the closest in size, spirit and function to Central Park and the Bois de Boulogne in the totality of escapism that it affords the Porteño. This is despite the fact that, just as you see the high-rises over Central Park South, so you can hear, in Parque Tres de Febrero, the rush of the trains heading west from Retiro. The park was originally established in 1879 by then former president Sarmiento on land once occupied by the home of Juan Manuel de Rosas. Its name commemorates the Battle of Caseros on February 3, 1852, when Urquiza defeated Rosas and sent him into exile. At that time the population of Buenos Aires was eighty thousand, and it was not immediately obvious that the city needed a park of this size, especially one relatively far from the city and still difficult to reach along highly inadequate roads. By the mid-1870s, however, the population had doubled, and many more Porteños were living in the north of Buenos Aires, in what is now the barrio of Palermo.

Great parks, like Tres de Febrero, have a narrative element to them. As they draw the walker through space, they seek to edify and divert him with a sequence of landscaped events. In the most populous section of Tres de Febrero you find an abundance of statues, a large lake where you can go boating and a formal garden, the Rosedal, that is joined to the rest of the park by a shimmering white bridge across the lake. The park is also a place of expansive fields and several late-Victorian brick buildings, one of them a museum of contemporary art.

High Society at the Hippodrome, c. 1904, from Caras y Caretas. *(Archivo General de la Nación)*

The other great site of the city's leisured class is the Hipódromo de Palermo, a mile-long racetrack modeled on Longchamp and Ascot. It differs crucially from either of these precedents, however, in being located entirely within the city's limits. The hippodrome originally opened in 1854 on marshland reclaimed from the Rio de la Plata, along the northern edge of the city. But it attained its present form only in the early 1900s. Known today mainly to the well-heeled residents of Palermo and Belgrano, it is a part of Buenos Aires that tourists tend not to visit or even hear about. That is a shame, since the Hipódromo boasts some of the best preserved, most abundant and most beautiful examples of Beaux Arts architecture anywhere in Buenos Aires, not to mention its fine restaurants, tea salon and, of course, the horse races.

Like most of the structures in the Hipódromo complex, the main building, from 1908, was the work of the French architect Louis Faure Dujarric. Despite a restrained rustication along the sides, the arcaded upper story in the center expands into five tall windows interspersed with Ionic columns and crowned by a florid cartouche bearing a coat of arms. Even the diminutive pavilion from 1912 that houses the Confitería Paris, a tea salon, is a work of stunning harmony. An oval tempietto conceived in the Ionic order, its entrance is flanked by two inset columns, while the flat roof is adorned with a dentilated cornice and a perfect trim of balustrades. Few buildings in the capital enshrine, to the same degree as those of the Hipódromo, the polished and elegant restraint of the École des Beaux-Arts at its very best. In these and other buildings on the campus of the Hipódromo, Dujarric did his job so well that he managed, almost alone among the architects of Buenos Aires in the Belle Époque, to break through the ornamental pastiche that defined so much of nineteenth-century classicism and to reach deep into the architectural power of its Baroque sources.

❋

THE CASE COULD BE MADE that 1910 was the most glorious year in the history of Buenos Aires, if not of the entire Argentine nation. It was the year of the Centenario, a massive twelve-month orgy of self-gratulation to celebrate the century that had passed since the country declared its independence from Spain. It was a time for taking stock, and never would taking stock prove quite as delightful as this. In 1810, Argentina had been a distant and fairly dismal outpost of the most backward kingdom in Western Europe, and much of its territory remained uncharted and unexplored. But now, a century on, it was the eighth-wealthiest nation in the world, after Italy and ahead of Canada and Australia.

Over that one-hundred-year period the population of Buenos Aires itself had increased forty-fold. Indeed, since Sarmiento's first census was taken in 1869, the city had grown from 178,000 to 1.7 million to become the largest urban center in Latin America and one of the largest in the world. And its economy, based on the export of meat and produce, was growing even faster than its population. For at least a decade, the world had been taking notice of this progress, and now, at the centennial, the city—and through it the nation—was to have its official coming-out party. This was the year when Buenos Aires assumed its place as one of a very select group of great urban centers, rivaling Paris, London and Rome in nearly every respect except ancientness. Only New York among the cities of this time had seen a commensurate expansion.

Buenos Aires had advanced mightily, not only in commerce but in culture as well. Two years before the centennial, the new Teatro Colón opened on Plaza Lavalle as a sumptuous Italian Renaissance palace, a hybrid of the Palais Garnier in Paris and La Scala in Milan. And it would attract some of the greatest names of opera's golden age, Caruso and Chaliapin among them. At the same time, Buenos Aires had certainly fostered, and may have invented, the tango, which had already taken Paris by storm—even if it remained marginal in Buenos Aires itself. This art form, to be considered in the next chapter, had the distinction of being the first cultural invention of the Rio de la Plata to conquer the larger world.

Meanwhile, restaurants and cafes like Café Tortoni on the Avenida de Mayo and the Confitería del Molino at the corner of Rivadavia and Callao were crowded with an international clientele supping on their exalted fare. Department stores like Gath & Chaves rose at the intersection of Bartolomé Mitre and Florida, which had become by this time one of the most frenetic commercial avenues in the world. Weeklies like *Caras y Caretas* emerged to make elegant sport of the high-flyers of the time, with such fervor that no Porteño could doubt that he lived at the center of everything.

This was the context in which the entire world, or so it seemed, showed up in Buenos Aires in 1910 to pay tribute, everyone from Georges Clemenceau and Anatole France to Isadora Duncan and Guglielmo Marconi, fresh from winning his Nobel Prize in physics. To this day the entire northern portion of the city, the showpiece of the capital, is awash in plazas and monuments that attest to the world's newfound admiration: the Plaza Francia, Plaza Italia, Plaza Alemania and Torre de los Ingleses, Great Britain's contribution in the Plaza Retiro, are only a few of them.

Like Paris and Vienna, Buenos Aires is a city of statues, whether seated, standing or on horseback, and many of the best were created on the occasion of the centennial or subsequently in response to it. The massive and relentless Monumento de los Españoles, a work of Agustín Querol, was commissioned by Spain for the intersection of Sarmiento and Libertador. From there its sixty-foot-tall marble mass, teeming with a promiscuous array of writhing bodies and surmounted by the female incarnation of Argentina itself, can be seen from miles in all directions. Many other sculptures arose at this time, among them Gustav Eberlein's statue of Cornelio Saavedra at the corner of Córdoba and Callao, Charles Cordier's statue of Miguel de Azcuénaga in Plaza Primera Junta, and perhaps the finest statue in the city, Arnaldo Zocchi's monument to Christopher Columbus in Parque Colón.

But the greatest monument of all was never built. Alvear and his successors had long felt that the grand axis of the Avenida de Mayo, with the Congreso at one end and the Casa Rosada at the other, was inadequate, that something more was needed. The monument that now rises along that axis, the fine neoclassical Pirámide de Mayo of 1811, seemed rather small to the imperious eyes of the oligarchs. In 1887 Alvear solicited and received permission to replace it with a far larger structure, but nothing came of the plan, and money grew scarce after the financial crisis of 1890. In anticipation of the centennial, however, the issue was revisited, and in 1909 a competition for the commission was won by two Italians, the architect Gaetano Moretti and the sculptor Luigi Brizzolara. If this project had been brought to completion, it would have been world-renowned, a marvel to compete with the Eiffel Tower, the Campanile of San Marco and the Statue of Christ the Redeemer in Rio de Janeiro. In the studies that survive, this titanic column of Carrara marble resembles a massive candle whose base is puddled in wax. With several individual sculptural groups at the base and a mounted equestrian statue of Argentina at the top, it would have towered over the city. But then the Great War came, and then another series of financial and political crises, and finally nothing was ever done.

The Infanta Isabela de Bourbon (right) with cow at the Exposición Internacional del Centenario, 1910. (Archivo General de la Nación)

The main event of the centennial celebrations was the great *Exposición Internacional del Centenario,* a kind of World's Fair in which the products and customs of many nations were on proud display from May to November of 1910, along a three-mile swath of the Barrio Norte. The fair extended all the way from the fine arts museum in the Plaza San Martín to the agricultural pavilions just west of the zoo and the transportation and science pavilions due west of that. It is a measure of how vast Buenos Aires had become by this time that the *Exposición,* although it stood in a relatively small corner of the city's northern limit, nevertheless extended over a space larger than the entire city of Buenos Aires during the presidency of Bartolomé Mitre. Officially opened by President José Figueroa Alcorta, the exposition offered such diversions as the first gas station in the country and balloon rides with Jorge Newbery, the country's first aviator and a national hero. The section devoted to agriculture, a matter of nearly universal fascination to the Argentines of the time, was held on the grounds of the Sociedad Rural, a major engine, then as now, of the nation's prosperity and one of the major forces behind the exhibition. A well-known image from the time—in which the exposition's guest of honor, Infanta Isabela de Bourbon, the stout aunt of the king of Spain, appears beside a prize Guernsey—will give some sense of the spirit of this part of the exhibition.

It was at the *Exposición Internacional del Centenario* that the Beaux Arts delirium of the oligarchs assumed its most extravagant form. Unlike the city's "real" architecture, the architecture of brick and masonry that had to answer to the pressing and practical needs of developers and occupants as well as all the dreary laws of physics, these structures were often intended to last no more than a few months. Structurally they required little more solidity than a few metal beams to which was affixed a wall scarcely more substantial than a theater curtain. The entrance to the transport section featured a large and presumably futuristic spheroid flanked by huge arches graced with what looked like irregular minarets. The pavilion commissioned by the Province of Buenos Aires bore

Pabellón de Fiestas, Correos y Telégrafos at the Exposición Internacional del Centenario, 1910. (Archivo General de la Nación)

glancing resemblance to the Castle in Disneyland. Meanwhile the Para-
guayan pavilion, shaped like a nave with two side aisles, was exemplary
in the decadent, fin de siècle energy of its looping lines.

But aside from the lovely Beaux Arts pavilions of the Sociedad
Rural—which still serve as the city's main convention center—little
architecture survives from the fairgrounds of the *Exposición*. One rare
exception is the *Pabellón de Fiestas, Correos y Telégrafos* (the Pavilion
of Fairs, Postal Service and Telegraphs). This was designed by Vinent,
Maupas and Jáuregui and took the form of a pale oval surrounded by
paired columns, with a gabled glass ceiling crowned by an elaborate
belvedere, in a style somewhere between French Baroque and Vienna
Secession.

It survives to this day, but few Porteños know about it, and fewer
still will ever see it. For it stands abandoned and hidden from view all
the way at the end of a narrow path that leads to the loading platform
of the local Jumbo, a huge retail outlet akin to Walmart or Target. But
if the intrepid tourist or architectural student manages to make it that
far, he will find that its exterior yet retains an air of faded, vandalized
majesty. Rather it is the interior that is so shocking, with its smashed-in
glass ceiling and floors that have rotted down to the foundations. There
is squalor everywhere, from the ruined floorboards all the way up to the
rafters. Weeds grow amid the volutes of the Ionic columns. Abandoned
for more than a century now, the pavilion has become the abode of feral
cats and nesting birds.

In the fate of this one building, it is tempting to see a sort of *Picture
of Dorian Gray* inversion of the dazzling, progressive visions of the entire *Generacion del '80* in its prime. Few of the oligarchs or proud Porteños who poured into the *Exposición,* who marveled at the palaces of the
Avenida Alvear and the Congreso on the Avenida de Mayo, could ever
have imagined that their city's ascent would be anything but boundless,
that it would be thwarted and even reversed by financial turmoil and by
more than fifty years of coups and anarchy. What seemed to be merely
the inception of their greatness was really its summit. This was their
Golden Age.

NINE

THE CITY OF
THE MASSES

(1920–1946)

IF THE GOLDEN AGE OF BUENOS AIRES, FROM 1880 TO 1920, was inspired by a dream of Paris, the age that followed found its inspiration in New York. While the former age sought to re-create, on the western bank of the Rio de la Plata, the classicism of the Old World, the latter was in thrall to the ecstatic hyperactivity of modern times. Put another way, the tango of San Telmo and the jazz of Luna Park began to drown out the strains of Tannhäuser that rose from the pit of Teatro Colón. The racing car and the football stadium confronted the Old World gentility of the hippodrome. In an age of mass media and mass movements, the common-man populism of Hipólito Yrigoyen, elected president in 1916, challenged the paternalistic detachment of his oligarchic predecessors. Skyscrapers in the Art Deco and modernist styles rose up beside the Beaux Arts palaces that, nevertheless, were still being built.

An entirely new cast of urban characters began to appear in the pages of such weeklies as *Caras y Caretas:* in addition to the top-hatted plutocrat one now encountered the slightly thuggish *compadrito,* the prostitute and the *estafador* or conman, perennial human types, to be

sure, but elevated, for the first time in Buenos Aires, to cultural consequence. And with them came important additions to the very language
of the Porteños: for a long time, the Spanish of the Rio de la Plata had
differed from that of Spain, but now it was infused with a vast new
vocabulary of slang, known locally as *lunfardo,* that arose among the
newly arrived immigrants who inhabited the docks and *arrabales,* or
outer barrios, which were thought to be of questionable repute.

But if there were sharp differences between Buenos Aires in its
Golden and Silver ages, it is impossible to separate too precisely the
cultural products of these two eras. Buenos Aires as we see it today is
largely the confluence or collision of their competing visions, the oligarchic vision of Beaux Arts palaces and Britannic efficiency and the
populist vision of La Boca and the electric nightlife along the Avenida
Corrientes.

The changes that Buenos Aires underwent at this time were the
necessary consequence of the exponential growth of its population. The
Golden Age had been the result of the native descendants of Spain—
assisted by artists and technocrats from England and France—exerting
themselves to re-create Europe in South America. This next phase of
Porteño culture was the consequence of Europe, in its millions, actually
reaching the banks of the Rio de la Plata. Although these immigrants
had begun to arrive as much as two generations earlier, only now did
they find their distinctive voice. And their Europe was a very different
place from the glittering continent of the oligarchs: it was the Europe
of Sicilians and Neapolitans, of poor Galician farmers and equally impoverished Russian Jews. Over the space of thirty years, between the
intendancy of Torcuato de Alvear and the presidency of Yrigoyen, they
would swell the population of the city to nearly eight times what it had
been under Alvear, from around 200,000 to something like 1.7 million.
This enlarged population was an infinitely more complex and evolving
organism than the earlier population of the city; now, an array of new
ethnic enclaves encountered one another on a daily basis. You were as
apt to hear Italian spoken on the streets of Buenos Aires as Spanish. But
there was also a good chance that you would hear French or German
or Russian or Syrian Arabic. Bookstores throughout the city catered to

these new arrivals, while newsstands offered local dailies in an array of foreign tongues: among those still in existence are the *Buenos Aires Herald* and the *Argentinisches Tageblatt,* both of which originated in the middle of the nineteenth century. And even if the food in restaurants like Munich in Recoleta or Herman's in Palermo or Edelweiss in Tribunales is now indistinguishable from that of any other Argentine steakhouse, their walls are still decked with deer mounts and images of happy Bavarians in lederhosen that attest to their ethnic origins.

The great centennial celebrations of 1910 had put Buenos Aires on the map, and now it became a magnet for pleasure seekers, intellectuals and political refugees from all over the world. Amid the chaos of the Spanish Civil War, everyone from Ortega y Gasset and Juan Ramón Jiménez to Rafael Alberti and Federico García Lorca sought the safety and stimulation of the city. As diverse a collection of humanity as Albert Einstein, Le Corbusier and Aristotle Onassis all gravitated to Buenos Aires, either as lionized celebrities or, in the case of Onassis, as a young man looking to make his fortune. Twenty years earlier, it would not have occurred to anyone simply to "show up" in Buenos Aires. Indeed, it is difficult to think of a single prominent citizen of the Northern Hemisphere, other than Darwin in 1832, who had visited Buenos Aires prior to the centennial celebrations. But now they began to arrive in significant numbers, and they, too, no less than the millions of immigrants, were to have a lasting effect on the character of the city.

For the first time, what might be called an art scene and a literary scene emerged in Buenos Aires. And it is interesting in this connection that, although the development of Buenos Aires and New York is parallel in many ways, it is not in this respect. For even if New York had relatively few distinguished painters in the nineteenth century, it had those few, and more importantly, it had an imposing structure of galleries, exhibitions, critics and academies—in short, an art world of sorts. This was largely, but not completely, lacking in Buenos Aires, where, until the 1920s, most successful artists were foreigners. But now that changed, as local artists began to rise to prominence, among them Antonio Berni, Lino Enea Spilimbergo and Benito Quinquela Martín. This last was the creator of many expressionistic scenes of port life in

Sculpture of Jorge Luis Borges (left) and Adolfo Bioy Casares in La Biela Café, by Fernando Pugliese. (Photograph by the Author)

La Boca; although little known outside of Argentina, they are highly appreciated in the capital, where the ever-nostalgic citizens find in them an expression of the vanished glories of La Boca in its prime.

There had been worthy writers in Buenos Aires throughout the nineteenth century, and they, unlike the more important painters and architects, were entirely homegrown. But they never consolidated their activities into anything that could properly be deemed a school, let alone a movement. In the 1920s, however, that changed, and the literary activities of the capital were played out between two opposing groups, the Grupo Florida and the Grupo Boedo. The former was so named because its informal membership tended to congregate at the Confitería Richmond on Calle Florida 468. (It closed in 2011, only to reopen as a clothing store.) The Grupo Boedo, by contrast, met in the cafes along the Avenida Boedo, about three miles southwest in the working-class barrio of the same name. If the Grupo Florida, which included Borges, Leopoldo Marechal and Victoria Ocampo, looked to Europe and to surrealism for its inspiration, the Grupo Boedo favored the more hard-bitten, down-to-earth style that appears in the novels of Roberto Arlt and that reflects the barrio in which they lived. Nevertheless, there was considerable overlap between the two groups.

At the same time, new forms of entertainment arose in Buenos Aires and with them new urban typologies. If many of the changes of this period were specific to Buenos Aires—the doubling of its population, for example—many more were the result of processes that, at that very moment, were playing out across the world. A brash, bright, giddily populist string of cinemas sprang up along Lavalle in that four-block stretch of the Microcentro from Calle Florida to Carlos Pellegrini, a stone's throw from the famed Obelisco. Here, where the earliest of the city's trains had passed from the river to the Plaza Lavalle and points west, more than a dozen movie theaters arose, mostly in the Art Deco style and adorned with the grandiose names that typify the genre: *Luxor, Monumental, Paris, Ambassadeur.* This stretch of Lavalle was the local answer to Times Square, Leicester Square and the Champs-Élysées.

Although Argentina produced its crop of movie stars, the heroes of the age were sports figures like Luis Ángel Firpo, the boxer whose match with Jack Dempsey in Manhattan's Polo Grounds, on September 14, 1923, was immortalized in one of the masterpieces of the great Ohio-born painter George Bellows. Firpo is buried in the Cemetery of Recoleta, where the entrance to his imposing tomb is distinguished by a life-sized bronze statue of the man, bare-chested in full boxing attire.

It was at this time as well that football—or soccer in American English—became the obsession of the city and the entire nation. The two main teams that divide the fervid and occasionally violent loyalties of the Porteños are River Plate and Boca Juniors, founded in 1901 and 1905, respectively. Their English names attest to the fact that the British brought this sport to Argentina, even though it now seems to the locals to be essentially Argentine. Aside from the fact that the sundry colors of the two teams, the blue and gold of Boca Juniors and the red and white of River Plate, suffuse the capital, their main architectural presence in the city is their stadiums. The River Plate stadium opened in 1938, while Boca Junior stadium, also known as the Bombonera, or

Chocolate Box, opened two years later. Unlike American baseball parks of the era, which at least tried to look imposing and impressive, these were and remain, architecturally speaking, entirely without distinction.

———————— ❋ ————————

SHOULD YOU WISH to annoy a Porteño, invite him to speculate that the tango may actually have originated in Montevideo, the capital of Uruguay. Where the popular dance began is one of the insoluble mysteries of this part of the world, and the question is surely beyond the scope of this book. But the aggrieved reaction of the Porteño will serve to underscore the centrality of the tango in Argentine, and especially Porteño, culture, and the considerable pride that the citizens take in it. Foreigners who have never visited the country, who know nothing else about it, nevertheless know that the tango is Argentine. The presidential plane (the equivalent of the U.S. president's *Air Force One*) is named *Tango One*. On summer days in the capital, many a corner of the Microcentro is clogged with locals assessing a young couple—the man with slicked-back hair and a zoot suit, the woman in a clingy black dress and stiletto heels—as they slink through one of the classic tangos. The tango is nothing less than the soundtrack of Buenos Aires: the slicing rhythms of the piano and *bandoneon* (a kind of accordion) as well as the warbled throb of a tenor resound in taxicabs and bars and can be heard skirling out of CD stores that sell nothing else and whose clerks cheerfully display an encyclopedic mastery of the subject. From all parts of Europe and North America, men and especially women abandon their jobs for a few weeks of each year and descend on Buenos Aires to find in tango a fulfillment that, they insist, can be found nowhere else.

Throughout its history, the nature of Porteño culture—with rare exceptions like the great poem "Martin Fierro" (1879) by José Hernández—has consisted in the adoption of someone else's culture. But the tango is different. Wherever it originated, it is universally associated with Buenos Aires. It is here that the dance developed and here that it encountered a citizenry of several million to propel it to world fame. And although the tango is danced throughout the country and the world, nowhere else does it make the kind of organic sense it makes on the streets and in the bars of Buenos Aires. It is an essentially urban dance, cynical, cunning and disabused, that percolated up from the Porteño underworld, from the brothels and dives of La Boca, from the docks where new arrivals encountered the already assimilated sons of Genoa and Bilbao.

Painting of Carlos Gardel, the famed tango singer, whose face is nearly ubiquitous in Buenos Aires. (Photograph by the Author)

The greatest exponent of tango music was the tenor Carlos Gardel, whose fame, by the 1920s, had spread throughout the world. Like Eva Perón and Jorge Luis Borges, he is one of the constantly recurring icons of the city, his distinct and yet very Argentine face appearing on the walls of cafes, the awnings of shops and even in graffiti. It is difficult to walk near the Cementerio de Recoleta or the Plaza Dorrego in San Telmo without encountering Gardel imitators in their fedoras and sharp suits. The souvenir shops along the Caminito are likewise stocked with statuettes of the man, and his distinctive, passionate warble is frequently within earshot. Gardel was not only the complete *tangista*, but the essential Porteño of his day: he was the embodiment of its popu-lism, with a hint of the demimonde and also of the Old World, since he seems to have been born in France, although that, like the origins of tango itself, is a subject of heated debate. In 1935, he died in an airplane accident at the age of forty-four and was mourned throughout Latin America, but in Buenos Aires most of all. In its three and a half centu-ries of existence, the city had never seen such an outpouring of grief on the part of the entire citizenry.

✳

IF THE WAVES OF IMMIGRANTS radically altered the cultural life of Buenos Aires, they altered its physical dimensions to the same de-gree. When the city incorporated the townships of Belgrano and Flores in 1887, it increased its physical territory more than eightfold but its population by only about sixty thousand inhabitants. That is to say that, between the traditional borders of Buenos Aires—roughly one and a half miles north, south and west of the Plaza de Mayo—and the area that had just been added, were large stretches of land that were at best sparsely inhabited. And yet by the start of the Second World War, that entire terrain would be filled in with a fairly continuous density of hu-man inhabitation. Some areas of Buenos Aires were and remain more populous than others, but there is no area that does not feel as if it were truly part of a great city. At no point do we sense, as we might in sec-tions of New York City like Far Rockaway or the outer reaches of Staten Island, that we are in suburbia, if not open country.

This process of urbanization occurred in Buenos Aires over the three decades from the election of Yrigoyen in 1916 to the election of Perón in 1946, and it had four main causes: real estate speculation, in-dustrial expansion, spontaneous growth and the extension of the means of transport.

The most critical cause was the improved means of transportation, since no one would have moved to Belgrano if he were required, twice daily, to make the two-hour walk between his home and his work in the Plaza de Mayo. As an article in *La Prensa* stated in 1886, "All it takes for an area to become inhabitable is for a distant street to be paved and for a tramway to pass nearby." New barrios rose up along the sides of the tramway and railway lines like vegetation along an irrigation course. To the west, beyond the preexisting town of Flores, Floresta and Liniers came into being along the Sarmiento Line; along the Pacific and Buenos Aires–Rosario lines Villa Crespo, Villa Malcolm and Chacarita appeared, together with half a dozen others; finally, the North and Central Line gave rise to Villa Alvear, Nunez and Saavedra. According to James Scobie, the number of inhabitants in the central-western part of the expanded city jumped, between 1904 and 1914, from 106,000 to 456,000, out of a total population of 1,575,000 in the latter year. Over the same period, and in the same part of the city, the number of individual houses rose from 16,000 to 58,000.

Some of these new communities grew piecemeal, as though through a natural and spontaneous process, while others were the consequence of real estate speculation, often targeted at the middle and upper middle classes. The nuclei of Villa Alvear—now known as Barrio Parque in Palermo Chico—and Villa Devoto were entire communities designed around 1900 by Juan Antonio Buschiazzo, who had been the favorite architect of Torcuato de Alvear. Another such development was Parque Chas, which has the distinction today of being the smallest barrio in the city. It shares with Barrio Parque another rare distinction of rejecting the pervasive Porteño grid in favor of a circular configuration, thus creating discrete pockets of curvature amid the checkerboard that dominates the rest of the city.

Other barrios were linked to industry. As noted, the northern section of the city had been favored by the wealthy—even if only for summer homes—from the late eighteenth century. With the large-scale movement of the upper classes to the Barrio Norte after the yellow fever epidemic of 1871, the slaughterhouses and brick factories that had stood there for generations moved to the southern extremity of the capital, along the Riachuelo. This lower-lying part of the city was prone to flooding and so was seen to be less desirable. And, as is the nature of real estate, this process of depreciation tended to reinforce itself. Thus, one or two generations later, when heavy industry arrived in Buenos

Aires, it settled in the south. This in turn made that part of the city unacceptable to all but its most disadvantaged citizens. Despite a few charming houses in the area, it has been among the poorest parts of the city for well over a century, and today it is home to the largest slum in Buenos Aires, Villa 25.

❋

AS ALWAYS, the most manifest and material expression of change in a society will be found in its architecture. And yet between this age and the preceding one, there was continuity as well as variation. Although the previous chapter examined Beaux Arts architecture and this one will examine early modernism—Art Deco and the first examples of rationalism—there was considerable chronological overlap between the two styles. The construction of two of the city's largest and most striking examples of Parisian taste, the Estrugamou from 1929 and the Alvear Palace Hotel from three years later, coincided with many of the early modernist buildings in the city. Indeed, two of the most classical structures in Buenos Aires, the Grecian temples of the Facultad de Derecho, or Law School, and the Fundación Eva Perón, were completed in 1949 and 1951, respectively.

In the passage from the Beaux Arts classicism of the oligarchs to the modernism of the next generation, Art Nouveau and the sundry stages of Art Deco played an important role. Much of the Art Nouveau in the city took the form of its Catalan equivalent, known as *modernisme*. A fine example, and one of the earliest, is the Galería Güemes, designed by the Italian architect Francesco Gianotti and inaugurated on December 15, 1915, on Calle Florida, then as now the city's main commercial avenue. Seen from the outside it is a curious and ungainly structure, consisting of two slablike forms that communicate by airborne bridges. It is crowned by a florid lantern, but this is almost invisible today due to the tall buildings that have clustered around it. Even at street level, it is nearly invisible, standing concealed behind a tasteless metallic annex from the 1970s. (The back door on San Martín, however, preserves some trace of its former glory.)

At nearly 250 feet tall, the Galería Güemes was for some years the tallest building in the city, perhaps in Latin America, and as such a source of considerable pride to the Porteños. Its beauty can best be gauged in the ground-floor gallery, inspired by the Galerie Vivienne in Paris and the Burlington Arcade in London. Like so much of the architecture of Art Nouveau, it is strongly influenced by natural forms, abstracted to a fine degree of geometric purity. These organic elements suffuse the very structure of the building, from the pendentives that support the dazzling dome to the dome itself, a twenty-foot-wide, wrought iron flower with petals of crystalline glass.

Palacio Barolo, designed by Mario Palanti in 1923, at
Avenida de Mayo 1370. (Archivo General de la Nación)

The Galería Güemes held the title of the tallest building in Buenos Aires for all of eight years, when that honor passed to the Palacio Barolo, an office tower on the Avenida de Mayo. This was the work of another Italian, Mario Palanti, one of the most interesting architects in Buenos Aires in this era. Both in Buenos Aires and in Montevideo—where he designed the wondrous Palacio Salvo—his work consists of a highly eccentric reinterpretation of classical structure according to his wayward intuitions about form. His work in both countries is marked by odd, bulbous accretions along the surface that he seems to have found beautiful. In fact, they were not. And yet, in their aggregate and against all the odds, they succeed in achieving a potent charm that only Le Corbusier managed to dislike.

As a patriotic Italian, Palanti was naturally a great admirer of Dante, and the Palacio Barolo is shot through with allusions, real or imagined, to the poetry of the dour Tuscan. At exactly one hundred meters tall it invokes the number of cantos in the *Divine Comedy,* while its triform massing alludes to the three divisions of the Dantean cosmos. Palanti oversaw every detail of this *Gesamtkunstwerk,* from the lamps and elevator cages to the Masonic patterns in the lobby's floor. This lobby is further adorned with rib vaults and a choice selection of Latin inscriptions—an Italian rather than Porteño impulse. Along its walls, at mezzanine level, a riot of balustrades is supported by vaguely Baroque extrusions that are surely without precedent in earlier architecture. All of it is in the worst possible taste, and yet it is a delight. Similar excess inspired Palanti's Palacio Roccatagliata, an apartment building at the corner of Santa Fe and Callao, and the house that he designed for himself in Palermo's Barrio Parque.

A later and more full-blown example of the Art Deco style is the Mercado de Abasto, on Avenida Corrientes 3247. As is often the case in Buenos Aires, this was the expansion or replacement of a nineteenth-century building of similar function on the same spot. In the present case, much of that building actually survives at the back of this newer and larger structure. The more recent addition, by the way, arose in response to the broadening of Corrientes in 1935, as part of the refining

*Mercado de Abasto, now Abasto Shopping,
designed by Delpini, Sulcic and Bes in 1936,
at Corrientes 3247. (Archivo General de la
Nación)*

of the grid that Rivadavia conceived in 1827 and that Alvear finally
initiated in the 1880s.

When the first Mercado de Abasto opened in 1889, it was to be one
of a number of such markets that sold meat and fresh produce in each
of the main population centers of the greatly expanding capital. One of
the best preserved of these is the Mercado de San Telmo, whose elaborate iron lattice construction is a curious cross between the primordial
rationalism that would soon give rise to modernism and that vaguely
ecclesiastical ornateness that the older generation demanded. The early
Mercado de Abasto was similarly conceived, and much of the original
structure still exists on Calle Lavalle. But in 1936 the far larger annex
was added along Corrientes to designs by the Slovenian architect Vik-
tor Sulčič. This granite-clad edifice is dominated by an unforgettable
sequence of five colossal arches, bloated and pneumatic in appearance,
that bounce down Corrientes with almost reckless abandon. The Mercado de Abasto functioned as a marketplace until 1984 when it was

Edificio Kavanagh, 1936, designed by Sánchez, Lagos and de la Torre.
(Archivo General de la Nación)

shuttered, only to be resurrected fourteen years later as that new Porteño typology, the high-end shopping mall.

If the Mercado de Abasto represents one of the pinnacles of the Art Deco style in Buenos Aires, the Edificio Kavanagh, which towers over the Plaza San Martín, can be seen as the link between that style and the full-blown modernism of the postwar era. Completed in the same year as the Mercado de Abasto, it is, at thirty-one stories, twice as tall as the Galería Güemes and remains a source of ongoing civic pride. The Edificio Kavanagh was one of the first examples of a reinforced concrete building in the capital, and it scrupulously avoids ornament throughout most of its facade. Only two earlier buildings in Buenos Aires, the Edificio Comega and the Edificio Saffico, both completed in 1934 on

Avenida Corrientes, achieved a comparable degree of denuded rational-ism. The Kavanagh is nearly twice the size of those predecessors as well, but its slightly more conventional mass has been disposed according to a rigid symmetry: five towerlike segments rise in a series of setbacks, their strong mural presence softened by threadlike bays of windows that extend the entire height of the facade. The Edificio Kavanagh was de-signed by the firm of Sánchez, Lagos and de la Torre, which also gave the city the similarly conceived Automóvil Club Argentino on Liberta-dor and the flagship building of the Banco de la Provincia de Buenos Aires, in the financial center.

✳

THE MOST FAMOUS STRUCTURE of this period, however, is not a building, but a monument. The Obelisco that stands in the middle of Avenida 9 de Julio, at the intersection of Corrientes, is the universal symbol of Buenos Aires. This is its Eiffel Tower, its Big Ben, its Wash-ington Monument. Granted, at 220 feet tall it is much shorter than those other monuments, but it serves its civic function admirably and can be seen for miles around. And far more than those foreign monu-ments, it is fully integrated into the rhythms of its city and its pedes-trian traffic. In its white simplicity it seems to be an example of the Art Moderne style, almost classical, but purged of all the fussiness of the École des Beaux-Arts. If we did not know its dates, we could believe that it had been built at any point in the nineteenth century. It is the work of Alberto Prebisch, a native Argentine of Polish parentage whose other famous work, the Teatro Gran Rex, stands a few blocks east on Corrientes.

The obelisk is rich in symbolism. It was completed exactly four hundred years after Pedro de Mendoza founded the first settlement of Nuestra Señora del Buen Aire, and it rises over the site where the church of San Nicolás de Bari once stood and where the first flag of a new and independent Argentina was hoisted in 1812. One of the ideas apparently considered for this site was a colossal statue of Hipólito Yrigoyen, twice elected president of the republic and only

The Obelisco, 1936, designed by Alberto Prebisch. (Photograph by the Author)

recently deceased. That proposal did not get very far, however, and the Obelisco was built in its stead. The dispatch with which it arose was as prodigious as its form: on February 3, 1936, exactly four hundred years to the day since the city's initial foundation, the legislature voted in favor of building the monument; construction began on March 20, and within thirty-one days it was complete. Today the obelisk is a beloved landmark so closely associated with the capital that few people realize that it was almost torn down. In June 1939, scarcely three years after its completion, the city council voted, by an astounding 23 to 3, in favor of demolition on the grounds that it was unsightly and unpopular. Only the last-minute intervention of the Intendente, Arturo Goyeneche, managed to save it.

———————— ❊ ————————

THE OBELISCO STANDS in the middle of Avenida 9 de Julio, and that avenue represents the single greatest change to the city in this period. It is invariably referred to by the locals, with a full measure of Porteño pride, as "the widest avenue in the world." It takes its name from the date July 9, 1816, when Argentina, having won its war against Spain, finally and definitively achieved its independence. Bounded by Carlos Pellegrini–Bernardo Irigoyen to the east and by Cerrito-Lima to west, it occupies one entire block of Juan de Garay's grid, 420 feet wide, that was systematically obliterated over the half century between 1934 and 1980. The avenue extends almost three miles, from Avenida Libertador in the north to Avenida Caseros in the south.

In one sense Avenida 9 de Julio is a phantom street. Pictures from before the demolitions began reveal that it looked much like any other north-south street in the capital: it had grand Parisian buildings and houses of worship, as well as numerous shops and houses. But all of that has vanished, like the tens of thousands of homes that evaporated when Robert Moses built the Cross Bronx Expressway in New York City. The essential point is that there was little that was remarkable about this street, among the hundreds of north-south streets of the capital. It was entirely typical—except that all three miles of it have ceased to be.

The original plan was very different from what we see today. As early as 1890 the Intendente Francisco Seeber proposed an avenue of the same length, but no broader than the Avenida de Mayo, which is one hundred feet wide. When Seeber made his proposal, the automobile for all intents and purposes did not yet exist, and the avenue was meant to serve pedestrians and horse-drawn carriages and trolleys. Such was the context in which the plan was approved by the legislature in 1912. And if it had been built in this form, it would have seemed more an inflection of the grid (like Avenidas Callao, Pueyrredón and Coronel Diaz) than the massive intervention that we see today. It would have resembled the Avenida de Mayo, the finest avenue in the city, but three times the length and adorned on either side with Beaux Arts buildings that rivaled its splendor.

Instead it became a line of brutal demarcation that separates one side of Buenos Aires from the other and that, in the process, has completely altered how Porteños experience the mile and a half from Alem to Callao, along the east-west axis, that forms the heart of the city. Indeed, the avenue is so large, comprising twenty traffic lanes, that even a fast walker cannot cross it in under two traffic lights or two minutes. It has subverted the logic of the city as it was before 1937, when the first stage of the work was completed; rather than that earlier continuum of streets stretching from Alem to Callao and beyond, you now have one part of the city that lies to the east of the avenue and the other part that lies to the west. So irresistible is the force of this avenue that it is nearly impossible for most Porteños, much less for tourists, to imagine the city in any other way than sliced in half by a superhighway. As such it is yet one more object lesson in that strange, almost hypnotic passivity with which pedestrians, throughout the world, accept their man-made urban environments as though they were the natural and immutable order of things. "*We shape our buildings; thereafter they shape us.*"

Certain anomalies, however, betray the earlier condition of the street. The Teatro Colón, for instance, is most visible from 9 de Julio, but it is oriented in the opposite direction. Only its back door faces 9 de Julio, recalling a time when it was just another street. And then there is the sharp diagonal of Lavalle, between Cerrito and Libertad, which seems entirely pointless and arbitrary until one recalls that it was originally planned as part of the Diagonal Norte, intended to pass directly from the Plaza de Mayo to the Plaza Lavalle.

Let this be said for 9 de Julio: on paper it would seem, at least to contemporary sensibilities, that a superhighway running through the historical center of a great city is an appalling idea. And yet the avenue is not without its charms: it has been expertly landscaped with jacarandas and two expansive parklike medians where the citizens can and do linger. And because there are pedestrian crossings at each of the streets that intersect with the avenue (some thirty of them from end to end), it has managed to weave itself with such thoroughness into the lives of the

Porteños that they have come to feel a kind of affection for it. Nonetheless, the construction of this avenue remains the single greatest mistake in the urban history of Buenos Aires.

And yet it was not the only major intervention in Garay's grid at this time. Buenos Aires differs from other cities like Rome and Paris, whose impractical tangle of medieval streets was energetically rectified at the behest of a monarch. Because Buenos Aires already possessed a grid with admirably broad streets, there was no real need to reconceive its street plan, other than to broaden a few avenues along both axes, as much for amenity as for ease of use. But the Porteños, in their desire for glory, went beyond these modifications to others that, whatever their ultimate success or failure, seem to have been motivated by little more than the fact that the municipality could afford them. There was no practical reason for the Avenida de Mayo to exist other than an aesthetic and patriotic impulse to create a display case for the city's newest Beaux Arts architecture. But in the eyes of the oligarchs, that one avenue, lovely though it was and remains, could not possibly suffice if Buenos Aires was to become the Paris of South America. As every visitor to Paris knows, one of its glories are those diagonal avenues that radiate from the Arc de Triomphe and the Place de la Nation and that greatly facilitate passage through the city. Thus it was decided that Buenos Aires, too, must have its diagonals. What function they would serve does not appear to have greatly interested the government.

And so, in what can best be described as a halfhearted gesture, projects for two such avenues, the Diagonal Norte and the Diagonal Sur, passed the legislature in 1907. Starting from the Plaza de Mayo, they did not extend for miles, as in Paris, but for only a few blocks northwest and southwest. Given the amount of destruction entailed by what was at most an aspirational rather than practical venture, one must wonder whether it was truly worth it. The actual design of both avenues was the work of a Frenchman, Joseph Bouvard, and although construction began in 1913, it was not actually completed until 1943. In fact, the Diagonal Sur was never completed at all; it ends, pointlessly and abruptly, only three blocks from the Plaza de Mayo and two blocks shy of its stated destination. The government, finding itself short of funds and having lost interest by that point, simply abandoned the project. In recent years there has been talk of completing the avenue, but that is unlikely to happen.

None of this is to deny that that these diagonal avenues look good, such as they are. They represent a welcome modification of the grid, and the uniform heights of the cornices along the Diagonal Norte produce a powerful visual effect. They reinforce a feeling that one often has amid the architectural and urbanistic enhancements of Buenos Aires in its Golden Age and its Silver Age: despite all the tribulations incurred, and with some exceptions, ultimately the magistrates and the citizens got what they paid for.

TEN

THE POSTWAR CITY

(1946–1983)

THE FOUR DECADES COVERED IN THE PRESENT CHAP-
ter, from the rise of Juan Perón to the fall of the dictators, are the sad-
dest and dreariest in the history of Buenos Aires. It may be that Perón,
who dominated Argentina for much of this period, raised up the working classes by providing them with housing and a better quality of life.
But it is difficult to dispute, from a purely urbanistic perspective, that
the drably rationalist structures that were built during his presidency
and that of his successors have, with all too few exceptions, diminished
rather than enhanced the capital.

And then there is the violence. On September 6, 1930, President
Hipólito Yrigoyen, who was nearing eighty and had been overwhelmingly reelected two years before, was ousted in a military coup led
by Lieutenant General José Félix Uriburu. In the sixty-eight years
since Mitre was first elected president of Argentina, a number of his
successors had resigned or died in office, but this was the first time
that a sitting president was removed by members of the armed forces.
The coup was significant in itself, of course, but even more significant
for what it presaged. To committed Peronists—and there are many
such in Argentina to this day—it was the beginning of the so-called

Década Infame, or Infamous Decade, a period of political instability that ended in Perón's becoming president in 1946 and in the restoration of order and prosperity. But if one is not a committed Peronist, then it spelled the beginning of half a century of ceaseless oscillation between authoritarianism and anarchy. In this reading, that troubled and violent era ended only with the collapse of the last military dictatorship in 1983.

But it is possible to take an even longer and even dimmer view of the matter and to extend the period of unrest in both directions. On the one hand, instability continues to this very day since, even after democracy was restored in 1983, respect for the separation of powers and the rule of law has been fluid and negotiable at best. On the other hand, the ultimate truth of Argentine history—much of it played out on the streets of the capital—is that the country has been in a state of greater or lesser instability since the last viceroy returned to Spain in 1810. Quite aside from the anarchy of the 1820s and the violence of Rosas up to 1852, even Bartolomé Mitre, that supreme democrat, the one who proclaimed that the worst election was better than the best military intervention, even he could be induced to take up arms against the legitimate election of Avellaneda in 1874.

Even the city's Golden Age, from 1880 to 1920, saw powerful upheavals. In 1890, the so-called Revolution of the Park, instigated against President Miguel Juarez Celman, was fought in Plaza Lavalle, midway between the present-day Palacio de Justicia and Teatro Colón. During the early years of the twentieth century, a number of immigrants from Italy and Russia, self-professed anarchists and communists, perpetrated and suffered acts of unspeakable violence. In the so-called *Semana Roja,* or Red Week, which began on May Day 1909, the chief of police, Ramón Falcón, ordered his forces to fire on 1,500 anarchists who were demonstrating in the Avenida de Mayo, resulting in dozens of deaths. Falcón was assassinated six months later at the corner of Quintana and Callao by a seventeen-year-old anarchist, Simón Radowitzky, who had only recently arrived from Ukraine. Anarchist bombs threatened the centennial celebrations of 1910, and in January 1919 the anarchists struck once again, and once again were brutally repressed by the new chief of police, Luis Dellepiane, in a week that is still known as the *Semana Tragica,* the Tragic Week.

Both the Semana Roja and the Semana Tragica have a curious urbanistic component. A street several miles long, running, with cruel irony, through some of the poorer sections of the city, is named for Ramón Falcón, while Avenida Teniente General Luis J. Dellepiane extends through still poorer neighborhoods as a major artery connecting two highways, the Autopista Ricchieri and the Autopista 25 de Mayo. In the affluent neighborhood of Recoleta two monuments have been raised to Ramón Falcón over the past century. The first is an elaborate classical sculpture near the famous cemetery: on a recent visit, one found, scribbled across the base, graffiti that read "Simón vive" (Simon lives), referring to Simón Radowitzky, together with an encircled A for "Anarchism." The second monument is a bronze plaque placed on the building that occupies the very corner where the commissioner was assassinated. As of this writing, the plaque, though placed fairly high above the street, has been doused with a well-directed volley of red paint that is meant to look like blood. It has been that way for over a year.

Argentina, like all the countries of South America, was forged through its wars of independence. But prior to the coup d'état of 1930, only one professional soldier, Julio Roca, became president (first in 1880 and again in 1898). At that point in the nation's history, the armed forces had only recently become a permanent and professional caste and had never directly intervened in politics. But all of that changed on September 6, 1930, when Yrigoyen, having become deeply unpopular due to the global downturn of the Great Depression, was overthrown by Uriburu. Thus ended exactly half a century of the peaceful transition of power since the disputed election of 1880. Thus began half a century of at best unstable democracy, frequently punctuated by coups and three times by military dictatorships, until democracy was finally restored in 1983.

Unlike ancient Rome, where emperors were created and deposed throughout a vast empire, each of the Argentine coups occurred in Buenos Aires itself, usually with a general standing over an elected president in the Casa Rosada and compelling him to sign a letter of resignation. That first coup of 1930 would be followed by five more, in 1943, 1955, 1962, 1966 and 1976. Following the coup d'état of 1943, four military men served as president in swift succession, the last being Juan Domingo Perón. He served for two terms, from 1946 to 1955, until he himself was ousted. For three years Lieutenant General Pedro Eugenio Aramburu governed Argentina until the free election, in 1958, of Arturo Frondizi, who was ousted in 1962. Four years later, Arturo Illia was ousted by Lieutenant General Juan Carlos Onganía. In 1973 Juan Perón returned from eighteen years of exile in Spain to begin a third term, but he died eight months later and was succeeded by his vice president (and third wife) Isabel Perón. She in turn was ousted in 1976 by a junta led by Lieutenant General Jorge Rafael Videla. This dictatorship endured until the restoration of democracy seven years later.

———— ❋ ————

JUAN DOMINGO PERÓN was a career military officer born in the province, but not the city, of Buenos Aires. Peronism, the political philosophy—if it is a philosophy—that is associated with him, has caused some confusion outside of Argentina, as though it were a mystery that only the native population could penetrate. In one sense it is quite complicated, when applied to Perón himself, and in another sense it is radically simple, when applied to his Peronist successors.

In the latter instance, it means little more than a vague but energetically expressed fealty to the memory of the man himself and an acceptance of the welfare state that he largely established and that no mainstream politician today in Argentina, or anywhere else, is likely to challenge. Beyond that, Peronism is a kind of tautology: a Peronist is someone who claims to adhere to Peronism, which is the corpus of political declarations of people who call themselves Peronists. In practice this can mean anything from the free market neoliberalism of Carlos Menem (president from 1989 to 1999) to the self-styled leftism of the current regime of Cristina Fernández de Kirchner, which claims to be implacably opposed to neoliberalism. Even the Montoneros, an armed

Marxist militia that terrorized the country in the 1970s, claimed to act in Perón's name *even as Perón gave the orders to gun them down.*

In the case of Perón himself, Peronism was a confluence of notions that were current in the world from the mid-1920s through the 1940s. Among these was the populism that was made possible by the emergence of mass media and that Hipólito Yrigoyen had introduced into Argentine politics, though in a far more restrained form. Perón borrowed from Italian fascism, which he had observed firsthand in Italy in the 1930s, as well as from socialism, insofar as its base of support was, like his, the working classes. But above all, Peronist populism was defined in practice by the attempt to override traditional institutions— whose built-in checks and balances had been conceived generations earlier in conscious imitation of the American Constitution—and to center power within the biological entity of Juan Perón himself. His second wife, Eva Duarte, an actress and vociferous supporter of Perón on radio even before they ever met, contributed to the movement in her own way. If Perón spoke for the working classes, she claimed to speak for *los descamisados* (literally, the shirtless ones), the poor and unemployed, the *lumpenproletariat*. And the public's reaction to each of them was correspondingly different. If there was an element of practical self-interest in the relation between Juan Perón and his supporters, there was something approaching religiosity, almost a secularized Mariolatry, in the public's embrace of his wife.

At the beginning of his first regime, Perón enjoyed high approval due to an economy propelled by Europe's hunger for the commodities of the pampas. Eventually, however, through Perón's incompetent stewardship and unsustainable benefits for workers, the economy began to falter. This produced dissent and then unrest, and so, through a process common to many populist regimes, in proportion as the initial benefits dwindled, they were supplanted by repression, which was seen as the only way for the regime to preserve order and hold on to power. When university professors became antagonistic to Perón, he dismissed more than 1,500 of them. Jorge Luis Borges, who had worked in the Biblioteca Nacional, was reassigned as a state "poultry inspector," a post that he declined to fill. Even the labor movement, the base of Perón's power, was not exempt from such purges. Cipriano Reyes, leader of the meatpackers' union, turned against Perón in 1947 for replacing the Labor Party with the Peronist Party. Reyes was tortured and held without trial for eight years—until Perón was overthrown in 1955. Many other union members experienced similar fates. Meanwhile, writers like Victoria Ocampo and musicians like Osvaldo Pugliese were imprisoned for speaking out against the regime, and the actress Libertad Lamarque was essentially blacklisted due to her rivalry—it has been suggested—with Eva Perón. At the same time, many opposition publications were shut down and two of the largest dailies, *Clarín* and *La Nación,* found their liberties severely curbed.

A further provocation was Perón's altering the constitution of 1853 to allow him to run for reelection in 1951. Although he won that election by more than 30 percent, opposition increased and soon violence accompanied it. On April 15, 1953, while he was holding a rally in front of the Casa Rosada, unknown conspirators carried out an aerial bombardment of the site, killing 6 and wounding 90 others, as well as doing damage to the Casa Rosada, the nearby Banco de la Nación Argentina and the Linea A of the Subte, which ran underneath it. On that occasion, Perón incited his supporters to ransack and set fire to the Jockey Club on Calle Florida, a bastion of the oligarchy. Two years later, on June 16, 1955, the opposition struck again when rogue members of the air force bombed and strafed another gathering of Perón's supporters in the Plaza de Mayo, this time killing almost 364 and wounding more than 700 others. Simultaneously they bombed the Palacio Unzué, Perón's residence overlooking Avenida Libertador, where the new Biblioteca Nacional now rises.

Although these attacks failed to kill him, Perón's days as president were numbered, and three months later he was on his way to Venezuela to begin a life of exile that would take him to Franco's Spain. Back in Argentina, the new government led by Eduardo Lonardi and then by Pedro Eugenio Aramburu, carried out a *damnatio memoriae* against Perón. A traveling exhibition sought to discredit him and Eva Perón, who had died in 1952, by revealing the almost regal splendor in which they had lived. Then a law was passed, the *Decreto Ley 4161 de 1956,* which made it illegal to mention Perón or his wife by name, to use words or phrases like *Peronismo, Peronista* or *tercera posición,* or to play the Peronist March.

Perón's exile lasted until June 20, 1973, when he finally returned to Buenos Aires and to power with his new wife Isabel, a nightclub singer thirty-five years his junior whom he'd met in Panama. But even as he arrived at Ezeiza Airport and was greeted by thousands of left-wing supporters from the Peronist Youth Movement and the far left Montoneros, right-wing Peronists opened fire on the crowd, killing at least 13 and wounding at least 365 (the numbers may be much higher).

But this *Masacre de Ezeiza* was only the beginning of the violence that would engulf the city and the nation over the ensuing decade. Shortly before Perón resumed the presidency on October 12, 1973, a group known as Triple A (the Alianza Anticomunista Argentina), essentially a death squad, was created by his advisers to attack the militant leftists of his own party. Most of the Triple A's activities were carried out during the administration of Isabel Perón. Having served as Perón's vice president, she succeeded him when, on July 1, 1974, he died of a heart attack at seventy-eight, only eight months into his new administration. With the Triple A began the Dirty War—Guerra Sucia—that would convulse Buenos Aires and the Argentine nation until the restoration of democracy.

There is a tendency to view the seven years of the military dictatorship as a neofascist assault upon the individual liberties of law-abiding, left-leaning college students. There was, to be sure, some measure of that, but the reality was far more complicated. During the one and a half years of the presidency of Isabel Perón, who was largely a figurehead, a situation approaching anarchy reigned in the capital and the country. The left-wing Montoneros and the Trotskyite Ejercito Revolucionario Popular (ERP) were essentially military organizations engaged not only in tactical acts of terrorism but also in pitched battles with the national army. As the journalist Paul Hoeffel wrote in 1976, before the dictatorship began, "Although there is widespread reluctance to use the term, it is now impossible to ignore the fact that civil war has broken out in Argentina."

In Buenos Aires itself political violence became almost routine. A bomb concealed as a bouquet of flowers was delivered on Valentine's Day 1972 to the home of Jaime Perriaux, a former justice minister. This resulted in the death of four police officers. On October 17 of that year, a bomb went off in the Sheraton Hotel, opposite Retiro Station, killing a Canadian woman, wounding her husband and causing panic among the hotel's seven hundred guests. At various times, leftist guerrillas kidnapped and murdered executives from General Motors, Ford and Chrysler. On one day, September 16, 1974, they detonated forty bombs throughout Argentina and hijacked two trains leaving the capital. Later they would hijack planes as well. On February 7, 1976, the Montoneros bombed the headquarters of the federal police, on Avenida Presidente Figueroa Alcorta, killing twenty-five and wounding many more. This was the context in which the military, working together with the right-wing Peronist Triple A, seized power.

As with the Rosas regime one and a half centuries earlier, the result was the emergence of an infrastructure of state terror in the city and around the country. This consisted mainly of Centros Clandestinos de Detención (CCD), or Clandestine Dentention Centers. Soon after the armed forces assumed power on March 24, 1976, 610 of these centers arose throughout the country, many of them of a very temporary nature. Over the next six and a half years, until the fall of the military regime on December 10, 1983, this number shrank steadily and drastically as the armed forces did their work with such exemplary efficiency that fewer and fewer people remained who, in the regime's estimation, needed to be "disappeared." After a few months the number of camps, across the nation, had shrunk to 364. In 1977 sixty remained; in 1978 forty-five; and in 1979 seven. By 1980 only two remained: El Campito in the Campo de Mayo, about eight miles beyond the limits of Buenos Aires, and the infamous ESMA (Escuela de Mecánica de la Armada, or Army Mechanical School), located in the capital itself in the northern barrio of Núñez, a quarter of a mile from the highway of Avenida General Paz. With its decorous redbrick buildings distinguished by columned porticoes, this tree-lined campus (now transformed into an arts center and memorial to the disappeared) resembles the quad of some liberal arts college in New England. This was the scene of detention, torture and execution of anyone the regime deemed suspicious or undesirable.

There were other CCDs in the city that did not have quite so pleasant a cast. These were somewhat closer to the center. A former bus depot, El Olimpo, in the barrio of Vélez Sársfield, is still standing today, as is the Automotores Orletti, a car repair shop in the barrio of Floresta. There is something infinitely dingy about these two sites that expresses in the most material terms the baseness of the regime that created them. A fourth site, the notorious Club Atlético at Paseo Colón 1200, was far closer to the center, near the stadium of La Boca, from which its name derives. It no longer exists, and its remains lie buried beneath the Autopista 25 de Mayo, a highway built under the dictatorship.

One of the means by which the victims of the repression were "disappeared" was the so-called *vuelo de la muerte,* the flight of death. The prisoners, heavily drugged and blindfolded, were taken in a van from one of the CCDs to the Aeroparque Jorge Newbery at the northern edge of Palermo, beside the Rio de la Plata. There they entered the special military airport at the main airport's southern end, where they were loaded onto a waiting Fokker F28 or Short SC.7 Skyvan. Once airborne, the plane headed several miles out, over the river, where the victim was pushed, still alive, from the fuselage. The hope was that, after the victim perished, his remains would be so thoroughly devoured by the fish that no trace would remain. Although this usually worked well enough, occasionally the regime was chagrined to learn that one of the bodies had washed ashore on the coast of Uruguay, directly across the river.

Today, one of the most serene spaces in the capital is the Parque de la Memoria, which opened in 2006 to honor the victims of the military regime. It is located a mile north of the aeroparque and just east of the Ciudad Universitaria, the main campus of UBA (the University of Buenos Aires), from which many young victims were taken. It is one of the few places in the capital that offers an unimpeded view of the Rio de la Plata, which was once so central to the lives of the Porteños. But in the midst of this peace, it is impossible not to think of those planes.

Few were the voices that spoke out against this state terrorism. One of the rare exceptions was a small-circulation English-language daily, the *Buenos Aires Herald,* under the editorship of Robert Cox, who risked his life to report on the forced disappearances. He worked together with Madres de la Plaza de Mayo, the Mothers of the Plaza de Mayo, who, starting in 1977, defied the regime by repeatedly protesting in front of the Casa Rosada in the hope of learning the fates of their vanished children.

❋

IN SUCH CIRCUMSTANCES, it might seem like a profanation to speak of architecture at all, but that would be an illusion. For life did go on through that dark period. Tango competitions were still held in Luna Park. The two main stadiums in La Boca and Belgrano were filled to the rafters with raving fans. The steak joints and movie houses along Lavalle, like the theaters along Corrientes, were teeming with a prosperous clientele, and children still begged their parents to take them to Italpark, the fairgrounds that used to stand on Avenida Libertador. And throughout this period, the city grew and evolved. But it did not flourish.

So undistinguished is the general mass of architecture over the forty years covered in the present chapter that one begins to wonder whether modernism, by its very nature, might be fundamentally incompatible with the dominant aesthetics of Buenos Aires as it had developed up to this point. Amid the abundance of newer buildings, some, to be sure, were more beautiful and energetic than others. But these are the exceptions. No writer on the modern architecture of Mexico City and São Paolo would deny its frequent excellence and originality. But in Buenos Aires, modernist buildings tend to be a dreary reenactment of something that was done better somewhere else. Part of the reason for so much modern architecture in the capital was the need to find housing for the working classes, and here, as elsewhere, modernist architecture offered a quick and relatively inexpensive way to meet that demand. But one suspects that there was another motive, which had been typical of the Porteños for over a century. It was a kind of collective cultural vanity and competitiveness with other world cities.

Assuming that I am correct in this generally depreciative assessment of the city's modern architecture, we must now ask why it was so. One reason, I suspect, is that this style almost never harmonizes with the sort of premodern architecture, richly historicist and highly ornamental, that predominates in Buenos Aires. A second, perhaps more powerful reason is that buildings in the capital are mostly derivative and, to put the matter delicately, not of the first rank. The glory of Buenos Aires consists in the cumulative effect of so much charming and eccentric architecture, more than in the pure formal power of any one structure in isolation. Now, it is in the nature of the Beaux Arts architecture that proliferates in the capital that it can achieve beauty and charm even if it is not of the highest formal power. This prerogative, however, has been denied to the architecture of modernism, especially to that endless sequence of rationalist boxes that forms so many of the city's residential blocks and office towers. And unless a modernist building is very well made—as few are in Buenos Aires—it will lose its luster very quickly, as opposed to most older architecture, which seems to be mysteriously enhanced by the passing years.

Modernism in Buenos Aires can be divided, a little arbitrarily, into two periods, from 1940 to 1960 and from 1960 to the mid-1980s. Mirroring the development of modernism around the world, especially in New York, this stylistic difference reflects its shift in status from something experimental and new to the official style of money and power.

If one had to assign a date to the initial stirrings of modernism in Buenos Aires, a good choice would be the first visit, in 1929, of the Swiss architect Le Corbusier. He had come to deliver a series of lectures at the instigation of Victoria Ocampo, the doyenne of advanced culture in the capital during the middle years of the last century. Given that Le Corbusier was no admirer of the Paris in France, it is fair to assume that few people on the planet were less disposed than he was to appreciate the Paris of South America. The more persuasive the Porteño reenactment of the Beaux Arts style, the more odious it all seemed in the eyes of Le Corbusier. Buenos Aires, he declared, was "a city in error, in paradox, a city that has not a new but an old spirit." The very structures that the Porteños had built with such pride and effort and expense over the previous two generations were the most detestable in his sight. These were the very things he had hoped to erase from the center of Paris, through his *Plan Voisin* of 1925, which advocated bulldozing most of the buildings on the Right Bank and replacing them with sixty-story cruciform towers surrounded by landscape. And now he advocated a similarly radical rearrangement of the Argentine capital, contracting it back to its 1880 borders and enhancing density by filling the area with 4 million inhabitants: they would live in high-rises built over the flattened building stock of what had once been San Telmo and Monserrat. At the same time, the entire governmental infrastructure would be moved to five man-made islands just to the east of the Dársena Sur.

Of course, nothing came of this plan, and both Le Corbusier and the initially adulatory Porteños to whom he had talked down grew tired of one another at more or less the same moment and to more or less the same degree. In Le Corbusier himself, this *état d'âme*—which he experienced often in his life—was coincident with his realizing that he was not going to get the lucrative commissions for which he had come in the first place. To make matters worse, Ocampo actually commissioned a convincingly Corbusian house that same year—the first such house in South America. And yet, the architect she chose was not Le Corbusier, but the prolific, versatile and local Alejandro Bustillo. This sheer white box of a building, shorn of all ornament, can still be seen at Rufino de Elizalde 2831 in the Barrio Parque section of Palermo. It has the distinction of being the first truly modern building in the city, a mass of interlocking blocks, short spurts of ribbon windows and at least one pylon, that signature of Le Corbusier's earlier style. The house seems especially remarkable when we consider that, less than a decade later, Bustillo would create the irreproachably classical temple front of the Banco de la Nación Argentina—Corinthian columns and all—on the Plaza de Mayo. Le Corbusier himself would go on to build only one project in Argentina or anywhere else in Latin America, and that was the Curutchet House in La Plata, the capital of the province of Buenos Aires. But that was in 1948, nearly twenty years after his initial visit.

The first truly modernist building in the center of Buenos Aires, the first to embody fully the official line of the International Style, was the Edificio Uruguay, designed five years later by Jorge Biraben and Ernesto Lacalle Alonso. Its fastidiously flat surface consists of alternating bands of concrete infill and ribbon windows, topped by four turret-like structures arrayed across the roof at forty-foot intervals. It is easy to imagine how this building must have struck the Porteños of the time, a mere two years after Leon Dourge completed the Palacio Duhau on Avenida Alvear. That distinguished but essentially typical Beaux Arts palace was decked out with all the Doric colonnades, the rustication and triangular pediments, the mansard roof and dormers, of Buenos Aires in its Golden Age. Yet, only a mile to the southeast stood this nine-story mass of almost truculent and undifferentiated flatness, whose staggered bands of windows and infill bore a striking resemblance to a zebra. Here was modernity made flesh. But today, one requires a vigorous historical imagination simply to notice this building. With the passing of the years, all of its polemical passion has been sucked out of it. In its battle against the received taste of its time, it, like the International Style that it represents, was the manifest victor. And for that very reason, it is now indistinguishable from three thousand other modernist buildings in the capital.

Despite the political turbulence of the *Década Infame* and the severity of the Great Depression, governmental architecture continued to arise in the capital, vast, monumental edifices of an expanding bureaucracy. Most of these were in the Art Deco style or, like the Banco de la Nación Argentina, essentially classical. As regards public housing, there had been some distinguished examples in the 1920s, such as Barrio Parque Los Andes in Chacarita, completed in 1928 to designs by Fermín H. Bereterbide. With its quaint redbrick houses and tiled roofs, it retains to this day an Arts and Crafts air. Many more such developments were planned in the next decade, but few of them were ever built.

That changed when Perón came to power in 1946 and the Argentine economy began to profit from the postwar commodities boom. Many of the larger projects completed at this time were of an infrastructural nature and were the necessary consequence of the city's rush to turn itself into a modern industrial city. Some of the most notable projects completed during Perón's regime were, in fact, initiated before he became president. Among these were the city's two airports, the domestic Aeroparque Jorge Newbery, built on landfill near the northern barrio of Belgrano, and Aeropuerto Internacional Ministro Pistarini, which stands outside the city limits in the partido, or county, of Ezeiza. This airport is universally referred to simply as Ezeiza. Work on both having begun in 1945, the aeroparque was inaugurated in 1947 and Ezeiza two years later. With the possible exception of Avenida General Paz, which defines the western limit of the capital and was completed in 1941, the first highway in the nation was the Autopista Ricchieri, which connects Buenos Aires with Ezeiza and was completed in 1948.

Workers' housing was very important to Perón, given that the working classes were his base of support. To this end he built, among other such developments, Barrio Residencial Cornelio Saavedra and Barrio Presidente Roque Sáenz Peña. Originally Perón had given them more self-serving names, but these were changed after he was driven from power. Though called barrios, they are in fact part of the legal barrio of Saavedra in the northwest part of the city, near Avenida General Paz. Both are also relatively rare examples of developments within Buenos Aires that were built according to a curving plan rather than a grid. They are made up mostly of one-story houses conceived in a quaintly vernacular style, with pitched roofs covered in red tiles. The greenery that surrounds them reflects, at some remove, the garden city aesthetic associated with the late nineteenth-century British urban planner Ebenezer Howard.

Two large-scale developments of this period were associated with Eva Perón: the Ciudad Evita and the Republica de los Niños (Republic of Children), completed in 1947 and 1951, respectively. Ciudad Evita, which lies about halfway between the city limits of the capital and Ezeiza airport, consists of workers' housing in the Mission Style, or what is known locally as the *chalet californiano* style, because of the whitewashed walls of the individual houses, each furnished with its allotment of greenery. As for the Republic of Children, it was and remains an amusement park based on the tales of the Brothers Grimm, with elaborate and brightly colored castles and other vaguely medieval forms. Although theme parks go back as far as Dreamland on Coney Island in 1904, the energy with which the Republic of Children sticks to its theme feels quite new, and may have been an inspiration for Disneyland, which opened four years later. The fact that it was built over the Swift Golf Club, which catered to a wealthy clientele, seemed to underscore the populist mood that defined so much of the Peronist regime. At the official opening, Perón himself could not resist inscribing the guest book with these words: "May this Republic of the Children teach the Argentines to be just, free and sovereign, so that they will never be able to accept the exploitation of their brothers or economic submission or political vassalage." In this way, the theme park was meant to serve as a propagandistic tool to instruct children in citizenship, but also to prop up the regime through subtle and not so subtle critiques of the entrenched power structure that opposed Perón. When he was ousted a few years later, the park was promptly stripped of its ideological trappings, though the Kirchner administration has put some of them back.

The style in which Perón's architects cast his public buildings can be called "fascist" due to a formal resemblance to roughly contemporary projects completed by Mussolini and Franco. In fact, it was a style that

Facultad de Derecho (Law School), inaugurated in 1949 at Av. Figueroa Alcorta 2263. (Archivo General de la Nación)

was not specific to any one political movement and that can be found everywhere from Warsaw to Washington. In each case it answers to the midcentury need to achieve monumentality within a context of pared-down classicism. Two eminent, or at least large, examples in Buenos Aires are the Facultad de Derecho (Law School) on Avenida Figueroa Alcorta and what is now the Facultad de Ingenieria on the Paseo Colón but was originally the Fundación Eva Perón. They were completed in 1945 and 1952, respectively. Both projects immediately drew criticism precisely for their unwelcome echoes of fascist architecture. Although the law school is the larger of the two structures, both have a square, or nearly square, footprint and are surrounded on all sides by Doric colonnades or, in the case of the law school, by Doric pilasters on the sides and blunt strips of masonry at the very back, facing the lowly train tracks of the Sarmiento Line. The Fundación Eva Perón was slightly more elaborate: when the ten columns of the entrance were deemed insufficiently glorious, each was topped with its own ugly statue that continued the line of the column's ascent. These statues were subsequently removed, to the great improvement of the building. A similar spirit, if somewhat less obviously classical, informs the four government ministries on the south side of the Plaza de Mayo.

Throughout the developed world, the four decades from the rise of Perón to the end of the dictatorship were a period of large-scale urban planning, of superblocks and master plans. Between the shoddy engineering of many of these projects and the neglect they have suffered in recent years, a certain gothic decrepitude seems to haunt them, a whiff of what one might find in the remoter republics of the former Soviet Union. Contemporary taste, wisely or not, finds a certain dingy fascination in these relics of discredited regimes, but that is a different satisfaction from the truer pleasures of real and effective architecture. A good example of Soviet-style architecture in Buenos Aires is the complex of buildings that fronts Plaza Houssaye at the southern end of Recoleta. These include the Facultad de Medicina (the medical school of Buenos Aires University, inaugurated in 1944) and the Hospital de Clínicas José de San Martín (inaugurated in 1962). Both present themselves to the pedestrian as vast expanses of reinforced concrete. The medical school

Hospital de Clínicas José de San Martín, inaugurated in 1962. (Photograph by the Author)

retains a strict symmetry that looks back to the Art Deco style and forward to Moscow State University and Warsaw's Joseph Stalin Palace of Culture and Science. The hospital foregoes even those contextualist adornments, and one would be hard put to name another important building anywhere else that is so thoroughly bereft of style.

Different in aesthetics, but every bit as oppressive, is the Ciudad Universitaria (University City) in the northern barrio of Núñez, beyond the aeroparque. Its campus is dominated by two nearly identical buildings designed by the local firm of Petersen, Thiele y Cruz and completed in 1967 and in 1971. These squat six-story hulks, like those of the medical complex, make liberal use of reinforced concrete, but now it is employed in the service of the Brutalist style. Grayish concrete bands are interspersed with ribbon windows that extend across the length of the buildings' four identical facades. The concrete core of the medical campus on Plaza Houssaye at least gave off an air of indestructible solidity, the sort that could withstand a nuclear assault. The two main pavilions of the Ciudad Universitaria, by contrast, convey a sense of underlying paltriness and fragility. The dreariness of these buildings is even more evident in their interiors, which are often plastered with posters and marked with graffiti. No light of day has ever entered these sepulchral atriums. The permanent dusk of their interminable corridors is relieved only by fluorescent lamps and the faded sheen of forty-year-old linoleum floors.

Perhaps the single most ambitious feat of urban planning in Buenos Aires in the forty years covered by this chapter was the development of Catalinas Norte in Retiro. Although the development of the site was first planned in 1956, little was actually built until the late 1960s. Over the succeeding decades Catalinas Norte evolved—and continues to evolve—into a complex of nineteen modernist buildings, mostly high-rise office towers stretching for half a mile along the western edge of Puerto Madero. The development takes its name from the Church of Santa Catalina de Sienna a few blocks away, at the corner of Viamonte and San Martín. The land was purchased by a German Argentine entrepreneur, Francisco Seeber, who also served as intendente of Buenos Aires from 1889 to 1890. Seeber constructed the last of the three great piers that extended into the Rio de la Plata, the Muelle de las Catalinas, as well as building a series of warehouses on the site that were called (in the original English) the Catalinas Warehouses and Mole Company Ltd. These undistinguished sheds survived into the 1940s, when the decision was made to develop the site with skyscrapers, and thus to furnish Buenos Aires with a skyline to rival New York's. Whether the city needed so many tall buildings in the first place was another question, and not one that many Porteños were inclined to ask. New York had a skyline and so must Buenos Aires.

The first building to rise, at the southern end of the site, was an initiative of Perón himself, the forty-two-story Edificio Alas. Completed in 1957, it was a drab, mixed-use residential and office tower whose reinforced concrete core recalls the Edificio Kavanagh from twenty years earlier. Although it remained the tallest building in Buenos Aires until 1995, stylistically it seemed behind the times even before it had been completed.

Edificio Alas, the first high-rise in Catalinas Norte, was completed in 1957 and remained, until 1995, the tallest building in Buenos Aires. (Photograph by the Author)

The real development of the Catalinas Norte began ten years later. At its northern edge, the Sheraton Buenos Aires Hotel & Convention Center dominates the space between the Plaza San Martín and the Retiro train station. This, surely, is one of the ugliest buildings in the capital. Designed by the firm of SEPRA (Santiago Sánchez Elía,

The Sheraton Hotel, part of the development of Catalinas Norte, c. 1971. (Archivo General de la Nación)

Federico Peralta Ramos and Alfredo Agostini) as a stolidly modernist slab of reinforced concrete, it is divided into eleven monotonous bays, each subdivided into two equally monotonous smaller bays. In spirit, it is not entirely dissimilar to the now demolished Rossiya Hotel in Moscow, though inferior even to that. The Sheraton was followed by five other modernist towers that arose in Catalinas Norte between 1973 and 1983: the Conurban, Carlos Pellegrini, Catalinas Norte, Madero and IBM Towers. But due to the economic hardships that followed the fall of the dictators, no further construction took place until nine more arose between 1994 and 2004. Although another decade would pass without any activity on the site, as of this writing three new towers are being completed. The five towers already mentioned were slightly better than the Sheraton and some of them showed a modicum of originality and initiative in their designs. Two of them stand out, if not for their excellence, at least for possessing some measure of originality: the Edificio Carlos Pellegrini, completed in 1974 to designs by the prolific local firm known as MSGSSS, and the Torre IBM, designed by Mario Roberto Álvarez and completed in 1983. Both of them, in their different ways, reveal a willingness, through color and anomalies in surface treatment, to play with and disrupt the uniform boxes of the International Style. Quite aside from the stylistic merits of each building individually considered, Catalinas Norte reveals the defects of large-scale modernist planning: not only is there no coherence between the buildings, but all of them, taken together, seem cut off and divorced from the rest of the city.

In the years just before the military seized power in 1976, there was a renewed interest in public housing, as is evident in two large low-income projects designed by MSGSSS, the Conjunto Rioja in Parque Patricios and the Barrio Comandante Luis Piedrabuena in the barrio of Villa Lugano, completed in 1973 and 1980, respectively. Unlike the garden city approach to public housing that was favored by Perón and his wife, these were Corbusian towers in a park. The efforts to vary and enliven this typology, through the introduction of colors and a certain inventiveness in massing and form, might have succeeded a little better if the materials used did not seem so shoddy and cheap.

The dictatorship, however, appeared to be more interested in infrastructure than in housing. In addition to sprucing up the capital in anticipation of the Mundial—the world soccer championship—of 1978, the mayor of Buenos Aires, Intendente Cacciatore, drew up plans in his book *La Ciudad Arterial* (*The Arterial City*) to build eight superhighways throughout the length and breadth of the city. These plans recall those of Robert Moses to crisscross the island of Manhattan with several elevated highways running through it from east to west. If Cacciatore's plan had been built, Buenos Aires would have had more miles of highways, per capita, than Los Angeles, and the entire character of the city would have been very different from what we see today. Avenida Pueyrredón and Avenida Santa Fe would have become superhighways, and another massive highway would have run straight down Avenida Leandro N. Alem, separating the citizens from the Puerto Madero. Today the entire area of Puerto Madero has been splendidly gentrified, but if the highway had been built, that would have been far more difficult. Ultimately, only two highways were built, the Autopista 25 Cinco de Mayo and the Autopista Perito Moreno. They run through already impoverished barrios, and any hope that those neighborhoods could be improved was rendered null and void by the relentless clamor of the cars and trucks and by the stench of their exhausts. At the same time, the earth that was dug up to build the highways was reused to form the nature preserve on the Costanera Sur, just east of the Puerto Madero. Although this preserve provides pleasant spaces for joggers and walkers, its most material effect was to place almost a kilometer of landfill between the bathing promenade of the Costanera Sur and the waters of the Rio de la Plata that once bordered it.

----------- ❋ -----------

IF THERE IS ONE ARCHITECT in Buenos Aires in this period who rises above the others through the power and originality of his vision, it is Clorindo Testa. When the Porteños wish to assure themselves that they do indeed have important modern architects, they point with pride to Testa, whom it would not be entirely wrong to call a national hero. Born in Naples, Italy, in 1923, he spent most of his life in Buenos Aires, where he died in 2013. One of his earliest works, from 1951, was Avenida Paseo Colón 819 in San Telmo, a graceful and well-proportioned modernist slab. Almost but not quite a continuous curtain wall, it is distinguished by a base made up of a two-story colonnade with square pillars. Though hardly a building of any striking originality, it nevertheless succeeds in drawing out whatever music the International Style might yet contain, and it is one of the rare buildings in Buenos Aires that succeeded in doing so.

Testa is known for two buildings in particular: his Banco de Londres, designed in 1959 and completed seven years later, and the still controversial Biblioteca Nacional, which, although designed in 1961, was not begun until 1971 and not inaugurated until 1992.

Both of these buildings are conceived according to the precepts of Brutalism and so are inspired to some degree by the later work of Le Corbusier. By far the better building is the Banco de Londres, at the corner of Bartolomé Mitre and Reconquista, in the heart of the city's financial district. Nowhere in Buenos Aires, and rarely anywhere else, has unadorned concrete been used to such refined effect. This project is one of the earliest examples of Brutalism in the capital, and Testa has designed it with an elegance that is rare for the style: far more typical of Brutalism is his National Development Bank (1979) a few blocks away. The Banco de Londres feels like a massive sculpture, an easily legible rectangular box whose supporting pillars have been pulled and perforated to the point of eccentricity. Unlike most of the works in the Brutalist style, this is not a sullen building; it is full of antic wit and an exuberance of personality. And in what amounts to a parody of the Porteño chamfered corner, or ochava, the main entrance to the building is a four-story overhang whose concrete mass looks as if it might come crashing down on anyone so rash as to enter. The interior consists of an equally complicated spatial game, its cavernous openness played out on shifting and intersecting levels. In its expansive freshness, the Banco de Londres represents a stunning counterpoise to the traditional banks that surround it and that, in keeping with their typology, were designed specifically to convey solidity and grandeur.

Testa's Biblioteca Nacional, which he designed with Francisco Bullrich and Alicia Cazzaniga, may well be the most famous and controversial work of modern architecture in all of Buenos Aires. It rises over one of the barrancas that descends toward Avenida Libertador, on the former site of the Palacio Unzué, the residence of Juan and Eva Perón. When Eva Perón died of cancer in 1952, at the age of thirty-three, the house became a site of pilgrimage for her supporters. For that very reason, after Perón was ousted in 1955, one of the presidents who succeeded him, Lieutenant General Aramburu, gave the order in 1958 for it to be demolished. Two years later, his successor, Arturo Frondizi, resolved to build a new national library on the site, far larger than the one that had stood on Calle Mexico since 1901. The library, however, displays none of the skill or wit or polish of the Banco de Londres. Resembling a robotic bug, it rises up on four massive pylons that contain the structure's elevators and circulation core even as they support the gray, monolithic bulk of the building that cantilevers in all directions and is pierced by a fairly arbitrary sequence of ribbon windows and curtain walls. As with so many examples of the Brutalist style, there is an almost truculent, bullying protestation of honesty, of truth to materials in this building. Projecting an air of authoritarian control, its very opacity—especially along the exterior—seems fundamentally opposed to that openness and enlightenment that we usually take to be the mission of a public library. Already the exterior is a mottled mess, scored by water seepage. Entire sections of the dingy interior are closed off in strong rains for fear that leakage from the ceiling will drop thirty feet onto the floor of the main reading room, infiltrate the computer terminals and start a fire. In front of the building, at the base of the barranca, stands a wispy, semi-abstracted sculpture of Eva Perón, commemorating the years she resided there.

As we review what was built in Buenos Aires from the 1940s to the 1980s, there is an overwhelming temptation to find in the shabbiness of the architecture an expression of the tawdriness of the regimes that created it. I can think of no good reason to resist this interpretation.

THE CONTEMPORARY CITY

DEMOCRACY RETURNED TO BUENOS AIRES AS SPRING-time returns to the earth, so gradually that one cannot say at which precise moment winter ends and spring begins. Science can determine to the minute when the axes of earth have tipped from one season into the next, and history informs us that the freely elected Raúl Alfonsín became president of Argentina on December 10, 1983. But that tells us little. As a matter of law, what happened on that day, at that instant, was the transfer of power from one president, Reynaldo Bignone, to another, Alfonsín: such transfers of power had happened before and would happen again. But the underlying transformation from one condition to the other was protracted and complex. There was no moment, like the fall of the Berlin Wall, when the Porteños suddenly understood that they had lost their shackles. The forced disappearances and *vuelos de la muerte* had ended a few years before, and most of the CCDs, or detention centers, had been closed for some time. The military had been so efficient in prosecuting its campaign against the Montoneros and the ERP that the citizens began to forget the mortal danger they had recently faced and the enthusiasm with which, at first, they had welcomed the military regime.

Furthermore, the dictatorship in Argentina, like similar regimes in every country it bordered, from Uruguay and Brazil to Paraguay,

Bolivia and Chile, was authoritarian rather than totalitarian. In this respect it differed from the Rosas regime nearly a century and a half before. Certainly books that were deemed subversive—Marx, Freud, Sartre and the like—were confiscated and destroyed. And even toward the end of the military regime, young men whose hair was too long or who looked as though they might be intellectually inclined could expect to be roughed up now and again by the police. But the average Porteño, whether going to the movies or tossing a bife de chorizo on his beloved barbecue, would not have noticed much difference between one regime and another. And while high school and university students, for the most part, did not dare to mock the regime openly, they felt fairly free to do so in furtive or not so furtive whispers.

For all of these reasons, when the generals announced, early in 1983, that free elections would be held on October 30, the Argentines were astonished; many had simply expected that the regime would remain in place for ever, surely to the end of their natural lives. One possible explanation for the generals' decision to hold elections was the fact that power resided in a group rather than in a single strongman determined to perpetuate his regime. A more immediate inducement, in any case, was the fact that they had started and then lost the Falklands War, or the Guerra de las Malvinas as it is known locally. This conflict lasted ten weeks, from April 2 to June 14, 1982, and when it was all over, the British had sustained 255 dead and 775 wounded, with 115 soldiers captured, while the Argentines sustained 649 dead and 1,657 wounded, with 11,313 soldiers captured. The generals' decision to invade the islands in the first place was a cynical but surprisingly effective ploy to distract an increasingly restive population from the disastrous state of the economy, from 90 percent annual inflation, falling real incomes and the impoverishment of the middle classes. The Porteños, like most Argentines, were whipped up into a frenzy of patriotism, a fact that they would soon come not so much to rue as to forget. Everyone from leftist labor leaders to the Montoneros themselves, the mortal enemies of the regime, supported the invasion of the Falklands.

It occurred to no one, apparently, with the exception of some of the Mothers of the Plaza de Mayo, that only a military defeat could precipitate the collapse of a military regime. And that is exactly what happened. Although the generals clung to power a little longer, at least they had the wit to understand that their hold on it was slipping and that the present situation was unsustainable. And so they called for free elections that Raúl Alfonsín won by 51 percent to the Peronist Ítalo Luder's 40 percent. This was the first time that a Peronist lost a presidential election in Argentina.

But the fear of dictatorship did not disappear from one day to the next. This voluntary demission from power had already occurred several times in recent Argentine history, in 1958, 1963 and 1971. It was not self-evident, then, that the military would not regroup and return a few years later. Such fear and uncertainty were expressed in the title of a celebrated report commissioned by Alfonsín, *Nunca Mas* (*Never Again*). The report tried to determine who was responsible for which crimes, all the way back to the 1950s. And when the report was delivered by Ernesto Sabato, the esteemed novelist and one of the most respected Argentine intellectuals of the day, it was inconveniently revealed that both sides, left and right, shared responsibility. On the same day that Alfonsín commissioned the report, by the way, he issued another decree that declared null and void the amnesty that the generals had granted themselves shortly before ceding power. In the fullness of time, more than five hundred military officers and some enlisted men would go to prison for the crimes committed under the dictatorship.

In the meantime, one of the most visible and immediate manifestations of public release came from the provocative Porteño artist Marta Minujín, who, shortly after Raúl Alfonsín was sworn in—but not before—constructed an armature, similar in size and shape to the Parthenon, in one of the medians of the Avenida 9 de Julio. Having invited the public to supply her with books that had been hidden from the authorities during the dictatorship, she mounted over thirty thousand of them onto the scaffolding in a temporary monument to freedom of expression. The books were afterward distributed to the public.

Today it certainly appears as though the specter of military intervention in Argentine politics is a thing of the past. Part of the reason is that the military has been underfunded for years, with a mere 0.8 percent of GNP going to the armed forces. Only one country in the Western Hemisphere, Suriname, spends less per capita on its armed forces. This fact, by itself, suggests that even if the public were more disposed to favor the military and even if some rogue generals were more inclined to dominion, they would lack the basic resources and manpower that they had through much of the twentieth century, when their profession was still held in the highest regard.

At the same time, there does not appear to be much Argentine soul-searching with regard to the dictatorship. The events of the 1970s and 1980s seem almost like something done to the Argentines rather than by the Argentines. Occasionally the national intelligence agency, the Secretaría de Inteligencia, is implicated in a crime scene or its aftermath, like the 1992 bombing of the Israeli Embassy at the corner of Suipacha and Arroyo, and the bombing, two years later, of AMIA, the Asociación Mutual Israelita Argentina, on Calle Pasteur 633. Such suspicions were stoked anew with the recent suicide—or murder—of Alberto Nisman, a prosecutor who was investigating the AMIA attack and whose lifeless body was found in his apartment in Puerto Madero. It is at such moments as these that one senses the presence of a shadow state that, through some malignant law of inertia, has perpetuated itself into the present day. But it would be wrong to suppose that it pervades the politics of the nation, let alone that it is the dominant, if hidden, fact about life in Argentina or its capital.

❀

AMONG THE MANY CHANGES that Buenos Aires has undergone since the fall of the dictatorship, not the least has been a shift in its legal status. In 1994 the national constitution was changed and Buenos Aires, which had been federalized in 1880, was now granted autonomy: instead of being ruled by the federal government, as had been the case for more than a century, it was given its own charter and constitution, which was passed in 1996. At the same time, it was allowed to elect its own mayor, instead of having the president choose an intendente to run the city. The first mayor so elected was Fernando de la Rúa, who went on to serve as president of Argentina from 1999 to December 2001. The fifth and current mayor, who also has presidential ambitions, is Mauricio Macri, soon to be succeeded by Horacio Rodríguez Larreta.

The physical transformation of Buenos Aires over the past three decades has been more incremental than fundamental. Surely the city looks different today from what it was thirty years ago, but the changes visited on the metropolis have generally preserved the structure and context that existed under the dictatorship and before. The greatest change has been the redevelopment and urbanization of Puerto Madero, which has become in the process the city's forty-eighth official barrio. Fairly soon after the port was completed in the 1890s, it proved to be insufficient for a new generation of ships with significantly larger drafts than it had been designed to accommodate. In response, a new port, the Puerto Nuevo along the Costanera Norte, was inaugurated in 1926. This is now the principle port of the capital, with some activity still occurring in La Boca. It is a fair guess that most Porteños will never visit the Puerto Nuevo and have little idea of what goes on there. Although it stands only a mile or so north of the densely populated residential towers along Avenida Libertador, it feels as if it were a world away. It is difficult to reach by public transportation and almost impossible to reach on foot. Between Avenida Libertador and the port lies roughly a quarter of a mile of train yards, followed by one of the largest and most dangerous slums in the world, which is itself sliced in half by the Autopista Dr. Arturo Umberto Illia, inaugurated in 1995. To traverse that one mile you must walk around it for nearly eight miles, seeing few signs of life other than huge trucks and truck repair shops. Once you arrive, however, you encounter a veritable feast of midcentury industrial architecture: container cranes, grain elevators, the astonishing Dr. Carlos Givogri Power Plant. This last was created in the 1930s as a palace, its centerpiece a huge arch flanked by elaborate bell towers and a central window that recalls the Baths of Diocletian in Rome.

But with the creation of this new port, the municipality was compelled to address the question of what was to be done with Puerto Madero. Like Darling Harbor in Sydney and the Hudson River on Manhattan's West Side, it was necessary, at the dawn of the twenty-first

New residential developments in the Puerto Madero, with the Bridge of the Woman, designed by Santiago Calatrava, in the foreground. (Photograph by the Author)

century, to reclaim in the name of leisure and recreation what had been built in the name of commerce. Even before the inauguration of the Puerto Nuevo, there had been talk of turning the 420 acres of the older port into a residential area. But it would take nearly seventy-five years before the first building, a Hilton Hotel designed by Mario Roberto Álvarez, opened in 1999, leading the way for ever more rapid development. Today the clump of buildings that define the Puerto Madero have formed the city's second skyline, a largely residential riposte to the office towers of Catalinas Norte in Retiro. Over the past twenty years, the streets have been extensively redesigned, but still according to the grid that defines the rest of the city. Along the east-west axis, each block lines up with the corresponding block in the original city to the west.

The present state of Puerto Madero recalls earlier stages in the development of that original city. At about a mile and a half wide along the docks of the Puerto Madero, and about a quarter of a mile deep along its east-west axis, it is roughly comparable in size and shape to the city of Buenos Aires before the establishment of the viceroyalty in 1776. Today it is the mirror image, nearly perfect in its symmetry, of that earlier stage of the city's evolution. At the same time, because the grid is not yet fully occupied and developed, because some of the blocks are mere topsoil and weeds, it recalls—with a bit of goodwill, admittedly—the condition of Buenos Aires after the grid was established in 1580, but before it was fleshed out three centuries later. Each of the streets is named for a woman, which explains why the newest bridge to span the waters of the Puerto Madero, a cable-stayed feat of engineering by Santiago Calatrava, is named El Puente de la Mujer, the Bridge of the Woman.

Some of the world's most renowned architects, among them Norman Foster, Cesar Pelli and Rafael Viñoly, have designed buildings for Puerto Madero. The renowned interior designer Philippe Starck reconceived, in his typically operatic fashion, the new luxury hotel Faena, through the adaptive reuse of a former grain warehouse built by the firm of Bunge and Borne. This building, whose deep-red bricks were imported from Manchester more than a century ago, had long been threatened with demolition. But through a new awareness of its cultural heritage that was almost nonexistent in Buenos Aires thirty or even twenty years ago, the structure was preserved, as was the nearby Faena Arts Center, conceived in a similar style.

There is something almost exhilarating in the speed with which the Puerto Madero has sprung into being. Fifteen years ago, one would have seen nothing other than a few abandoned warehouses and here and there a hole in the earth where construction workers were laying the foundations for the first towers. Over that period, however, this second skyline has emerged as though out of thin air. From a distance, its inordinately tall towers seem huddled together, but on closer view they are fairly spread out, and so can be viewed in greater isolation than is the case with the skyscrapers of Chicago or New York.

One of the finest and tallest of these towers is the work of Cesar Pelli, a New York–based native of Argentina. Completed in 2008, his Torre YPF, unlike most of the new high-rises in the Puerto Madero, is an office building whose main tenant is the state-owned energy giant YPF. Constructed out of reinforced concrete, it nevertheless presents itself as a shimmering, if somewhat opaque, tower of finely detailed glass. Structurally, its distinguishing trait is the way in which the main portion of the building appears to be set into a surrounding frame, while a lofty five-floor chunk of its western exposure has been ingeniously conceived as an airborne atrium. Pelli's firm is also responsible for two of the newer skyscrapers in Catalinas Norte, the Torre BankBoston, completed in 2001, and the rather more interesting Edificio República from 1996, a magnificent reinterpretation of that tired modernist typology, the slab. Pelli has given it a curving, parabolic facade and articulated its curtain wall with fine ivory-like string coursings that recall the Bloomberg Building in midtown Manhattan, which this firm also designed.

Most of the new buildings in the Puerto Madero, however, are residential towers, which, like the Torre YPF, are not only taller than those of Las Catalinas, but exhibit far greater sensitivity in design and far greater skill in engineering. Even a work of fairly standard postmodern contextualism like the three-building Torres Le Parc complex, designed by Estudio Aisenson with Estudio R. Iannuzzi & G. Colombo, possesses a basic charm that is entirely lacking in the drab towers of the 1970s. Some of the other towers in Puerto Madero exhibit an almost extravagant postmodern inventiveness, as though channeling the futuristic dreams of designers from the 1920s. One finds this in two of the tallest buildings in Buenos Aires, the Torres Mulieris, conceived by the prolific local firm of MSGSSS, which was responsible for several of the earlier buildings in Catalinas Norte. But it is especially evident in the towers of the Torre El Faro development, two nearly identical buildings completed in 2003 to designs by Dujovne, Hirsh. These are connected every ten or so stories by sky bridges. The bridges seem to be more ornamental than anything else, but there is an enchantment to them, all the same.

As yet, Puerto Madero remains a work in progress, and it is too early to judge its ultimate success. It still feels incomplete, and the overwhelming tendency to build up and to encircle each plutocratic tower with security gates and guards to monitor them—a tendency increasingly found in other affluent barrios like Palermo and Belgrano—has resulted in broad avenues that often feel deserted. They offer little more than a few dry cleaners and convenience stores that serve the affluent inhabitants of the towers. These men and women may sleep in Puerto Madero, but they live their lives to the west, in the clamorous heart of the traditional city. And although there are many excellent and expensive restaurants along the eastern and western sides of the docks, they never achieve that almost euphoric buzz of excited activity that makes Palermo, Recoleta and the Microcentro such exhilarating theaters of urban interaction. One suspects that, in part, this is due to pedestrians having to traverse a layer of infrastructure roughly a third of a mile wide, whether by bus or on foot, in order to reach Puerto Madero from Leandro N. Alem. Its connection to the rest of the city feels forced and inorganic, a little like Roosevelt Island in New York's East River, though decidedly more pleasant and better conceived.

Puerto Madero surely has its detractors. As Pope Francis, who was himself born in the working-class barrio of Flores, recently told an interviewer, "One thing that scandalizes me, that used to scandalize me when I was in Buenos Aires, is the new Puerto Madero. How lovely, all of it won from the river, on one side those enormous buildings and 36 restaurants where they charge you an arm and a leg! And then a slum!" He was referring to the comparatively diminutive slum that has arisen on the Costanera Sur, just south of the Reserva Ecologica.

❋

IN PART, THE POPE'S COMMENT registered a measure of anxiety that is quite common among his fellow Porteños. One of the phrases heard frequently of late in these parts is *primer mundo,* first world. When a restaurant in Palermo is conspicuously chic in a way that recalls London or New York, the Porteños will register their appreciation by pronouncing it *muy primer mundo,* very first world. When the decrepit century-old subway cars of the Linea A were finally replaced in 2013 with gleaming yellow cars from China, with such amenities as air-conditioning (a first for the metro system), computer-generated signage and a decipherable public address system, the mayor, manifestly pleased, declared the whole thing to be *muy primer mundo.* This, of course, is not something that one would ever say in London or New York. It is a comment that arises out of a longing to be part of the first world and a certain nervousness about falling short.

Today Buenos Aires presents itself as a paradox, like an optical illusion of a box, drawn in perspective, that appears simultaneously to advance and recede in space. It is a city of great beauty and great ugliness, of great refinement and great abjection. But is it a great and beautiful city with pockets of abjection, or is it an abject city with a veneer of first-world order? Is it part of Europe or part of South America? This indeterminate status haunts Argentina in general, but it is especially acute in Buenos Aires itself. To achieve what today we would call first-world status was the ambition of Porteños since the days of Rivadavia in the 1820s. And around the time of the great centennial celebrations of 1910, they seemed to have finally attained it. For this reason, the Porteños of the 1920s, 1940s or 1960s do not appear to have troubled themselves greatly with this question. It was implicitly assumed that they were members in good standing of that larger, brighter world. But after half a century and more of coups and rampant corruption (which was largely nonexistent among the Argentine political class before 1930), it has fallen in status. Argentina is not a third-world country, and Buenos Aires is not a third-world city; but neither of them could now be called entirely first-world either. That indeterminacy, no less than the awareness of having lost the status that it once possessed, defines the collective character of Buenos Aires today.

You can spend days, even months, in the capital and see only the first-world city and be fully taken in by the glistering spectacle. As you enter the boutiques on Calle Florida, the grand hotels on Posadas and Alvear, the trendy, high-concept restaurants in Palermo Viejo, you notice a polish to the wood, a sheen to the brass accents, a sharpness to the general design that seems to leave no doubt that this is the equal of Europe or the United States, that it is indeed part of the first world. Large chain stores have begun to dominate retail along Calle Florida, although not to the same degree as in American cities, while chain bookstores, like Ateneo, Cuspide and Distal, have installed cafes—in self-conscious imitation of Barnes & Noble and Waterstones—where readers come to sip lattes and peer into their mobile devices. Throughout the city, or at least its middle-class neighborhoods, you will also find such fixtures of American consumption as Starbucks, McDonald's and Subway (all three a sign of gentrification in these parts).

*One of the better examples of recent architecture, Torre
Prourban, designed in 1984 by MSGSSS. (Photograph by the
Author)*

In the past generation, four high-end malls, known as *shoppings* in
Spanish, have altered the way in which Porteños spend their money.
In addition to the Abasto Shopping, mentioned previously, three were
created by the firm of Juan Carlos López y Asociados. The earliest was
Patio Bulrich in Retiro, a mid-nineteenth-century structure for cattle
auctions that was reconceived as a mall in 1989. This was followed by
Alto Palermo in 1990 and by Gallerías Pacifico in 1992. Perhaps the
most impressive is the last, which inhabits an Italianate palace on Calle
Florida, similar in style to the Casa Rosada and designed by Emilio
Agrelo and Roland Le Vacher in 1888, but completed a decade later.
Only Alto Palermo is an entirely new structure. Conceived in a pared-
down postmodern style, it achieves distinction through its sensitive use

Galerias Pacifico on Calle Florida, the city's main shopping stretch. (Photograph by the Author)

of stone on the facade as well as the daring volumes of its central drum, best seen on Avenida Coronel Diaz, and of the grand entrance whose sprawling semicircular atrium opens directly onto Avenida Santa Fe.

First-world Buenos Aires extends to Palermo Viejo, the local equivalent of the Marais in Paris and the West Village in New York. Formerly a middle- and working-class area, it has preserved its two-story homes from the turn of the century and now offers small-scale boutiques, fledgling art galleries, artisanal ice-cream parlors and scores of high-concept restaurants that strive to be very different from the asados, or steakhouses, that pervade the rest of the city. This part of Palermo, no less than the Puerto Madero, is affluent, but it feels far younger, and more bohemian than plutocratic.

First-world Buenos Aires also dominates the city's art scene. Since the year 2000, not only has the Porteño art world expanded, but a number of museums have opened, mostly devoted to contemporary art: MALBA (the Museo de Arte Latinoamericano de Buenos Aires) opened in 2001, followed by the Fundación Proa in La Boca in 2008 and the Fortabat Art Collection in the Puerto Madero in the same year. Soon afterward, a gut renovation was carried out on the Buenos Aires Museum of Modern Art in San Telmo in 2010; and the Faena Art Center, near the Faena Hotel, opened a year later. There is also a huge art fair, Arteba, that has taken over the pavilions of La Rural every year since 1991.

All of this belongs to Buenos Aires, the first-world city, the city of the Porteño middle class, which in many ways resembles the middle class throughout the world. But in one crucial sense it is quite different: it is poorer than the middle class elsewhere because of the general incompetence of the governments that it has consistently elected. Between the hyperinflation of 1989, which reached 12,000 percent, and the *corallito* (the run on the banks) in December 2001, when the nation defaulted on its debt, a good part of the wealth of this class, perhaps as much as two-thirds, evaporated overnight. And the fortunes of the middle class have hardly improved under the current national administration. Although better off, surely, than they were in the immediate aftermath of the default, they are still far below the standards of the middle class in most of the other developed countries of the world. One of the preferred pastimes of the middle class in recent years has been the *Cacerolazo,* from *cacerola* or pot. It is a form of protest in which the middle- and upper-middle-class inhabitants of Recoleta, Palermo and Belgrano take to the streets while banging pots and pans to protest the regime of Cristina Fernández de Kirchner. Even in the wealthier portions of the Barrio Norte one sees telltale signs that all is not as it appears. Electrical outages in summer, cracked and uneven pavements, entire outer walls of Beaux Arts buildings covered in graffiti, all give the lie to the European aspirations of the citizens.

At the same time, the passage from the first world to the third, from Europe to South America, is often a matter of only a few blocks in any direction. Less than a quarter of a mile north of the wealthy Avenida Libertador, with its elevated towers and river views, lies one of the largest slums in the world, Villa 31. It is one of a dozen such slums that have arisen over the years in the interstitial spaces of the capital. The biggest is Villa 21 in Barracas, while one of the smaller slums, in Puerto Madero, has already been mentioned. But the oldest and most famous is Villa 31, which has occupied the space between the Retiro rail yards and the bus terminal for over eighty years, since the Great Depression. Today it is home to more than forty thousand souls. According to a 2009 governmental census, half of them are natives of Paraguay, Bolivia and Peru, while the rest are Argentines from the northern provinces. Their presence points to a demographic shift that has taken place in Buenos Aires over the past generation. Although the population remains largely European in origin, you now see many more indigenous inhabitants than would have been the case twenty years ago. These are the base of Kirchnerite support in the city, or what there is of it, and they can often be seen attending staged demonstrations intended to block traffic in the center of the capital. Such blockades have become a fact of life under the present regime.

Like the Cemetery de Recoleta, Villa 31 reads like a mad parody of the Argentine capital. Rather than a grid, it has developed in an organic fashion that mimics the evolution of Paris or Rome. It is an unregulated agglomeration of makeshift houses, some of them rising three stories and fashioned from cinder-block, corrugated iron and any other materials found amid the discarded rubbish of the capital. When seen from the air, or on Google Earth, the density of the buildings in this slum, as well as in all the other slums in the city, produces a distinct visual pattern that is very different from the orderly grid of the rest of the city. But even in some of the more established areas of the city, in Balvaneras and especially in the southern barrios of La Boca and Barracas, century-old buildings in the *estilo frances* are in a state of such manifest decay that one wonders how they remain standing at all. Whole chunks of their masonry surface, scored and scoured with graffiti, have fallen away. Wrought iron balconies sag and metal poles that once supported a reinforced concrete substructure now stand illogically exposed to the elements.

In many respects, Buenos Aires today resembles New York City as it was in the 1970s. There are parts of the capital that no foreigner and few locals would be advised to visit without an escort. Although many

Abandoned bank on Avenida Almirante Brown, corner of Suarez. (Photograph by the Author)

Graffiti or Arte Callejero (Street Art). (Photograph by the Author)

Plaza San Martín. (Photograph by the Author)

parts of the city, especially in the northern half, rival Paris or New York
in the degree of their order and cleanliness, the state of filth and der-
eliction in other parts can be disturbing to first-world sensibilities. But
if the example of New York provides some perspective, perhaps it will
also provide hope. Cities can sustain almost unimaginable degrees of
mismanagement and ruination and yet revive to equal or even surpass
their earlier condition. A more competent national administration than
the present one would greatly aid in the achievement of that goal. At the
same time, it must be said that the local administration has done what
it could under difficult and trying circumstances, and that, throughout
this period, the parks and transportation infrastructure within the city
are superior to what they were in New York in the 1970s, and superior
perhaps to what they are today.

❋

IF BUENOS AIRES RESEMBLES New York as it was forty years ago, it also calls to mind Rome under Constantine the Great. When we think of Ancient Rome today, we are thinking of that moment, around 325 A.D., when the city attained the dimensions that are now so familiar to us, when it finally felt perfect and complete. Nearing the five hundredth anniversary of Pedro de Mendoza's first settlement on the banks of the Rio de la Plata, Buenos Aires as well feels essentially complete. At every previous period in its history, the capital was clearly striving to achieve some as yet latent potential, to provide some pressing infrastructural enhancement or to fill out its grid or ennoble the building stock in a way that would enable the Porteños finally to feel that their work was done. That time has come. Although there remain many areas of the capital that are ripe for development, and although aspects of the city's infrastructure are in urgent need of improvement, the great work of creating Buenos Aires is now finished. Hereafter change will come as the refinement and elaboration of what already exists, as the restoration of whole neighborhoods that have fallen into decay, and as the full reintegration of the city, and the nation, into the wider world.

ACKNOWLEDGMENTS

I WOULD LIKE FIRST TO THANK MY EDITOR, ELISA-
beth Dyssegaard, for the skill and sensitivity that she brought to the
task of editing my manuscript and for her serene patience. My thanks
go as well to her able assistant, Laura Apperson, for the many tasks she
undertook in the service of my book, to Donna Cherry for her solicitude
in overseeing its production, and to Bill Warhop for the skill and care
with which he copyedited my text. I cannot thank enough my esteemed
agent Angela Miller, who believed in this project and exerted all of her
considerable agenting skills on its behalf. Although I have benefited
from the help of too many people to list here, I would like especially
to thank Jorge Tartarini, Catalina Lascano, Margarita Gutman, David
Jacobson, Rosita García Carillo and Adriana da Cunha. My thanks as
well to the staffs of the Archivo General de la Nación, the Biblioteca
Nacional and the library of the Museo de la Ciudad. Finally, I must
thank the anonymous forces behind two superb websites, Moderna
Buenos Aires and Arcón de Buenos Aires, for their devoted and tireless
sense of mission in elucidating, respectively, the recent and the remoter
past of one of the world's great and undersung cities.

SELECTED
BIBLIOGRAPHY

Acarete du Biscay. *Relación de un viaje al Río de la Plata*. Buenos Aires: Alfer and Vays, 1943.

Andrews, George Reid. *The Afro-Argentines of Buenos Aires, 1800–1900*. Madison: University of Wisconsin Press, 1980.

Berjman, Sonia. *La Plaza Española en Buenos Aires 1580–1880*. Buenos Aires: Kliczkowski Editores, 2001.

Bernand, Carmen. *Historia de Buenos Aires*. Bogotá: Fondo de Cultura Económica, 1999.

Borges, Jorge Luis. *Cuaderno San Martín*. Buenos Aires: Editorial Proa, 1929.

Borges, Jorge Luis. *El Aleph*. Buenos Aires: Editorial Losada, 1949.

Borges, Jorge Luis. *Evaristo Carriego*. Buenos Aires: Gleizer Editor, 1930.

Borges, Jorge Luis. *Fervor de Buenos Aires*. Buenos Aires: Imprenta Serantes, 1923.

Borges, Jorge Luis. *Luna de enfrente*. Buenos Aires: Editorial Proa, 1925.

Brown, Jonathan C. *A Brief History of Argentina*. New York: Facts on File, Inc., 2011.

Brown, Jonathan C. *A Socioeconomic History of Argentina, 1776–1860*. Cambridge: Cambridge University Press, 1979.

Cabeza de Vaca, Álvar Núñez. *Relación de los naufragios y comentarios*. Madrid: Librería General de Victoriano Suárez, 1906.

Concolorcorvo (Alonso Carrió de la Vandera). *El Lazarillo de Ciegos Caminantes*. Buenos Aires: Stockcero, 2005.

Cox, David, and Robert J. Cox. *Dirty Secrets, Dirty War*. Charleston, SC: Evening Post Publishing Company, 2008.

Cuerva, Jorge Ignacio García. "La Iglesia en Buenos Aires Durante La Epidemia de Fiebre Amarilla de 1871." *Revista Teologica* 11 (2003): 115–47.

Echeverría, Esteban. *El Matadero-La Cautiva*. Madrid: Catedra, 1990.

Fletcher, Ian. *The Waters of Oblivion: The British Invasion of the Rio de la Plata, 1806–1807*. Tunbridge Wells: Spellmount Ltd., 1991.

Foster, David William. *Buenos Aires: Perspectives on the City and Cultural Production.* Gainesville: University Press of Florida, 1998.

Galeano, Diego. "Medicos y policías durante la epidemia de fiebre amarilla (Buenos Aires, 1871)." *Salud Colectiva* 5, no. 1 (April 2009): 107–20.

García, Juan Agustín. *La ciudad indiana: Buenos Aires desde 1600 hasta mediados del siglo XVIII.* Buenos Aires: Hyspamerica, 1900.

Gorelik, Adrián: *La Grilla y el Parque: Espacio publico y cultura urbana en Buenos Aires, 1887–1936.* Quilmes, Argentina: Universidad Nacional de Quilmes, 1998.

Gutiérrez, Ramón. *Buenos Aires: Evolucion urbana, 1536–2000.* Buenos Aires: Cedodal, 2014.

Gutiérrez, Ramón. "Buenos Aires: A Great European City." In *Planning Latin America's Capital Cities 1850–1950,* edited by Arturo Almandoz, 45–75. London: Routledge, 2002.

Gutman, Margarita, and Jorge Enrique Hardoy. *Buenos Aires, 1536–2006.* Buenos Aires: Ediciones Infinito, 2000.

Hanon, Maxine. *Buenos Ayres desde las quintas de Retiro a Recoleta (1580–1890).* Buenos Aires: Olmo Ediciones, 2014.

Herz, Enrique German. *Historia de La Plaza Lavalle.* Buenos Aires: Cuadernos de Buenos Aires, 1979.

Johnson, Lyman L. *Workshop of Revolution: Plebeian Buenos Aires and the Atlantic World, 1776–1810.* Durham, NC: Duke University Press Books, 2011.

Koolhaas, Rem. *Delirious New York.* New York: Monacelli Press, 1994.

Luna, Felix. *Buenos Aires y el país.* Buenos Aires: Editorial Sudamerican, 1982.

Luqui-Lagleyze, Julio. *Buenos Aires: Sencilla historia.* Buenos Aires: Librerias Turisticas, 1998.

Lynch, John. *Argentine Caudillo: Juan Manuel de Rosas.* Oxford: Rowman & Littlefield Publishers, 2001.

Lynch, John. *The Spanish-American Revolutions, 1808–1826.* New York: W. W. Norton, 1973.

Lynch, John. *Spanish Colonial Administration 1782–1810.* University of London: Athlone Press, 1958.

Machain, Ricardo de Lafuente. *El barrio de la Recoleta.* Buenos Aires: Cuadernos de Buenos Aires, 1962.

Machain, Ricardo de Lafuente. *La Plaza Tragica.* Buenos Aires: Cuadernos de Buenos Aires, 1962.

Machain, Ricardo de Lafuente. *El barrio de Santo Domingo.* Buenos Aires: Cuadernos de Buenos Aires, 1956.

Marechal, Leopoldo. *Adán Buenosayres.* Buenos Aires: Editorial Corregidor, 2013.

Maroni, Juan José. *Breve historia fisica de Buenos Aires.* Buenos Aires: Cuadernos de Buenos Aires, 1969.

Maroni, Juan José. *El Alto de San Pedro.* Buenos Aires: Cuadernos de Buenos Aires, 1969.

Mitre, Bartolomé. *Rimas.* Buenos Aires: Imprenta y Librerias de Mayo, 1876.

Morrison, Samuel Eliot. *The European Discovery of America: The Southern Voyages A.D. 1492–1616*. New York: Oxford University Press, 1974.

Municipalidad de la Ciudad de Buenos Aires. *La arquitectura en Buenos Aires 1850–1880*. Buenos Aires: Cuadernos de Buenos Aires, 1972.

Pando, Horacio Jorge. *Historia urbana de Buenos Aires*. Buenos Aires: Diseño, 2014.

Podalsky, Laura. *Specular City: Transforming Culture, Consumption, and Space in Buenos Aires, 1955–1973*. Philadelphia: Temple University Press, 2004.

Rapoport, Mario, and María Seoane. *Buenos Aires, historia de una ciudad*. Buenos Aires: Planeta, 2007.

Romero, Jose Luis, and Luis Alberto Romero, eds. *Buenos Aires, historia de cuatro siglos*. Buenos Aires: Altamira, 1983.

Ross, Stanley R., and Thomas F. McGann, eds. *Buenos Aires: 400 Years*. Austin: University of Texas Press, 1982.

Sargent, Charles S. *Spatial Evolution of Greater Buenos Aires, Argentina, 1870–1930*. Tempe: Arizona State University, 1974.

Sarlo, Beatriz. "Cultural Landscapes: BA from Integration to Fracture." In *Other Cities, Other Worlds: Urban Imaginaries in a Globalizing Age,* edited by Andreas Huyssen. Durham, NC: Duke University Press Books, 2008.

Sarmiento, Domingo Faustino. *Facundo o civilización y barbarie en las pampas Argentinas*. Buenos Aires: Siglo XXI Editores, 2004.

Scobie, James R. *Argentina: A City and a Nation*. New York: Oxford University Press, 1971.

Scobie, James R. *Buenos Aires: Plaza to Suburb 1870–1910*. New York: Oxford University Press, 1971.

Scobie, James R. *Revolution on the Pampas: A Social History of Argentine Wheat, 1860–1910*. Austin: University of Texas Press, 1964.

Schávelzon, Daniel. *Arqueología de Buenos Aires*. Buenos Aires: Emecé Editores, 1999.

Schiavo, Horacio. *Palermo de San Benito*. Buenos Aires: Cuadernos de Buenos Aires, 1969.

Schmidl, Ulrich. *Ulrich Schmidls Erlebnisse in Südamerika*. Straubing: 1962.

Shmidt, Claudia. *Palacios sin reyes: Arquitectura pública para la capital permanente: Buenos Aires 1880–1890*. Rosario: Prohistoria Ediciones, 2012.

Tartarini, Jorge Daniel. *El Palacio de las Aguas Corrientes. De Gran Depósito a Monumento Histórico Nacional*. Buenos Aires: AySA, 2012.

Timerman, Jacobo. *Prisoner without a Name, Cell without a Number*. New York: Alfred A. Knopf, 1981.

Walter, Richard J. *Politics and Urban Growth in Buenos Aires, 1910–1942*. Cambridge: Cambridge University Press, 1993.

Wilson, Jason. *A Cultural Guide to the City of Buenos Aires*. Oxford: Signal Books, 1999.

Zabala, Rómulo, and Enrique de Gandía. *Historia de la Ciudad de Buenos Aires*. Buenos Aires: Municipalidad de la Ciudad de Buenos Aires, 1980.

INDEX